Beyond NAFTA:
An Economic, Political
and Sociological
Perspective

Beyond NAFTA:
An Economic, Political and Sociological Perspective

**edited by
A. R. Riggs and Tom Velk
North American Studies
McGill University**

The Fraser Institute

Vancouver, British Columbia, Canada

HF
1746
B49
1993

Printed in Canada.

Canadian Cataloguing in Publication Data

Main entry under title:

Beyond NAFTA

Based on papers presented at a conference held at McGill University in March, 1993.
Includes bibliographical references.
ISBN 0-88975-162-5

1. Free trade—North America—Congresses.
2. North America—Commercial treaties—Congresses.
I. Riggs, A. R. (Alvin Richard), 1931–   II.
Velk, Tom, 1938–   III. Fraser Institute
(Vancouver, B.C.)
    HF3211.B49   1993   382'.917   C93-091765-0

Contents

Section V: What's in it for Mexico and the Hemisphere?

Section VI: Law and Dispute Settlement

Afterword—A Summary

Preface

Michael A. Walker

THIS BOOK IS PART OF A SERIES of eight books and 21 monographs that form part of a Fraser Institute project entitled **The North American 20/20 Project**. The purpose of this project, which has been funded by the Lilly Endowment of Indianapolis, is to undertake a multidisciplinary and multinational analysis of the requirements for and impacts of economic integration in the hemisphere. In accomplishing this ambitious program of research, The Fraser Institute has been very pleased to collaborate with institutions and individuals in Chile, Colombia, Costa Rica and Brazil as well as, of course, in Mexico, the United States and Canada. One of these collaborating institutions is the North American Studies program at McGill University, which itself has established a high reputation as a source of informed comment on North American economic and social issues.

The current volume is the reflection of a conference held at McGill University during which a wide range of opinions and positions were presented to an audience that reflected the many constituencies who have an interest in North American Free Trade. The editors have done a marvellous job of assembling most of the presentations delivered at the symposium, and have preserved them in this volume for those who want better to understand the North American Free Trade Agreement, for those who would seek to emulate it, and for those who wish to understand what will be its implications for the future. The Fraser

Institute has been pleased to sponsor both the conference and this volume as part of the North America 20/20 Project and to assist the editors and their authors in making their views better known to a wider audience. It is the opinion of the Institute that public policy will be improved by the broadest possible discussion of issues of this kind. While we have been pleased to sponsor the work of the editors and the authors, that work has been conducted independently and may or may not reflect the views of the membership and trustees of The Fraser Institute.

Acknowledgements

THIS VOLUME PRESENTS THE RESULTS of the third free trade symposium arranged by McGill's North American Studies Programme since 1987. All have been generously funded by Mrs. George Packer Berry of Princeton, New Jersey. Over the years the Gerald Wilkinson endowment has allowed us to explore a variety of issues of academic interest and public policy.

We wish in particular to thank as well Michael Walker and the Fraser Institute for their generous aid as co-sponsors of our conference, "NAFTA Between Elections" (March 18-20, 1993), a "North America 20/20 Event." The Centre for International Studies, University of Toronto, also offered much-needed encouragement for so ambitious a program, and McGill University provided us with its usual hospitality. Both Principal David Johnston, who has done much for hemispheric cooperation, and NAFTA itself, have inspired North American Studies to expand its intellectual and teaching frontiers in anticipation of a more cosmopolitan world.

About the Contributors

ALAN S. ALEXANDROFF is a professor with the Centre for International Studies, the University of Toronto.

THOMAS D'AQUINO is President and Chief Executive Officer of the Business Council on National Issues, composed of the directors of 150 leading Canadian corporations.

STEPHEN BLANK is Associate Professor, Lubin School of Business, Pace University, and Director, Canadian Affairs, Americas Society, New York, N.Y.

CARLOS A. BRAGA is a trade economist with the World Bank, Washington, D.C.

DONALD V. COES is Professor, Anderson School of Management and Latin American Institute, the University of New Mexico, and Consultant, Latin American Technical Department, the World Bank.

BRADLY J. CONDON is a barrister and solicitor, Faculty of Law, the University of Calgary, Calgary, Alberta.

ANDREW COYNE is a member of the Editorial Board, the *Globe and Mail*, Toronto.

ARMAND DE MESTRAL is Professor, Faculty of Law, McGill University, Montreal.

ROBERT M. DUNN, JR., is Professor of Economics, George Washington University, Washington, D.C.

EARL H. FRY is Endowed Professor of Canadian Studies and Political Science, Brigham Young University, Provo, Utah.

JOHN W. GALBRAITH is Associate Professor of Economics, McGill University, Montreal.

GEORGE W. GRAYSON is a professor with the Department of Government, College of William and Mary, Williamsburg, Virginia.

M. TERESA GUTIÉRREZ-HACES is with the Center for Research on the United States, the National Autonomous University of Mexico (UNAM), Mexico City.

ANTHONY HALLIDAY is with the Parliamentary Centre for Foreign Affairs and Trade, Ottawa.

JAMES L. HUFFMAN is Professor of Law, Lewis and Clark School, and Bradley Resident Scholar, The Heritage Foundation, Washington, D.C.

JORGE JURAIDINI is Deputy Representative to Canada for NAFTA Negotiations, Government of Mexico.

COLLEEN MORTON, formerly Director, the U.S.-Mexico Business Committee, Washington, D.C., is Vice President, Institute of the Americas, La Jolla, California.

JOHN O'GRADY, an independent consultant on labour market and industrial relations issues, is also an Associate Fellow of the University of Toronto's Centre for International Studies.

SUSAN KAUFMAN PURCELL is Vice-President for Latin American Affairs, the Americas Society, New York, N.Y.

EDUARDO F. RAMIREZ, an attorney, is with the Research Center on North America at the National Autonomous University of Mexico (UNAM), Mexico City.

A. R. RIGGS is Associate Professor of History and Director of North American Studies, McGill University, Montreal.

MALCOLM D. ROWAT is a Project Adviser with the World Bank, Washington, D.C.

BRIAN R. RUSSELL is a lawyer and Director of the U.S. Policy Studies Group at Dalhousie University, Halifax, Nova Scotia.

STEPHEN A. SCOTT, of the Quebec Bar, is a professor in the Faculty of Law, McGill University, Montreal.

RODRIGUE TREMBLAY is Professor of Economics at the Université de Montréal.

GIL TROY is Assistant Professor, Department of History, McGill University, Montreal.

TOM VELK, Associate Professor of Economics, McGill University, Montreal, is also a freelance television journalist.

MICHEL VILLENEUVE is Senior Manager, Trade-Finance, at the Canadian Imperial Bank of Commerce.

MICHAEL A. WALKER is Executive Director of the Fraser Institute, Vancouver, British Columbia.

WILLIAM G. WATSON, Associate Professor of Economics, McGill University, Montreal, is also a columnist for the *Financial Post*, Toronto.

THE HONOURABLE MICHAEL WILSON is Minister of Industry, Science and Technology, and Minister for International Trade, Government of Canada, Ottawa.

Introduction

A. R. Riggs and Tom Velk

THIS COLLECTION OF PAPERS CONTAINS the opinions, predictions and informed analysis of 32 widely separated economists, business leaders, historians, political scientists, bankers, legal and constitutional experts, journalists, politicians and diplomats. They came to Montreal from Canada, the United States and Mexico, March 18-20, 1993, to discuss and debate the North American Free Trade Agreement (NAFTA), effective (if passed by the three legislatures) on January 1, 1994.

Co-sponsored by the Fraser Institute, Vancouver, Canada, and McGill University's North American Studies Programme, the symposium was arranged for and attended by a general audience. This volume is therefore both a record of scholarly proceedings and a layman's guide to the workings and controversial issues of NAFTA.

An intelligent layman unfamiliar with the NAFTA debate might have expected our conference questions and answers to be obvious. Have not economists since David Hume in the 18th century been telling us that free trade is beneficial? Is not voluntary exchange necessarily advantageous for all, since traders would hardly incur the costs and trouble of interaction otherwise? And is not the policy implication just as obvious as the theory—government should get out of the road so traders and the public are not asked to pay the transaction costs imposed by political boundary lines?

But as Stephen Blank of the Americas Society says, NAFTA is not essentially a free trade arrangement. If it were, it would be one sentence long, and its policy prescription would be "fire the customs agents, burn the tariff schedules and throw open the borders." In fact, NAFTA contains 2,000 pages and it was not intended for bedtime reading.

As a result, in one conference paper after another, blackboard-easy puzzles were accompanied by tough questions without clear answers. In his summing up of our conference, McGill economist John W. Galbraith laid out the core explanation for NAFTA's complexities. First, NAFTA is not a direct move toward free trade. Its rules for regional trade preference build up a new regulatory overlay. The resulting trade flow, while less confined and more efficient than before, is still restricted. The gains lost by this potential to divert trade away from the very best pattern (only possible if the world's trade blocs meld into one) should remind us of the pay-off from a long-run commitment to an ever-expanding trade frontier.

Second, the division of free trade gains among the players presents a political and organizational challenge. The poorest will do best. Real Mexican per capita income, assuming the necessary investment in human capital takes place, will grow by an order of magnitude. Chile, a future prospect for NAFTA, on the strength of present economic performance and potential, has perhaps the brightest growth prospects of any nation on earth.

Another ameliorating force is the flow of overseas investment into the poorer nations in amounts sufficient to lift all boats by adding an extra quantity of productivity and income to the entire trading bloc. But an improvement in income distribution within Canada and the United States also depends upon new investment. Low income earners, those with skill levels no better than their new competitors, must bootstrap their skills.

Third, the regional quality of the existing deal gives ample room— too much room—for regulatory complexity. Quibbles over rules of origin, jurisprudence, and regulatory co-ordination are themselves wasteful, or at least expensive. We have arranged questions and answers concerning these and other NAFTA issues under six headings or sections: Background and Prospects; What's in it for Canada?; What's in it for the United States?; What's in it for the Business Community?;

What's in it for Mexico and the Hemisphere?; and Law and Dispute Settlement.

There is agreement among those who monitor politics in Mexico City, Ottawa and Washington that the most significant threat to passage of NAFTA now lies in the United States. Colleen Morton, until recently with the U.S.-Mexico Business Committee (where she lobbied in Congress) rates NAFTA's chances at 50-50. She wishes the agreement could have been finessed as the FTA was, and she says the question is, "How much political capital will President Clinton be willing to spend?" With recent changes in committee membership, much support has evaporated in Congress.

Tom Velk and A. R. Riggs have studied the effort in Congress to brush away trade barriers in the 1930s, when a trade-off in favour of expedient political unity postponed the time of economic integration until the present. Gil Troy, of the history department, McGill, believes that the president has much room to manoeuvre now, since the NAFTA was a "phantom issue" in the late elections.

Susan Kaufman Purcell of the Americas Society disagrees. She points out that more than 60 new members of Congress campaigned against NAFTA. (Today she would have added the apparent defection of the new House Majority Leader, Richard Gephardt, and a challenge in federal courts regarding an environmental impact statement.) They constitute a formidable threat, and the ambivalent position of the president and of Labor Secretary Robert Reich has been of little help. Organized labour, she warns, still has clout in the Democratic party. So far as side agreements on labour and the environment are concerned, she wonders how far Mexico can be pushed.

Participants agreed that Mexico is enthusiastic about NAFTA, as we saw in an address by Jorge Juraidini, Deputy Representative to Canada for Trade Negotiations, who argues that Mexico is a small economy and cannot harm the larger, developed nations to the north.

It may sound strange to speak of Canada as a trading colossus. Early debates are predicted in Ottawa by Anthony Halliday of the Parliamentary Centre for Foreign Affairs and Trade, with the spotlight on the position of the Liberal party. Alan S. Alexandroff of the Centre for International Studies, the University of Toronto, argues that NAFTA has deeply divided the Liberals (and will continue to divide them), but that the extreme nationalists cannot avoid, in his opinion, what they call "the trap of continentalism."

Continentalism is most strongly supported today, of course, by Mexico. The question then becomes, "What's in the NAFTA for Mexico?"

The answer is, "a lot." Academics from UNAM (the National Autonomous University of Mexico), Eduardo Ramirez and M. Teresa Gutiérrez-Haces, reminded the symposium that in addition to trade advantages, Mexico has much to gain politically and socially from NAFTA. Ramirez, an attorney, discussed profound changes already advancing—a transition from civil to common law, for example—as Mexico opens its borders and encourages harmonization with Canada and the United States. Gutiérrez-Haces says a "limitless will" exists for change in Mexico, but that the transition process is very difficult.

George W. Grayson, a political scientist at the College of William and Mary, Williamsburg, is interested in the impact of NAFTA on Mexico's "authoritarian" political system. He concludes that the advantages of NAFTA for Mexico include a diminishing of repressive rule, decentralization, an undermining of the power of labour chieftains, and far less corruption.

Conferees seemed generally to agree that the biggest winner in a three-way arrangement, at least for the time being, should be Mexico, with a prediction of significant long-term growth in Gross Domestic Product (GDP) of 11.4 percent. Why then should Canada and the United States be interested in adding a partner to their FTA?

Thomas d'Aquino, president of Canada's Business Council on National Issues, concentrates on opportunities for business, because, he says, we are going to achieve a "level playing field." Michael Walker, who heads the Fraser Institute in Vancouver, agrees that access to markets and government procurement will aid Canada, and he denies that job loss in manufacturing is a special function of international trade agreements. Service production is the way of the future for advanced economies, he says.

Robert M. Dunn, Jr., an economist at George Washington University, got the most press play when he concentrated on the job-loss issue. Dunn claims the loss will be serious among unskilled and semi-skilled workers as manufacturing moves south. He argues that the agreement should be adopted, but with compensation in the form of job retraining and earned income tax credits for losers. A possible offset is a flow of investment capital into Mexico. William G. Watson, McGill Economics, agreed that there will be some zero-sum trade diversion, some diminishing of sovereignty, and job losses. Watson agrees with Dunn that governments in Canada and the United States should aid workers in the loser category.

John O'Grady, a consultant on labour market and industrial relations in Toronto, however, would like to scrap NAFTA. His argument cites the Cox and Harris real income gains for Canada of less than one percent, high adjustment costs, changes in income distribution, plant closures and poorly enforced environmental and labour standards in Mexico.

Some of the participants in our extended seminar took issue with the O'Grady assessment. Rodrigue Tremblay, of the Economics Department, Université de Montréal, says that job losses from the Canada-U.S. FTA would have been fewer had Canada a planned and well-coordinated policy on trade. The bulk of job losses in Canada's manufacturing sector, he says, is a result of the recession of 1990-91, and the currency exchange rate was also deeply involved. Canada's trade minister, Michael Wilson, claims that 118,000 jobs have been created in 1992, and he notes that the trade surplus in Canada rose 27 percent from 1991 to 1992. Michel Villeneuve, of the Canadian Imperial Bank of Commerce, was also optimistic about NAFTA, but cited a need for efficient export financing mechanisms. Armand De Mestral, of the Faculty of Law, McGill, spoke of NAFTA from his experience on FTA dispute settlement panels. He was pleased that the dispute avoidance and dispute settlement aspects have been extended with NAFTA, and should work pretty well.

A number of our participants addressed the question, "What's not in the agreement for everybody involved?" Andrew Coyne, of the Toronto *Globe and Mail*, agrees that free traders should support NAFTA, but he notes that agriculture and culture, for example, are exempted and that there is no subsidies code.

Subsidies are going to create problems. Brian Russell, a lawyer and director of the U.S. Policy Studies Group at Dalhousie University, specifically addressed the issue of subsidies. He warns about President

Clinton's recent allusions to government assistance to high-tech companies. If this becomes policy in the United States, he says, the issue is bound to worsen national and global trade warfare.

Earl Fry, a political scientist at Brigham Young University, cautions that too little attention has been given to 91 state and provincial governments, two federal districts, six major territorial governments, and countless county and local jurisdictions. Non-national governments must become energetic supporters, he says—not reluctant partners—of NAFTA. Stephen A. Scott, of the Law Faculty, McGill, notes that the federal government in Canada might have to use its constitutional authority to enforce NAFTA against the provinces.

James L. Huffman, a lawyer presently with the Heritage Foundation, Washington, heroically tackled the water transfer question, another neglected item, and proposed a "North American Water Market Foundation" as an adjunct to NAFTA.

Carlos Braga, of the World Bank, complains about neglect of intellectual property rights, an issue that will be with us for years to come. Bradly Condon, of the Faculty of Law, University of Calgary, dealt with NAFTA and environmental policy implementation, and concluded that environmental laws are likely to withstand challenges brought under NAFTA. In fact, he says, NAFTA provides more protection for genuine environmental laws than does the Canadian constitution.

Three of our participants speculated about the future of the NAFTA (assuming that it is passed). Malcolm D. Rowat, a trade lawyer with the World Bank, believed that Chile may join NAFTA, despite its environmental problems. Chile and Mexico, he notes, are the two Latin American countries making the greatest progress in macro-economic adjustment, trade liberalization, privatization and decentralization. It appears unlikely that Chile will join MERCOSUR, the Southern Cone common market.

Donald Coes, also with the World Bank (and the University of New Mexico), stresses that MERCOSUR is dominated by Brazil. Brazil might do a lot better outside than in, but would lose some of its hegemony in South America. Facing environmental and other major problems, Brazil might eventually join NAFTA, while it remains a member of the South American Common Market.

Stephen Blank, of the Americas Society, believes that if NAFTA passes there may be discerned an "emerging architecture of North America," where borders disappear in favour of "pooled sovereignties," together with the eroding of central governments' power to manage national economies. In addition, the growing regionalization of the North American economy, he warns, could lead to fragmentation, regional trade barriers, or even efforts to revive old sovereignties. This, he implies, is the greatest long-term threat to NAFTA, and may not derive from congressional protectionists in Washington, but from the cohesive qualities of federalism itself.

In the end, conference participants gave reason to hope these complexities do not bar the way to eventual progress on trade. Most interesting was the new enthusiasm for free markets. Progress was reported from the front in Chile and Mexico, and tough issues such as property rights under law and constitutional limits on free trade initiatives were found to be solvable, both in theory and practice. The balance of force seems everywhere to be with those who are willing to take the risks associated with change.

Section I
NAFTA: Background and Prospects

Free Trade Patriarch: Cordell Hull and Inter-American Trade Barriers

A.R. Riggs and Tom Velk

SIXTY YEARS AGO, FRANKLIN D. ROOSEVELT stood before the governing board of the Pan American Union and asked that the republics of the hemisphere "abolish all unnecessary and artificial barriers and restrictions which now hamper the healthy flow of trade."[1] Behind the American president's request of April 12, 1933, lay the lifelong efforts of his secretary of state, Cordell Hull, who viewed the tariff as "the king of evils," and "the largest single underlying cause of the present panic."[2]

---

1   Samuel Rosenman, ed., *The Public Papers and Addresses of Franklin D. Roosevelt* (New York: Random House, 1938), II, p. 131.

2   Quoted by Robert Dallek, *Franklin D. Roosevelt and American Foreign Policy, 1932-1945* (Oxford: Oxford University Press, 1979), p. 33.

Cordell Hull passionately believed that efforts by countries to alleviate the Great Depression with protective tariffs and other barriers to international trade had only made matters worse. In 1932, Britain's Imperial Preference system barred the United States from Commonwealth markets in Canada, Australia and South Africa. Germany would shortly begin to negotiate exclusive barter arrangements in Europe and Latin America that ruled out competition. Nor did Hull spare his own country, the greatest culprit of them all, for setting off world economic warfare with its Hawley-Smoot Tariff of 1930, the highest in United States history with average rates of more than 50 percent.

This paper deals with the free trade obsession of Secretary Hull, who may be termed the true father of negotiations going on today to eliminate trade barriers in the world, and especially in the Western Hemisphere. Unfortunately, the culmination of his efforts at freeing clogged channels of trade in the Americas came at a Buenos Aires conference of 1936, where a combination of world events and specific national objectives (including those of the United States) dealt a crushing blow to his crusade.

A crusade it was, and in the light of recent developments the time has come to reconsider the efforts of Cordell Hull as visionary and constructive. The secretary of state recalled with satisfaction in his memoirs that in his maiden speech to Congress in 1898, he had pleaded for lower tariffs and fewer trade restrictions. On the same page he boasted that 34 years later he co-authored a demand for reciprocal tariff agreements in the New Deal Democratic Platform of 1932.[3] Although historians have long recognized that Secretary Hull used the standard of freer trade to judge all his ventures in diplomacy between 1933 and his retirement in 1944,[4] they have been less than satisfied with his single-minded mission. Robert Dallek, in his prize-winning book, *Franklin D. Roosevelt and American Foreign Policy, 1932-1945*, noted drily that

---

3   Cordell Hull, *The Memoirs of Cordell Hull* (New York: The Macmillan Company, 1948), I, p. 352.

4   Richard Pollenburg and Walter La Feber, *The American Century* (New York: John Wiley & Sons, 1979), p. 233.

Hull's "air of harmless benevolence masked a vindictive evangelism which he put at the service of economic internationalism."[5] Irwin Gellman in *Good Neighbor Diplomacy*, also published in 1979, wrote that "Hull's fixation on reciprocity forced the State Department to devote too much time to a program of limited value" that came out of Hull's "outdated Wilsonian free trade beliefs."[6]

Outdated or not, the first item on the Hull New Deal agenda, a proposal for the World Economic Conference—scheduled for June 1933 in London—called for a truce on further tariff increases and an across-the-board reduction of ten percent by all countries participating. At preliminary discussions in Washington, Hull secured the assent of Britain and France, but the tariff question became moot when President Roosevelt torpedoed the conference by refusing to accept an agreement on currency stabilization.[7]

After the London fiasco, Hull's hopes for freer trade rested upon continuing support from his president, actions by the United States Congress and on establishing a common front, under the rubric of The Good Neighbor Policy, between his own country and the republics of Central and South America. Representatives of the 21 nations were scheduled to meet at Montevideo, Uruguay, for the Seventh International Conference of American States on December 3, 1933. There the delegates would be confronting the ghost of the last Pan American conference at Havana in 1928, which ended in a spirit of rancour and mistrust over the issue of "Yankee imperialism."[8]

The Roosevelt-Hull Good Neighbor Policy sought to reverse 35 years of United States intervention in the affairs of Latin America.

---

5   Dallek, p. 33

6   Irwin F. Gellman, *Good Neighbor Diplomacy: United States Policies in Latin America, 1933-1945* (Baltimore: The Johns Hopkins Press, 1979), p. 58.

7   Hull, I, pp. 249-52.

8   Dallek, p. 82. The standard work on New Deal Latin American diplomacy is Bryce Wood, *The Making of the Good Neighbor Policy* (New York: Columbia University Press, 1961).

Between 1898 and 1920, United States marines, soldiers, and naval personnel invaded the states of the Caribbean region no fewer than 20 times. In addition to military intervention, the United States consistently used its economic power and influence to control Latin American economies and governments.

The major diplomatic objective of Latin Americans at the Montevideo Conference of 1933 was to obtain a guarantee from the United States that this kind of interference would end. With some reservations, Cordell Hull was ready to renounce unilateral intervention, but he also harboured other plans for the Montevideo conference that he failed to discuss with President Roosevelt. Aboard ship for South America, the Secretary prepared a complicated economic resolution favouring bilateral or multilateral negotiations for eliminating barriers to trade, abandonment of special trade preferences and import and export prohibitions, and equality of treatment based on an unconditional most-favoured-nations clause.[9]

The secretary knew, however, that nothing could be accomplished in the area of freer trade at Montevideo without the approval of Saavedra Lamas, foreign minister and head of delegation from Argentina. In his memoirs, Hull singled out Saavedra Lamas as the leader of anti-American forces whenever a conference was held. Señor Saavedra Lamas wished to take the lead in arbitrating the so-called Chaco War between Bolivia and Paraguay with an anti-war pact.[10]

Initially, Secretary Hull did not favour the Lamas peace initiative because the United States was committed to the Kellogg-Briand Pact (1928), which was based on the premise that wars could be prevented by getting every nation of the world to promise not to make war. Hull was mainly interested in appeasing Argentina without relinquishing United States hegemony. At the same time he hoped to sell his economic plan and convince the conferees of American commitment to the Good

---

9   Hull, pp. 319-21, 353.

10   *Ibid.*, pp. 325-26.

Neighbor Policy. He found the political atmosphere at Montevideo extremely hostile, "like a blue snow in January."[11] According to Hull,

> One of my first sights from the ship was billboards with the huge words: "Down with Hull." And some of the newspapers shown me spoke of the "big bully" who had come down from the North, and wondered what he was up to now. Most of the press of Montevideo and Buenos Aires across the Plata River raw-hided our country and our delegation, called us names, and threw out the idea that we were down there, as usual, for purely selfish, narrow purposes.[12]

Only at the last moment did Argentina send a delegation headed by Lamas. Hull practically beat them to their hotel, and met Lamas at once. Señor Lamas was cool, Hull patronizing. With ego-building attention, the American secretary prepared a proposal on peace for Lamas to deliver at the conference, and Hull quoted the Argentinian as saying, "We shall be the two wings of the dove of peace, you the economic and I the political."[13] This was an abrupt turn-around. As the conference closed, Hull reflected that "the American delegation had succeeded in all its plans."[14]

There could be no doubt about which plan Hull considered the most important. Fresh from his triumph in South America and armed with the endorsement of practically the entire hemisphere, the secretary of state wasted no time in turning trading principles into law. A draft of a Reciprocal Trade Agreements Bill was in the hands of President Roosevelt by February 1934. It passed Congress by huge majorities, and the president signed it on June 12, 1934.[15] Renewable at three-year intervals, it provided for reciprocal, bilateral agreements with other nations and

---

11　*Ibid.*, p. 324.

12　*Ibid*, p. 324.

13　*Ibid.*, p. 329.

14　*Ibid.*, p. 338.

15　*Ibid.*, p. 357. See also, John E. Findling, *Close Neighbors, Distant Friends: United States-Central American Relations* (New York: Greenwood Press,

gave the executive the power to alter tariffs by as much as 50 percent on an unconditional most-favoured-nation principle. During 1935, Hull's State Department concluded bilateral agreements with Brazil, Colombia, Haiti and Honduras, and was negotiating with nine other Latin American countries.

By 1935, however, the State Department in Washington was already alerted to impending world crisis, and in the words of Secretary Hull, "the newborn friendship among the American Republics required solidifying."[16] Hull lobbied now for an extraordinary conference of the 21 Inter-American States, to be convened at Buenos Aires on December 1, 1936. The danger to hemispheric security was obvious. Civil War in Spain, representing a fascist threat to democratic government, aggression by Mussolini in Africa, the stance of Hitler in Europe and Japan in China demanded a response. Germany was engaged in a concerted effort to deprive the United States of its markets and influence in Latin America.

Nobody was more concerned about fascist penetration of Latin America than Secretary of State Cordell Hull. Nazi Germany, he believed, had become the dominant influence in South America.[17] One artifice of the Berlin government was to undermine United States trade with Latin America. Under a plan worked out by Hitler's advisers, Germany accepted barter as a method of payment in international trade. It paid for goods in scrip, which could only be used for the purchase of German goods. Much of what Germany exported was armaments, and it became the main supplier to Latin America by far.[18]

Considering the Nazi hysteria in the United States at the time, Hull probably exaggerated the extent of German influence in Latin America, but, more significantly, the threat to American security was genuine,

---

1987), p. 89.

16   Hull, p. 493; Dallek, p. 122.

17   Hull, p. 495.

18   *Ibid.*, p. 496.

and it was a major reason Hull wanted to convene a Buenos Aires conference. Now the free trade issue was to be integrated with a geopolitical agenda, and if Secretary Hull expected to see a lining up of the 20 other delegations behind his proposals, he was sadly mistaken. A different South America greeted him from the one he had left at Montevideo three years earlier, and even the presence of Franklin Roosevelt at the opening session could not help him. Leading countries of the Americas, unlike the United States, had begun to prosper, and they now held the bargaining cards.

When the Great Depression struck in 1929, Latin American economies were devastated. Largely without industrial bases, they depended on resource and agricultural exports to buy the manufactured goods they required. The economic disaster was compounded by the United States tariff. Because of the depression, Chile defaulted on its national external debt, but so did many other countries of Latin America. Defaults began in 1931, and by 1934 only Argentina, Haiti, and the Dominican Republic continued normal servicing of their external debts.[19]

Brazil defaulted with others, but by 1930 it had begun a vigorous industrialization process that was the envy of its neighbours. Unlike the United States and numerous other countries, Brazil by 1937 reached a level of per capita income higher than that of 1929.[20] Argentina suffered perhaps the least economically among Latin American countries. By 1935, the Argentinian economy had reached its mid-1929 levels, something the United States had not accomplished.[21] Argentina, in fact, was prepared to contest the United States in its traditional role as leader of the hemisphere.

At the Buenos Aires Conference of 1936, Saavedra Lamas, having just received a Nobel Peace Prize (with a boost from Hull) for ending the Chaco War, was elected permanent chairman. There he did his best

---

19   Carlos P. Diaz Alejandro, "Latin America in the 1930s," in Rosemary Thorp, ed., *Latin America in the 1930s* (London, Macmillan, 1984), p. 20.

20   Luiz Bresser Perevia, *Development and Crisis in Brazil, 1930-1983* (Boulder: Westview Press, 1984), p. 234.

21   Arturo O'Connell, "Argentina in the Depression," in Thorp, ed., p. 199.

to deter American aims and promote his version of the Drago Doctrine of nonintervention.[22] As a result, discussions on the "Maintenance, Preservation and Reestablishment of Peace," were accompanied by an "Additional Protocol Relative to Non-intervention."

The Protocol was what Latin America, led by Lamas, had been attempting for many years to force on the United States: a binding guarantee that the United States would respect the autonomy of the Latin American countries.[23] Of the proposals for peace, only the Protocol received an unqualified endorsement by all delegates.

A further blow to Hull's initiatives came when the Conference considered his favourite project, the lowering of trade barriers, and rejected a proposal for a multilateral truce.[24] By the time the conference closed, the atmosphere was so intense that delegations were flinging about such words as "pigs" and "liars." Because of a diplomatic cold, Hull's closing address was read for him, and Lamas failed to offer the usual courtesy of seeing him off.[25]

The Eighth International Conference of American States at Buenos Aires in 1936 was no success for the United States. Rejection of Hull's "tariff truce," a demand that first surfaced during the London Economic Conference of 1933, signalled the beginning of the end of his international crusade for free trade talks. Weakened because it needed unanimity or nothing, the United States compromised with a bloc of resentful Latin Americans, who held all the good cards: healthy economies in key nations, alternative sources of export and import, the Argentinian challenge and a threat of global war that endangered hemispheric security.

---

22   Hull, p. 499.

23   *Report of the Delegation of the United States of America to the Inter-American Conference for the Maintenance of Peace, Buenos Aires, Argentina, Dec. 1-23, 1936* (Washington: Government Printing Office, 1937), p. 19.

24   Gellman, p. 67.

25   Dallek, p. 134; Gellman, p. 67.

A threat of war, now preoccupying the State Department, failed to deter Hull from his dogged pursuit of trade agreements. On November 17, 1938, he finally persuaded Great Britain to alter its Imperial Preference system. Canada and Britain signed a trade agreement with the United States.[26] In December, at the Ninth International Conference of American States in Lima, Peru, the delegates agreed to a stronger declaration of solidarity, and Hull prevailed upon them, once again, to reiterate his pronouncements on freer trade.[27] Three months after war erupted in Europe in 1939, Secretary Hull was back in Congress to urge renewal of his Reciprocal Trade Agreements Act. In his words, it would "serve as a cornerstone around which the nations could rebuild their commerce on liberal lines when the war ended."[28] When Congress renewed the law the United States had reciprocity agreements with 21 nations covering about two-thirds of its trade.[29]

Again, in 1943, when the United States had agreements with 27 countries, Hull rejoiced in a two-year renewal that was to reach beyond his retirement in 1944. And when news of Franklin Roosevelt's death reached the former secretary on April 12, 1945, he was dashing off a letter to the Ways and Means Committee of the House of Representatives that urged them to extend, once again, the Reciprocal Trade Agreements Act of 1934.[30]

Reciprocal agreements alone, however, would never satisfy Cordell Hull, who settled in the '30s and '40s for a trade-off in the face of a foreign policy dilemma. Great Power conflict dictated that he use the limited coercive and persuasive clout of the United States to cut Latin America free from German influence. The trade-off was, do you desire

---

26   Hull, *Memoirs*, p. 530.

27   *Ibid.*, p. 610.

28   *Ibid.*, p. 746.

29   Arthur Link and William B. Catton, *American Epoch* (New York: Alfred Knopf, 1980) I, p. 447.

30   Hull, *Memoirs*, II, pp. 1211-12; 1721.

long-term economic integration, or political unity in the short-run, where Great Power concerns so often dominate?

Perhaps a similar process was at work worldwide in the Cold War era, when Great Power conflict allowed free trade opponents to create a similar dilemma. The recent emergence of the United States as the single great power remaining could assist free trade forces. Danger lies, however, in new special interests, operating now on a global level. Protectionists who carry the banner of environmentalism and a list of work-place standards are already presenting trade-off demands.

Free Trade and the Future of North America

Michael A. Walker

THANK YOU, MR. CHAIRMAN, for the opportunity to join in these discussions about the North American Free Trade Agreement. The Fraser Institute has been very pleased to co-convene this event.

NAFTA will be perceived by historians as one of the most important treaties of this century because of what it promises for the future, not only for North America, but also for the hemisphere. We held a conference recently in Central America that attracted representatives from all over Latin America, as well as Canada and the United States. It is fair to say that there is enormous enthusiasm for securing a hemisphere-wide trade agreement. I believe that NAFTA is an important step in that direction.

I would like to accomplish two things in my address today. One is to talk briefly about negotiating strategy, or what we were trying to achieve in the agreement, and the extent to which we were successful. The second is to deal with what is, in the end, going to be one of the key issues in determining whether people will support this free trade agreement or not, namely, what happened under the free trade agreement of 1988 with the United States. There is a lot of support in Canada for the complaint that with the FTA we shot ourselves in one foot. People say we lost many jobs, and that the deal had a significant negative impact

on our industrial sector. Why would we then turn around and add
Mexico to this agreement and effectively shoot ourselves in the other
foot? Why not just get rid of the FTA and return to the happy circum-
stance that prevailed before we got involved in all of this? An answer
to this question will form the major portion of the latter part of my
analysis.

First of all, why did Canada get involved? It is fair to say that at one
time there was no support politically for entering into NAFTA. The
government of Canada originally rejected the notion of negotiating a
free trade agreement with Mexico. The political reaction was exactly as
I have pointed out. We ran into political difficulty with the FTA. Why
would we go ahead with another round of political punishment with
NAFTA?

Fortunately, what I would refer to as the saner heads prevailed. The
cabinet agreed to go along with a free trade arrangement with Mexico.
I believe there were two reasons for this change in attitude. The first was
a recognition that Mexico and the United States could do whatever they
wished, and, it appeared, were determined to proceed with a deal.

Such an agreement implied that Canada would face a new competi-
tor for our products in the U.S. market. The United States is our single
largest customer, and the FTA that we had negotiated granted us
superlative access to its market. We had obtained better access than any
other country in the world. Now, if the Mexicans negotiated a bilateral
agreement with the United States, this would cause us harm. There
would be some investment diversion from Canada to Mexico. It also
meant for us trade diversion. We stood to lose because of an agreement
that we could not influence.

The opportunity that existed for us was to get on board, to get inside
this agreement, instead of drawing up a bilateral pact with Mexico to
access its market and retrieve some of the benefits we stood to lose.
These benefits are significant. But here in Canada we are told time and
again that Mexico is a poor country. Why would we want to expand our
market access there? Why should we be concerned about getting access
to Mexico in order to reduce losses we would suffer as a result of the
United States being penetrated more aggressively by Mexico?

The reality is that Mexico is the largest trading partner for North
American industry. The average Mexican, although very poor, buys

about $500 worth of North American produced products from outside Mexico, namely from Canada and the United States. By comparison, the average Japanese buys only $425 worth of North American products, and the average European about $300 worth. So Mexicans are undeniably very significant trading partners right now for Canada and the United States. Admittedly, Canada's activity in the Mexican market today is very small. With NAFTA, however, we have an opportunity to expand our access to the Mexican market.

I think the number one reason why we argued for Canada to become involved was to offset potential losses. True, this may not be a very edifying rationale for pursuing such an agreement, but it is very pragmatic and an important reason for doing so. There is a second consideration that helps to explain why we rejected a bilateral trade deal with Mexico. Why should we encourage what certain economists (Paul and Ronald Wonnacott and Richard Lipsey) have called the "hub and spoke" model of North American economic integration, with the United States at the hub and each of the other countries out on the spokes? Eventually all of the countries of the hemisphere would be out on the spokes, the only country having access to all markets being the United States. It should be apparent that this is not a sensible way to organize things, for it reduces the negotiating power that each trading partner would have in striking a deal with the United States. It also makes little sense with regard to the unstated political considerations that accompany a trade arrangement. A trilateral or a multilateral arrangement eventually linking countries together is obviously preferable to allowing the United States to dominate each nation individually in trade relations or in other relations through time. For both of those reasons, it was strongly argued that Canada should pursue a NAFTA, that Canada should opt for a multilateral kind of integration in the hemisphere, with the completion of the agreement as the first step.

What are Canada's key objectives? I will cover them quickly so as not to steal Trade Minister Michael Wilson's thunder in discussing them. Moreover, I need to talk about them a little bit to justify my mentioning our just-released book on the subject. I heartily encourage you to peruse it, as it collects the opinions of outstanding Canadian, American and Mexican analysts. Entitled *Assessing NAFTA: A Trinational Analysis*, it looks at the deal from the point of view of all three countries to determine what their motives and objectives were, and then measures their success in a number of different sectors as well as in an overall sense.

From Canada's point of view, what did we gain? First, we gained tariff-free access, after ten years, for all Canadian exports to Mexico. This is very important because at the moment, although Mexicans have almost untrammelled access to the Canadian market, we face extraordinary barriers in getting into Mexico: import licensing difficulties in exporting our forest products and mining services and impediments to investing in its mining sector, which is very important in Canada. Mexico has rich mineral ore deposits. We would not have ensured access to develop these or to supply services to others engaged in their development unless we could negotiate an agreement with regard to services and export our products related to mining and these other areas.

A free Mexican market is also important to encourage things such as the importation of paper. A number of years ago I was doing a marketing survey in Mexico that involved a board game called "Poleconomy," which had been selling very well in Canada through the Fraser Institute. It is a game that teaches people how the economy functions. We were trying to produce it in Mexico and found that it was very expensive to do so. In fact, it was much more expensive to produce the game in Mexico than in Canada, and we could not understand why because everything else is so much cheaper to produce there. The reason, as it turned out, was the cost of paper.

Paper was very expensive in Mexico. Paper was, in fact, subject to import licensing. Apart from the fact that Canada is the world's largest exporter of paper, and such barriers are of great economic interest to us, the fact that access to paper supplies in Mexico is controlled relates directly to the freedom of the press. Here a seemingly straight economic issue of Canada not being able to export its forest products into Mexico relates in a fundamental way to Mexico's emergence as a democratic and free country. The elimination, over time, of these tariffs and other barriers is going to mean more than just swifter economic development in Mexico and a better market for paper and other materials. It is going to have an impact on a lot of other things as well.

With NAFTA, we have attained eventual elimination of import licensing requirements. Additionally, we have opportunities to bid now on major Mexican government procurement contracts. Mexican industry, in particular the energy industry, which is one of the largest in Mexico, is still very much a government-owned enterprise. The fact that we have obtained the right to bid on government procurement is very important in that industry and in other areas as well.

Under NAFTA, Canadian financial services companies will be able to open subsidiaries, invest in and acquire financial institutions in Mexico; i.e., banking, securities, and insurance. As some of you may know, Canadian banks are among the largest in the world. It is very important that we secure access to those markets for our financial services products.

There has been a major liberalization of the restrictive Mexican investment regime. In the past there were rules and counter trade requirements and all kinds of strings attached to investments. These have been essentially wiped out by the North American Free Trade Agreement, making it much more possible for Canadians and their agents to invest in Mexico on a secure basis.

We will, for example, have the opportunity to demand extra-national adjudication in the event that the government of Mexico should seize some part or impair the asset value of some investment made by a Canadian in Mexico. Disputes will be settled by a third party outside the Mexican government. The Mexican government has agreed to be bound by this kind of adjudication.

Most important of all is that, in terms of developing more trade with Mexico, Mexico has agreed to be bound by the trinational disputes settlements mechanism, which was a first for the Free Trade Agreement between Canada and the United States. Prior to the FTA, if the U.S. government, through its Commerce Department, took some action against a Canadian exporter into the U.S. market, then the U.S. political system, through the International Trade Commission, was the route by which a Canadian could seek redress. There was a final appeal to the U.S. court system but this was a lengthy, expensive, and uncertain course subject to the vagaries of legal delay.

With the FTA with the United States, there are, for the first time, binational panels wherein two Americans, two Canadians and a fifth person chosen at random from a list agreed to by both, settle disputes between the two countries. This has proved to be extraordinarily important. As you know, the case of wheat and pigs is an issue that went to the very highest levels—which is where this issue belongs! In the case of pigs, it went to the very highest level of adjudication and was settled in Canada's favour. In other words, we have found in this binational panel system a way of taking the politics out of international trade. This has been extended to the Mexico-Canada-U.S. agreement.

Most important, the Mexicans have agreed, in order to make compliance with the adjudications process possible, to reform their own judicial system, to go to the evidentiary-based process that is used both in Canada and the United States. Therefore, we will have Canadian activities in Mexico governed by a judicial process with which we are all familiar. Of course, this will not stop with Mexican commerce. It will spread throughout the whole of Mexican judiciary. In due course, it will have profound implications for the nation domestically.

We achieved all of these things, in terms of getting access to the Mexican market, that we have hoped for. In the meantime, we did not lose anything. In fact, we improved some of the conditions we had already achieved in the Canada-U.S. Free Trade Agreement, including improving this binational dispute mechanism that has now been made permanent. Earlier, it was just a temporary provision.

I wish now to return to the NAFTA background issue that I mentioned at the outset, namely the popular complaint, "Why should we sign this agreement with the Mexicans when we have lost so much with the agreement with the United States?" Is it because of the FTA of 1989 that employment and manufacturing have slumped in Canada? You will hear time and time again that in manufacturing we have lost 300,000 to 400,000 jobs. The employment statistics displayed in Chart 1 go back to 1970 and take us up to 1992. We see from the chart that a reduction in manufacturing employment as a fraction of total employment, as a recent occurrence in Canada, is not unusual. In fact, it is not unusual relative to our history, and neither is it unusual relative to what is happening in the United States.

The FTA between Canada and the United States has had very little to do with the progress of manufacturing employment as a fraction of total employment. To strengthen this argument, I want to survey the

Chart 1: Manufacturing Employment as a Percentage of Total Employment

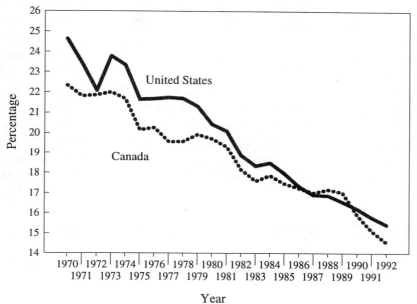

Source: Statistics Canada, *The Labour Force*, various issues.

history of Canadian unemployment back to 1911, and discuss unemployment shares in services, in agriculture and in other goods production, including manufacturing, mining, logging and all of the things involved in goods production. These employment data are presented in Chart 2.

Since the 20th century began, Canada has taken half of its labour force out of agriculture. Only 4 percent of our labour force is now employed on farms. Our task during the century has been to raise productivity by getting most people off the farm and into other occupations so that we could raise our standard of living.

In other words, we have witnessed a fantastic enhancement of our standard of living because we got people out of agriculture and into service production and manufacturing activities.

What have we learned about the decline of manufacturing? Considering all goods production activities, there has been a steady decline since the mid 1950s in those kinds of activities. We should not be surprised to find that during 1989, 1990, and 1991 they have also gone down. This is the ultimate direction in which the economy has been heading for a very long time, and it will continue to move in that direction.

The charts portray an ineluctable impression that goods production is the way of the past. Service production is the way of the future. Since 1900, we have greatly improved our standard of living as we have transformed our labour force, largely from goods employment, towards service employment. We should never allow ourselves to think that this represents a movement towards low wage and low quality kinds of

Chart 2: Historic Employment Shares (Census Years)

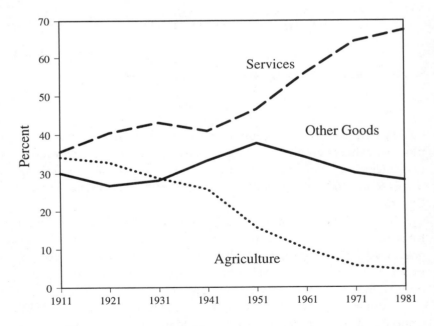

Source: Herbert G. Grubel and Michael A. Walker, *Service Industry Growth: Causes and Effects*, The Fraser Institute, 1989.

employment. If true, how could we have transformed our society from a largely goods-producing entity to a services-producing economy while simultaneously increasing our standard of living?

In 1946, for example, goods production encompassed 60 percent of our labour force, while only 40 percent were employed in the service industry. Today, about 25 percent are employed in goods (including both those which are manufactured and those which are not) and 75 percent in services. Consider this. How could we have raised our standard of living so substantially if all service jobs involve changing beds and washing floors? They are nothing of the sort. Service jobs include transportation, telecommunications, a small number of computer service jobs, a large number of financial services, real estate and insurance jobs, as well as legal, accounting, and health care service jobs, which are highly skilled and high paying. These jobs are a part of a lifestyle that has changed considerably since the 1940s.

The final message is that in terms of where we are heading, both as a society and internationally, we are going to find ourselves increasingly trading to get the manufactured goods that we want from other countries who are in an earlier phase of their development. This is perfectly natural, and it should not be deplored. The trade agreement with Mexico is an opportunity to take advantage of this natural and inevitable historic development.

The Emerging Architecture of North America

Stephen Blank

The Intent of the Canada-U.S. FTA

IT IS EASY TO MISUNDERSTAND the fundamental nature of the Canada-U.S. Trade Agreement (FTA), to see it as a trade agreement and starting point for U.S.-Canada economic integration. In reality, the FTA was not the beginning of the process of economic integration between the United States and Canada, and it is not concerned primarily with trade.

Rather, the agreement marked the recognition by both countries of the high levels of bilateral economic integration that had already been achieved. It was less an effort to stimulate new trade than to stabilize an emerging environment in which vast and rapidly increasing interdependencies made each side vulnerable to actions by the other. Finally, it acknowledged the need to develop new rules and practices that would lessen the danger that the gains of wider markets would be eroded by unilateral actions.

If high levels of economic integration preceded the FTA, the agreement nonetheless intensified the process of building new political, administrative and regulatory structures and practices for managing a relationship that transcends national control over national economies. With the new dispute settlement mechanism, we see the emergence, however modest, of a binational system of law, precedent and practice. And by raising levels of confidence that the process of bilateral economic integration will not be interrupted, the FTA has also been a powerful stimulus to cross-border corporate reorganization and rationalization.[1]

A "North American economic space"

As we have noted, in a fundamental sense, the Canada-U.S. FTA was not about trade. Much, probably the largest share, of Canada-U.S. trade occurs within companies. It is more accurate to talk about complex, cross-border production and marketing networks than trade in a classic sense of arm's length transactions across national borders. What results is a much "deeper," more "structural" integration that builds upon trade-based linkages of the "GATT era."[2]

Research now being carried out by the Americas Society on the changing structure and strategy of U.S. firms in North America throws some light on the nature of this emerging economic system.[3] Canada's

---

1   See Isaiah Litvak, "U.S. Multinationals: Repositioning the Canadian Subsidiary," *Business in the Contemporary World*, Autumn 1990, and Joseph D'Cruz and James Fleck, *Yankee Canadians in the Global Economy* (London, Ontario: The National Centre for Management Research and Development, The University of Western Ontario, 1988).

2   See the notion of "Complex interdependence" developed by Robert O. Keohane and Joseph S. Nye in their *Power and Interdependence: World Politics in Transition* (Boston: Little, Brown and Company, 1977). But Albert Bressand adds a much deeper understanding of the changing nature of corporate networks. See, for example, the various essays in "Project Promethee," *Perspectives*, No. 9: "1991: The Global Challenge, Promethee," Paris (1989) or Albert Bressand, "Beyond Interdependence: 1992 as a global challenge," *International Affairs*, 66:1 (1990).

3   We have recently completed a series of Working Papers dealing with various aspects of changes in corporate structure and strategy.

manufacturing industries are undergoing extensive rationalization and restructuring. Subsidiaries of U.S. firms operating in Canada—key agents in Canada's rise to the world's highest standard of living—have been profoundly affected.

Canadian branch plants of the 1960s and 1970s have essentially withered and died in the face of the new competitive dynamic. Strategies to "Canadianize" management, decision-making, and production and marketing strategies—the essence of "good Canadian corporate citizenship" in the 1970s—have been overtaken by the changing nature of technology, competition, and globalization in the world economy.[4]

Powerful forces are redirecting Canada's economy from an East-West to a North-South orientation.[5] Canadian subsidiaries are now less likely to produce solely for Canadian markets. No longer defined nationally, markets are now seen in global or continental terms or in terms of cross-border regions.

These developments are hardly new, although the pace of change has quickened markedly in the past two years. First, instead of economic isolation, Canadians have opted for wholesale economic liberalization with their major trading partner; the FTA and NAFTA have codified this, going far beyond the sectoral route taken with the Auto Pact. Second, change is being driven by forces that reach far beyond the influence of Canadian elites. Globalization, worldwide lowering of tariffs through the GATT, rising levels of international competition, and new technologies and innovations in production and management are the forces driving change in Canada and elsewhere around the world.

---

4 See Joseph LaPalombara and Stephen Blank, *Multinational Corporations and National Elites: A Study in Tensions* (New York: The Conference Board, 1976) for an analysis of the environment for U.S. firms in Canada in the mid-1970s and of their responses.

5 See Thomas Courchene, *In Praise of Renewed Federalism* (Toronto: C.D. Howe Institute, 1991).

The nature of restructuring

Change in the structure and strategy of U.S. firms operating in Canada should be seen as a response to global change. In turn, the response of these firms (as well as Canadian-owned firms) has driven structural change in the Canadian and U.S. economies.

Evidence suggests strongly that the U.S. branch plant manufacturing sector in Canada has given way to subsidiary operations that must survive within the production web of their parent firms. The role of Canadian subsidiaries, like that of all units within firms, increasingly emerges out of the competition among entities within the firm for access to mandates, capital, and the development of new products. Rationalization in the strategy and structure of their operations is likely to continue, becoming a permanent part of the subsidiary's day-to-day operations. Canadian firms have changed as well, reacting in similar ways to the same forces as foreign-owned firms in Canada.

Intensive rationalization and restructuring of the manufacturing industries is not a phenomenon that affects Canadian subsidiaries alone, however. The restructuring of Canadian industry is a dimension (relatively limited from the perspective of many American headquarters) of a pattern of corporate restructuring and rationalization on a continental and global basis. What is often viewed from Canada as an isolated and U.S.-engineered restructuring of the Canadian economy is in reality a part of a much wider process.[6]

Often the reorganization of firms is explained only in terms of location of production. Canadian critics of the FTA (and U.S. critics of NAFTA) have argued that the FTA provides foreign-owned firms the

---

6   This is not to suggest, however, that restructuring is not particularly painful in Canada. The lack of adjustment in Canadian manufacturing industries in the middle-1980s was responsible for a sharp divergence in American and Canadian productivity growth in this period. "This inferior productivity performance, combined with a further deterioration in relative wages and the near-30 percent appreciation of the dollar (from trough to peak) generated a colossal unit-labour-cost disparity" with the United States. Thomas Courchene, "Mon pays, c'est l'hiver: reflections of a market populist," *Canadian Journal of Economics*, November 1992, p. 764.

perfect incentive to cease manufacturing in Canada. In what might be called the doomsday scenario of the FTA, U.S. firms, after having withdrawn production and displaced Canadian workers, would then simply supply Canadian markets from plants in the United States. Instead of being a country of U.S. branch plants, Canada would become a country of U.S. warehouses. This scenario is based primarily on the view that the location of production is determined largely by the cost of factors of production, particularly labour, and the regulatory environment. In this light, Mexico is an industrialist's dream: cheap labour and a questionable commitment to environmental protection.

While this scenario has been played out in some cases, it will not reach the proportions opponents of the FTA and NAFTA predict. Because the entire production process is undergoing change in response to global competition, it is simply wrong to think that what determines locational decisions are how cheap workers are and how much a company can get away with environmentally. If that were the case, Canada would have been "warehoused" a long time before the FTA ever came into force.

Firms will continue to develop and manufacture in the United States and Canada because these countries already possess the human capital—people with skills, knowledge, experience, and commitment to business success—that more than makes up for any cost advantages Mexico and other low-wage countries have. If there are any big losers, they may be the Newly Industrializing Countries (NICs) of Asia.

In our view, the restructuring occurring today is more complex, affecting the fundamental tenets of industrial production and business management. The proper analogy is the change in production and corporate systems in the 1880s and 1890s, which led to the rise of technologies of mass production and the system of industrial capitalism. Then, the entire system shifted. Today we are experiencing another paradigm shift, and the evidence is not hard to find. The corporate giants of the United States—companies like GM and IBM, viewed as the symbols of U.S. post-war industrial capitalism—are entering into struggles that go well beyond the problem of weak markets. Even as economic recovery gains force, many of North America's most important firms are struggling to find the strategy and organizational structure that will ensure their competitiveness (and in some cases survival) in the new global business dynamic.

One need only look to the business page to find the hard evidence of the restructuring. The magnitude and scope of job losses is staggering, affecting not only production but management positions as well. Evidence confirms that these losses are structural rather than cyclical, that they are not likely to be recreated when economic conditions improve, and that more downsizing can be expected. A recent survey of more than 800 companies by the American Management Association found that one in four companies is planning work-force reductions by the middle of 1993. That is the highest level in the six-year period of the survey.[7] Clearly, restructuring in North America has not yet ended.

An "emerging North American jurisprudence"

Allan Gotleib, a former Canadian ambassador to the United States and a noted legal scholar, recently suggested that the integration of economies in North America is making international law in its traditional sense increasingly irrelevant.[8] Relations between the U.S. and Canada are much less structured by international rules and regulations, he stated, than by domestic policies that shape trade and investment flows and influence competitive advantage. Gotleib notes the economic integration gives rise to an increasing number of regulatory incongruities. If we have free trade, he argues, regulatory arrangements based on national sovereignty must be revised, and the same rules should apply to all when they are dealing in the same markets.

Gotleib speaks of the general emergence of a "new jurisprudence," the beginnings of which are already visible in the Canada-U.S. dispute settlement process. This new jurisprudence builds on the domestic legal

---

7   Steve Lohr, "Big Companies Cloud Recovery by Cutting Jobs," *The New York Times* (December 17, 1992).

8   "International Law in a North American Economic Space," Lecture delivered at the Americas Society/Canadian Affairs, November 21, 1992.

structures of the two nations, but constitutes a substantially new addition to their legal systems. He sees in the future a tri-level legal and political structure in North America: an overarching North American framework, with national systems and strong regional systems within it.

American and Canadian firms are evolving new strategies and structures for new North American markets. For many businesses, it makes much sense for a division in Southern Ontario or New York to supply a region composed of Eastern Canada and the Northeastern states rather than to ship across the continent to Vancouver. The economic logic of an emerging North American economic space is eroding the political logic of national economies.

A new "architecture" of North America

Developments in North America suggest that the conventional state-centred approach is now inadequate to an understanding of emerging political, economic, legal, and corporate systems. This is not meant to suggest that those proponents of "globalization" are accurate when they contend that borders are becoming irrelevant in a world characterized by increasingly widespread markets.[9] Rather, notions of sovereignty that have structured thinking about international relations and the international economy since the late 19th century, and particularly since the end of World War II, must be revised in light of current developments.[10]

---

9   Kenichi Ohmae is probably the best known advocate of this view. See his *The Borderless World* (New York: Harper Collins, 1990) or "Managing in a Borderless World," *Harvard Business Review*, May-June 1989.

10   See Andrew Schoenfield's view that one of the key characteristics of the postwar era was the increased control over national economies by public authorities and the "pursuit of intellectual coherence" in the form of "long-range national planning." *Modern Capitalism; The Changing Balance of Public and Private Power* (Oxford: Oxford University Press, 1965), pp. 64 and 67.

Kenichi Ohmae urges countries to join "the interdependent and borderless interlinked economy" forming around the world.[11] But we are not moving toward Ohmae's "borderless" world. We are heading toward a world of multiple borders, many of which are overlapping, and political authorities on different levels that increasingly share (and compete to control) functions. The outcome of present trends will not be the simple erosion of the state-system either upward, into some sort of North American sovereign entity, or downward, to the independence of various sub-national regional entities, but rather the emergence of a more complex system of "linked loyalties" and "pooled sovereignties."[12]

Stronger regions within North America

Trade and investment flows have not grown evenly across borders. Instead, flows of goods, services, capital, and people have deepened between particular areas in each country. Thus, at the same time as we see the emergence of an overarching Canada-U.S. FTA, we also see heightened regional differentiation within North America.

Freer and vastly increasing trade and investment flows give regions within nations much greater choice in economic development. Freer trade with the United States, rather than leading to the "Americanization" of Canada—so feared by Canadian economic nationalists—has really opened up the door to greater differentiation within the Canadian and American economies.

Canada is one of the world's most trade-based economies, but Canada's economy is really four distinct regional economies: British Columbia, the Prairies, central Canada (itself an increasingly uncertain

---

11 Kenichi Ohmae, "The Interlinked Economy," *Chief Executive*, October 1990, p. 50.

12 See, for example, William Wallace, *The Transformation of Western Europe* (London and New York: Council on Foreign Relations Press, 1990) for a view of similar developments in Western Europe.

amalgam of Ontario and Quebec), and Atlantic Canada. And Canada's economic performance from the mid-1970s onward shows the impact of these regional diversities. International economic integration has intensified the tendency for Canada's regional economies to relate to each other as a zero-sum game in which good times for one region are achieved at the expense of the others. When international commodity prices boom, central Canadian manufacturers complain. When natural resource prices fall, the resource-producing regions in Canada's West suffer while Toronto feels no pain at all. This regionalization of economic trends stimulates internal migration flows that further add to regional imbalances.

The internationalization of the American economy has also intensified regional disparities. U.S. states, no less than Canadian provinces, compete increasingly for foreign investment and to promote local exports.[13] More broadly, American states seek to create competitive advantage with new mixes of extractive and distributive policies, by reorganizing administrative structures and by launching new initiatives in support of education, science and advanced technology.[14]

What these developments suggest, following Michael Porter's notion of "clusters of excellence,"[15] is that clusters are more likely to develop

---

13   See James D. McNiven, "Challenge and Response: The Rise of State Export Development Policies in the U.S.," Centre for International Business, Dalhousie University: Discussion Papers in International Business, No. 80, April 1989; Japan Economic Institute, "Globalization, Economic Realities Force States to Reassess their Overseas Programs," JEI Report: Washington, No. 19A, May 15, 1992; and Earl Fry, "The U.S. States and Foreign Economic Policy," unpublished paper prepared for the Conference on "Managing Foreign Relations in Federal States," Australia House, London, March 11-12, 1992.

14   See Jurgen Schmandt, "Regional roles in the governance of the scientific state," in Jurgen Schmandt and Robert Wilson, eds., *Growth Policy in the Age of High Technology: The Role of Regions and States* (Boston: Unwin Hyman, 1990).

15   Michael Porter, *The Competitive Advantage of Nations* (New York: The Free Press, 1990), Chapter 4.

for many industrial sectors at regional and local rather than national levels, and that a North American economic geography is emerging, characterized by increasing specialization and competition among sub-national and cross-border regions.

Economics more than ethnicity help us understand developments, for example, in Quebec. Rita Dionne-Marsolais, a leader of the Parti Quebecois, writes that "while the rest of Canada believes Quebec's aspirations are basically cultural, in reality they are strongly economic." As barriers to trade and investment have declined and trade and investment volumes increased, Quebec, she says, has learned that its destiny lies increasingly in its economic relationships outside of Canada.[16]

Regionalization of our economies accounts for the growing importance of cross-border entities such as "Cascadia" (made up of Oregon, Washington, British Colombia and Alaska) or "PNWER"—the "Pacific Northwest Economic Region," an association of state and provincial legislators from Alberta, British Colombia, Alaska, Oregon, Washington, Montana, and Idaho.[17] NAFTA's impact, for example, will be felt mainly in the Mexican states that border the Rio Grande and in California and Texas. Even without an agreement, a new, cross-border economic region is emerging: "We're moving towards the integration of Texas and northeast Mexico into a single region," says Socrates Rizzo, the governor of the state of Nuevo Leon,[18] and hundreds of Texan and Mexican companies have poured across the border to open offices, start up joint ventures, or set up distribution arrangements.

The new architecture is not oriented solely on a north-south axis. Japanese and Pacific trade and investment flows are also shaping the new North American architecture. About 40 percent of all U.S. exports to Japan, for example, originate in three states—California, Washington,

---

16   Rita Dionne-Marsolais, "The FTA: A Building Block for Quebec," *The American Review of Canadian Studies*, Vol. 21, Nos. 2/3, Summer, Autumn 1991.

17   Terry Brainerd Chadwick, "Hands Across the Border: The Pacific Northwest Economic Partnership," *The New Pacific*, Fall 1989.

18   *The Economist*, June 27, 1992.

and Oregon. The interests of these states are influenced substantially by this deepening Pacific relationship.

Implications of the new architecture

One critical implication is the eroding capacity of central governments to "manage" what are no longer national economies. In both Canada and the United States, economic globalization reduces the capacity of the central government to protect regions from the impact of changes in international price movements or to create durable prosperity.[19] In both countries—not just in Canada—changes in the federal system are shifting many new responsibilities and powers to states and provinces.

Both countries confront serious institutional frictions that are accentuated by this shifting balance of power between central and state/provincial authorities. In Canada, the failure of central governmental institutions to represent regional interests has long been a source of frustration among non-Central Canadians,[20] and demands for institutional reform have increased dramatically in recent months.

On the U.S. side, state governments are often poorly structured to bear the kind of social and fiscal responsibilities they now confront. Archaic state fiscal systems and state legislatures, which heavily overrepresent rural interests, are common problems. Alice Rivlin, one of the most highly regarded American economists, has recently laid out a "blueprint for pushing power down to the states and cities."[21] She feels the federal government should manage social insurance, foreign affairs,

---

19 See Stephen Blank, Marshall Cohen and Guy Stanley, "Redefining Sovereignty for the 21st Century," *The American Review of Canadian Studies*, Vol. 21, Nos. 2/3, Summer/Autumn 1992.

20 See R. Ken Weaver, "Political Institutions and Canada's Constitutional Crisis," in R. Ken Weaver, ed., *The Collapse of Canada?* (Washington: The Brookings Institution, 1992), and Peter Brimelow, *The Patriot Game; National Dreams and Political Realities* (Toronto: Key Porter Books, 1986), Chapter 2.

21 See Alice Rivlin, *Reviving the American Dream: The Economy, the States and the Federal Government* (Washington: The Brookings Institution, 1992), Chapter 6.

and areas where activities cross state borders, as well as finance the health care system. States should be responsible for a productivity agenda that includes education, training, community development, housing, and the infrastructure. She suggests that some fiscal and policy responsibilities might be exercised by groups of states working together.[22]

It is inappropriate, however, to try to conceptualize these changes simply in terms of transfer or devolution of authority within existing federal systems. What is going on is more complex than this. The direction of change is not toward a "borderless" world but toward more complex political organizations. As national borders no longer define the boundaries of social systems, those boundaries will assume a rather wider range of shapes. For example, efforts to heighten competitive advantage are more likely to be undertaken successfully, at least for many sectors, at local and regional rather than national levels and, similarly, most observers feel that education is more likely to evolve as a local or regional rather than a national responsibility. But many environmental issues transcend regional or even national borders and few would deny the need to maintain national or international rules that ensure economic openness.

In this sense, what is happening in North America may well be moving us closer toward what Europeans call "subsidiarity"—that decisions should be devolved to the lowest level of government capable of handling them—than to more traditional definitions of federalism.[23]

It is clear that a general trend toward devolution will also create substantial needs for re-centralization of authority in certain areas. Standards and rules are required to maintain a "level playing field," for example, in terms of trade, treatment of investment, and fair competition. In the emerging system of governance in North America, national

---

22   "Shifting Power Out of the Beltway," *Fortune*, June 29, 1992.

23   B. Guy Peters, "Bureaucratic Politics and the Institutions of the European Community," in Alberta M. Spragia, ed., *Euro-Politics: Institutions and Policymaking in the "New" European Community* (Washington: The Brookings Institution, 1992) pp. 110-111.

sovereignty will be unbundled both downwards and upwards, and the boundaries of new systems of authority will differ from traditional national borders.

What all of this suggests, finally, is that competition among authorities for control over different systems is likely to increase and could well dominate politics for the foreseeable future. Rivlin emphasizes the need "to sort out functions of government—both between the federal government and the states and within the states—to clarify missions and make sure everyone knows who is responsible for which activities."[24] Sorting it out would be difficult at the best of times. These are not the best of times.

First, all parties bring a certain "baggage" with them into the game. Globalization has disrupted long-established patterns of social relationships. The import-substitution-based economy of John A. Macdonald no longer exists and, without this, many Canadians fear that they possess insufficient common interests to maintain Canadian identity and cultural coherence.[25] Less profoundly, but still painfully, the effects of the integration of the U.S. economy into global markets are taken by many Americans as evidence of a national decline.

As national sovereignty and the capacity of central governments to guarantee prosperity both erode, it is scarcely surprising that there is a strong economic nationalist/protectionist backlash. Nor should it be surprising that this movement unites groups on the Canadian left and the American right and much of the North American labour movement. The grinding recession, the battering American and, even more, Canadian firms have taken, and the escalating number of lost jobs all keep eyes focused on shares of a shrinking pie.

---

24 Rivlin, *op. cit.*, p. 180.

25 For an excellent review of Canadian second thoughts about the Free Trade Agreement, see Gilles Gherson, "Canadian Continentalism and Industrial Competitiveness," in Fen Osler Hampson and Christopher Maule, eds., *Canada Among Nations 1992-93: A New World Order?* (Ottawa: Carleton University Press, 1992).

The pain is more intense because the impact of globalization comes on top of an ongoing revolution in the way we make things. Driven by slow growth, heightened global competition and the availability of new technology, the structure of production and employment is changing in the 1990s in a way comparable only to the revolution of mass production in the 1880s and '90s. What this means is that many of the most secure North American workers in the post-World War II world—our core middle class of high school educated, unskilled, blue collar industrial workers and the vast service economy that grew around them and their factories—are being left high and dry as firms struggle to compete by adopting new capital-driven technologies.

One cannot deny, finally, there is danger that political systems could lurch in unexpected directions. History is not short of ironies. Economists from Adam Smith to Karl Marx were sure that the thrust of capitalism was fundamentally international and that it would destroy the surviving remnants of medieval state systems. But the world of the 20th century and modern industrial capitalism was shaped far more by statesmen such as Bismarck, by "gas and water" socialists such as the Fabians and by Meiji reformers, all of whom saw the rising industrial system in the service of the modern state. The emergence of the new industrial era at the end of the 19th century coincided not with a new internationalism driven by international markets or by international classes, but rather by intense and vicious nationalism.

The danger is that the growing regionalization of the North American economy could lead to fragmentation, regional trade barriers, and exclusiveness, or to efforts to revive old national sovereignties. But the opportunities are enormous: enhanced efficiency, more rapid growth, and greater regional variety and autonomy.

Transition Without Rules? Mexico Between a Trilateral Agreement and an Effective Implementation of NAFTA

M. Teresa Gutéirrez-Haces

THE MEXICAN DEBATE OVER NAFTA has opened discussions about other profound changes in the country's political, economic, legal and social policies. We must wait for history to unfold to know the consequences—for now we can only discern a limitless will to transform.

NAFTA negotiations are concluded. The numerous clauses contained in the two-volume agreement lay the foundations for a new commercial future in North America, but are encoded in a way so complex as to be understood only by a select group of experts.

I begin with my first impressions of the final document. Remember, NAFTA was written and negotiated piecewise, and final negotiations fell to a small number of political officials. What's more, it does not answer what is justly any Mexican's first question: "How is NAFTA going to affect me?"

The agreement was part of a broad spectrum of demands for substantial change in the Mexican economic and social situation. My paper addresses the transition—institutional, legislative, economic, and political—necessary to move Mexico from its protectionist past to a free trade future.

Even without considering the problems of implementation and parallel agreements, this domestic transition is the greatest challenge to the Salinas administration's plans for modernization. The changes are part of a general criticism of the protectionist model and reflect Mexican hopes for the new market ideal. I am surprised that criticism of the old economic model, the current initiative for change and the new model proposed all come from the same political party.

Since 1982, debate has been dominated by those who view the market as an efficient allocator and those who believe that excessive regulation by the state led Mexico into an acceleration of its economic crisis. But in Mexico, presenting a free market alternative is a false choice, for the state has always applied overwhelming influence on economic reality.

In this case, the priorities as well as some of the actors have changed, but we cannot speak of a weakening of the state. Privatization, the creation of a new constitutional framework, a social policy embedded in programs such as Pronasol (the national solidarity program), etc., are elements of a transition that leads to what has officially been labelled state reform.

International and domestic changes are interwoven. Mexico faces growing protectionism on various fronts, from GATT to U.S. courts. Mexican citizens are bewildered by the contrast between a promise of untrammelled international commerce and the reality of accusations and penalties applied to key export markets for tuna, shrimp, steel, and cement. Perplexity grows when a public accustomed to nationalistic and official anti-American rhetoric hears foreigners (Canadians and Americans) complaining that Mexico is robbing them of jobs. How can a commitment to the New Order be confirmed in the midst of such confusing signals from abroad and high transition costs at home?

Commercial protectionism may strengthen the American social pact, but it does not help in a transition process so difficult for Mexicans. Trade challenges have inflicted costs upon numerous Mexican exporters, from those in the broom industry to the giant Cimentos de Mexico (CEMEX). This firm, which controls 68.2 percent of the market in Mexico, recently lost $502 million in a trade-related dispute with the United States.

Mexico's problems were exacerbated when President Bush and Prime Minister Mulroney left office, creating an uncertain and perhaps distrustful political environment, one which will severely test leadership and the strength of the North American trade alliance. It will force the Mexican government to redesign its lobbying policy.

Within Mexico, there has been an undeniable rush to dismantle protectionism. On the positive side, Mexican industry has become more efficient, and consumers have benefited from the withdrawal of state sponsorship of favoured monopolies. Entrepreneurial imagination now extends to the United States and Canada. On the other hand, the adjustment costs can be significant, especially for small business and agriculture.

Mexico's strategy of modernization has attracted international attention. But it is important to distinguish between strong entrepreneurs and industrialists, with ample sources of foreign investments and clear development strategies, and the large number of small, ill-prepared business people who employ 70 percent of the country's work-force.

I believe that these subtle adjustments should be regulated by government, which can best ameliorate the troubles caused by plant-closings, capital flight and unemployment. It is clear to me that the cost of change is unequally borne, depending as it does upon the size and importance of the economic unit.

Mexico's serious problems are not solely the result of the end of protectionism. Some are related to foreign and domestic investments that concentrate economic power. Twelve groups control 32 percent of manufacturing and monopolize the production of copper, glass, corn flour, cement, aluminium, and cellulose, among others. Eleven branches of the most dynamic industrial sectors are controlled by one to four companies.

In 1992, 20 financial groups were consolidated; they absorb 97 percent of total bank deposits and control 89 percent of all brokerage house stock, as well as 84 percent of leasing companies' investments and 79 percent of all factoring. (All this information can be found in Mexican

Stock Exchange—MSE—reports). I think such oligopolistic power translates into an ability to set the rules during the evolution toward NAFTA.

Although all business in Mexico must buy technology, those unconnected with powerful economic groups will have a hard time of it. About 90 percent of all companies (they being the small ones) have done practically nothing to apply the National Agreement to Raise Productivity and Competitiveness that was signed by the government, entrepreneurs, and union officials. For example, despite the creation of a Competitiveness Triangle—an alliance between government and productive sectors—and an announcement by President Salinas to eliminate import duties on agricultural machinery, farm activity actually decreased 1.3 percent and overall growth was only 2.4 percent in 1992.

The changeover has been accompanied by a $25 billion trade deficit, a natural consequence of the inflow of investment capital, a thing desirable and necessary for the revitalization of the economy. But the deficit is also driven by a 4.19 percent increase in consumer imports between 1986 and 1992.

Foreign investment in Mexico is rising rapidly. Amounting to more than $50 billion by 1993, 57 percent was found in the Mexican Stock Exchange. More than half was channelled to Tel*fonos de M*xico. The Ministry of Commerce and Industry (Secofi) promotes foreign investment as well.

The Foreign Investment Commission (FCI) authorizes shares purchasable by foreigners. Since 1989, Mexico has permitted foreign investment in its stock market, and in four years has attracted more capital investment than in all previous history. The Automatic Investment Regime offers a way around the FCI. As a result in 1992, only 14.9 percent of new investments required approval. Eighty percent of the 906 new foreign investment societies were authorized by the new system.

Mexico's large corporations find investment capital in international markets, resulting in a private external debt of approximately $21 billion. This is a dynamic sector of the economy that attracts favourable international attention, although, in my opinion, it benefits a small fraction of the population. Moreover, government wage and inflation policies have favoured the growth of an underground sector in the Mexican economy.

I have sketched an outline of the most important changes that the new order has brought to Mexico. The challenges that I see emerging are the following:

The legal and normative challenge. Laws have been passed respecting weights and measures, imports, and exports. Taxes have been reconciled to the rules of the GATT, and taxes, and rules have been adjusted in fisheries, communications, mining, finance, and power generation. More changes are forthcoming. The challenge lies in how far these new laws will go and how permanent the reforms will be.

The institutional challenge. Mexico has many bureaucrats. Their support will be essential, and winning it will not be easy.

The ethical challenge. The extensive bureaucracy must not fall prey to corruption. The challenge is to redefine the rules for a new social behaviour.

The political challenge. The new order must be established and justified without the official sanction of NAFTA. The political market must become as free and open as the economic one. Citizens must be free to choose goods and leaders. Economic policy must also take into account adjustment costs.

The international challenge. Traders in the United States and Canada must support a North American Social Fund, which will offer financial aid to those experiencing onerous adjustment costs. The key point of the transition in Mexico lies in the political will to rally a society that confusedly supports change. Gaining social consensus for economic modernization, the new utopia, could be hampered by a poorly regulated period of adjustment.

Section II
What's in it for Canada?

NAFTA in Canadian Politics: Chihuahua Turns Pit Bull?

Anthony Halliday

T O EXPLAIN THE TITLE'S ADMITTEDLY strained metaphor, it should be observed that the chihuahua is a small canine of Mexican origin that can only nip the ankles. Pit bulls, on the other hand, are ferocious dogs, unpredictable and potentially lethal—even for their owners.

From a Canadian perspective, NAFTA seems to have undergone a comparable transformation. When the accord was completed in August 1992, we confidently predicted that George Bush would be in the White House for four more years, and that by judicious use of the "foreign policy imperative" he would steer the agreement through Congress. Moreover, he was committed to presenting the implementing legislation early in his second term. By now we should have known the fate of NAFTA in the United States.

There was, of course, a risk that the Bush administration would fail to persuade a Democratic Congress, but this, we believed, would present no problem for the government in Canada. The bilateral Free Trade Agreement would remain in force. What went wrong? The pit bull is running amok, disrupting the political process in the United States, doubtlessly worrying Mexicans and leaving Canadian politicians scrambling for cover. Bill Clinton was elected, and his support for NAFTA is highly conditional. He wants to conclude side deals before presenting implementing legislation to Congress.

By holding out the prospect of further negotiations, the president has unleashed powerful domestic forces in Canada as well as the United States. There is probably no negotiable side deal on labour standards that can satisfy the union movement in either country. Moreover, it is improbable that all U.S. or Canadian environmentalists will support an eventual side deal. Yet the views of environmentalists in particular will determine many votes, if and when the NAFTA implementing package is brought before Congress.

The need to negotiate side deals has delayed the U.S. approval process to the point that they will be hard-pressed to present and obtain approval for the NAFTA implementing bill in time for the agreement to enter into force on January 1, 1994. While the U.S. administration determines its negotiating positions on the side deals and assesses what is needed for a majority of congressional votes, the Canadian government has had to scramble to cope with the domestic political fall-out. For the Mulroney government and its successor, the pit bull is on the prowl.

Legislative timetable

The politics of NAFTA in Canada may be treated under three heads: the timing of the legislation; the content of the side deals; and the role of the agreement in the upcoming election. Whatever its presentational convenience, this triptych is a somewhat artificial construct; there is considerable overlap between the three components in terms of timing and substance.

Unfazed by the uncertainties of the Washington scene, the government of Canada is proceeding with legislation to implement NAFTA. The government intends to have legislation passed by both Chambers and ready for royal assent by the end of June at the latest. Given its majorities in the Commons and the Senate and its determination, if required, to curtail debate, the government's timetable would seem quite feasible.

In pushing for legislation at this time, the government is obviously proceeding on the assumption that the side deal negotiations will in no way affect the text of NAFTA itself. There is justification for this assumption, since the U.S. administration has emphasized that negotiations on the supplemental agreements will not involve any fundamental changes in the NAFTA text.

However, there are certainly major disadvantages in seeking to legislate at this time. Traditionally, Canada's governments have waited for Congress to approve legislation to implement trade agreements before presenting their own bills to Parliament.

Why then did Mr. Wilson and the government decide to break with tradition and proceed now with a NAFTA implementing bill? Here we could well take the government's explanation at face value. According to Trade Minister Michael Wilson, Canada needs to have the legislation in place before the Tory leadership convention on June 11, 1993. He notes that Parliament may not sit in the summer and that an election in the late fall would leave little time for Parliament, even if sitting, to implement the agreement so that it can enter into force on January 1, 1994. Proponents of this rationale forget that in 1988, Canada was able to rush legislation through Parliament in December to implement the Free Trade Agreement.

It has been suggested that there may be another, more partisan, reason for proceeding now with Bill C-115; to remove it as an issue in the election. This view is based on the assumption that in an election the Conservatives would, if at all possible, wish to avoid being drawn into a debate on the merits of NAFTA and, by extension, the FTA, which is widely perceived to have caused job loss.

This hypothesis overlooks the fact, elaborated below, that the Liberals, more than the Conservatives, would be vulnerable to an intense scrutiny of their policy positions in this area. Moreover, the role of NAFTA in the election will depend on whether the New Democrats succeed in making it an issue; not on whether there is legislation waiting to be proclaimed.

The side deals

For Canadians, the side deals should pose few substantive problems. They are evidently intended to address issues on the U.S. agenda relating to Mexico. In fact, for Canada, there is no compelling interest in sitting at the negotiating table. Our participation will make little or no difference to the final shape of the accords.

In practice, however, the government is impelled by the logic of a tripartite NAFTA to participate in the side deal negotiations. We cannot afford to promote the idea that the U.S. can, without reference to Canada, pursue its interests with Mexico, and, in the future, with Chile, and who knows what other NAFTA aspirants. Moreover, the government would find it difficult to explain its absence from the negotiating table to the Canadian labour and environmental movements. They would certainly assert that there are Canadian interests to be pursued.

We are thus condemned to another round of negotiations, the shape of which remains far from clear. The United States is plainly the "demandeur." It has posted its initial negotiating goals but may have to modify its proposals as the administration conducts its other negotiation—with Congress.

What then are the prospects for the successful conclusion of negotiations on the side deals, at least on the environment and labour, this summer? There are grounds for optimism. Negotiations have been initiated. Bracketed texts are being prepared, at least on the environment issues.

Moreover, the U.S. position on the substance of the environmental side deal is edging in the direction of realism. Belatedly but commendably, U.S. Trade Representative Mickey Kantor has discovered that trilateral commissions armed with extensive powers to investigate— even the right to subpoena witnesses—to issue binding recommendations, and even to impose trade sanctions, would intrude on U.S. sovereignty as much as on that of its partners.

How would side deals play politically in Canada? Labour will undoubtedly reject them as inadequate. This reaction would tend to be discounted because it is entirely predictable. Whatever the content of the labour side deal, the Canadian union movement will not buy into NAFTA.

The reaction of the Canadian environmental movement is less predictable and is likely to be mixed. To some extent, Canada's "greens" will take their cue from their American ideological "soulmates." An optimistic scenario would have a consensus among Canadian environmentalists that the negotiated side deal represents a major advance, and that an international reconciliation of conflicts between environmental and trade objectives would best be left to future GATT negotiations.

Failure to negotiate side deals that satisfy Congress cannot, however, be precluded. If President Clinton adheres to his "condition," this would mean the end of NAFTA. What, then, would be the implications for Canada? Substantively Canadian economic interests would not be significantly harmed by the failure of NAFTA. Unlike Mexico, we have a bilateral agreement to fall back on. The major Canadian political casualty in these circumstances would be the credibility of the government for pushing ahead its early legislation.

However, on the basis of U.S. proposals to date, it seems likely that the negotiation of side deals for environment and labour will succeed, and that perhaps as early as Labour Day, the U.S. administration will be in a position to present a NAFTA implementing package to Congress.

NAFTA in the 1993 election campaign

The third dimension of NAFTA's place in Canadian politics is the role it will play in the Canadian election, which will likely be held in September or October. Examination of this issue requires a working assumption as to the status of NAFTA in the United States at the time of the election.

It is highly unlikely that Congress will have enacted NAFTA implementing legislation by the time of a Canadian September or October election campaign. Thus, some uncertainty over U.S. intentions will persist during the Canadian election. If the implementing bill has been formally submitted to Congress for a vote under "fast-track" procedures, however, it will be generally assumed that the administration and the Congressional leadership have cut the necessary deal and are assured that there are enough votes for passage.

Thus, the most likely working assumption for prospects of NAFTA at the time of the Canadian election is that the agreement will, irrespective of Canada's position, enter into force between the U.S. and Mexico. The question for Canadians to ponder will be whether Canadian interests will be served by adherence to a "done deal." As the only unqualified supporters of NAFTA, Conservatives will obviously seek to persuade voters that Canada's economic interests require access to a growing Mexican market. The NDP, as the only unqualified opponents of NAFTA, will lay claim to the votes of a majority of Canadians who, the polls tell us, are opposed to NAFTA. An interesting question is, then, "How will Liberals handle NAFTA in the election?"

It should be no great revelation to restate that the Liberals are deeply divided on the merits of NAFTA, and indeed on the position the party should take, when in power, on the FTA itself. To paper over these differences, the party has adopted the "renegotiation" option for NAFTA. Leader Jean Chrétien has made it clear that failure to negotiate changes would lead to a Liberal government's withdrawal from NAFTA.

In an election, the Liberals would have to signal whether they considered the side deals as adequate to meet their concerns on labour and the environment. This would still leave them with a commitment to renegotiate in the area of subsidies, trade remedies, and energy.

This is not the occasion to critique the suitability of the "renegotiation" option. Should NAFTA become a major issue in the Canadian election, however, it may be expected that both the Conservatives and the New Democrats, as well as the media, will demand that the Liberals reveal their objectives: negotiating coinage that can be deployed; the consequence of failure for Canada's membership in the FTA as well as NAFTA; and whether negotiations would be initiated prior to or after January 1, 1994. We may predict that the Conservatives as well as the New Democrats will gain if the NDP succeeds in making NAFTA an important election issue.

Prognosis

Providing no one is taking bets, here are some concluding predictions on the political impact of NAFTA in Canada. They are based on the assumption that there will be no accidents on the U.S. side that would cast doubts on the willingness of Congress to implement it.

Canadian implementing legislation will be through both Houses of Parliament by the end of June, and will receive Royal assent shortly before dissolution.

The side deals will be successfully concluded and will cause little political fall-out in Canada.

NAFTA will not emerge as a major election issue.

The Canadian government taking power after the election will proclaim the implementing legislation, and Canada will be ready to join the U.S. and Mexico in NAFTA on January 1, 1994.

The pit bull will resume the dimensions and attributes of a chihuahua and retire to its diminutive kennel. The nation can then get on with its other business.

The Social Side of NAFTA: Labour Adjustment, Income Distribution and Labour Standards

John O'Grady

Introduction

I WANT TO COMMENT BRIEFLY on three aspects of NAFTA: the problem of labour adjustment, the implications for income distribution within Canada, and the question of labour standards.

Any trade agreement must be compared to the status quo. For our purposes, the status quo is the current GATT agreement and the Canada-U.S. Free Trade Agreement. The case that is being made by the proponents of NAFTA is that Canada would be in a substantially better position if we agreed to set aside the FTA and replace it with NAFTA. I regard that case as fundamentally undemonstrated.

Many of you are familiar with the econometric literature. You will know that the estimated gains that accrue to Canada from scrapping the FTA and moving into NAFTA are quite small. Those of you who are familiar with the Canadian debate on the FTA will recall the important role played in that debate by the Cox and Harris model. Their model generated the highest—some would say implausibly high—estimates of real income gains for Canada from the FTA. Cox and Harris, as many of you are aware, have modelled the effects of a shift from the FTA to NAFTA versus continuation of the FTA with the United States going it alone with Mexico.[1] They found that the real income gains to Canada of implementing NAFTA would be less than 3/100s of 1 percent per annum after equilibrium has been established. Some might say that is close enough to zero to call it zero.

In my view, in its present form NAFTA is seriously flawed and should not be ratified. I draw some comfort from the recent statement of the U.S. trade representative, Mickey Kantor, that without significant supplemental agreements, NAFTA will not be approved by the U.S. Congress.

NAFTA, as drafted, is a standing invitation to companies in Canada that want to produce for the North American market under far less stringently enforced environmental, health, safety, and labour standards, to relocate to Mexico. It is surely ironic that on this issue Canadian workers' interests are currently being better represented by Mickey Kantor than by Trade Minister Michael Wilson.

There are many critics of NAFTA who are opposed in principle to a trilateral trade agreement. While I respect that view and find some of its arguments attractive, it is not my own view. Rather, my argument is as follows:

- The adjustment costs will be higher than are currently being predicted by the advocates of NAFTA. Trade liberalization, I believe, should only be introduced in tandem with a quantum leap in active labour market policies for which the bench-marks are the open economies of Northern Europe. Safeguards in trade agreements and active labour market policies are, at least in some sense, substitutes for one another.
- The consequences for income distribution of trade liberalization have been perverse and will continue to be so. To counter-

---

1   Cox and Harris' findings are summarized in Drusilla K. Brown, "The Impact of a North American Free Trade Area," in Nora Lustig et al., eds., *North American Free Trade* (Washington: Brookings Institution, 1992).

balance these trends requires social policies, labour standards, and labour rights innovations to which most advocates of NAFTA are ideologically opposed.

- Trade agreements cannot be neutral with respect to labour standards. Trade agreements by their very nature are either instruments to leverage up labour standards or to leverage them down.

Labour adjustment

The benefits of trade liberalization flow disproportionately to smaller economies. Thus, it is no surprise that in the case of the FTA, econometric findings were unanimous in discovering that the potential benefits to Canada exceeded those to the United States. The other side of the coin is that the adjustment costs associated with trade liberalization are also borne disproportionately by smaller economies.

Our point of departure should be the estimates of dislocation pursuant to the Canada-U.S. Free Trade Agreement. All of the econometric studies estimated that job losses would be comparatively modest. Moreover, those losses would be spread out over the ten-year implementation period. In general, plants would reorient themselves to the North American market and achieve significant productivity gains through specialization. The scope for productivity gains attendant upon such specialization would give rise to an increase in business sector investment in plant and machinery. That, at any rate, was the scenario.

I do not dispute that this scenario constitutes part of the real story—but only part. The forecasts of the FTA's impact clearly underestimated the scale and the pace of production rationalization that would occur. The forecasts clearly underestimated the scale of plant closures that would occur, mainly among branch-plant operations and principally in southern Ontario.

For more than fifteen years now, the Ontario Ministry of Labour has maintained a data series on permanent lay-offs involving 50 or more workers. That data series distinguishes three categories of lay-offs: those arising from a reduction in operations, those arising from a permanent but partial closure of a plant, and those lay-offs arising from a complete plant closure. We can take the lay-offs arising from partial and complete closure as a proximate indicator of adverse rationalization.

It is useful to compare the experience of the 1982 recession with the present recession. In the last recession, only 24 percent of lay-offs were caused by partial or complete plant closures. In the current recession, that proportion has increased to 67 percent.

The workers affected by these closures are predominately semi-skilled, blue-collar people. Their skills are typically much more job-specific than are the skills of white-collar workers. We can anticipate the labour market experience of these workers by looking at what happened during the last recession. A Statistics Canada study tracked the labour market experience of the roughly one million workers who were permanently laid off between 1981 and 1984. By 1986, well into the recovery, only 57 percent had obtained full-time employment. Of those who obtained re-employment, just under half experienced a wage loss on re-employment. The average wage loss was 28 percent.

If by successful adjustment we mean re-employment on a full-time basis with a wage loss of 10 or less percent, then the rate of successful adjustment was less than 35 percent. Much of this, of course, is attributable to the marginal role of active labour market programmes in Canada. Among the permanently laid-off workers, only 4.8 percent received government supported training. If active labour market policies are a substitute for safeguards in trade agreements, then in Canada we can only conclude that they are a pretty sorry substitute.

Income distribution

Trade liberalization between economies such as Canada and the United States on one hand and Mexico on the other cannot help but see a shift to Mexico of production that is comparatively more labour-intensive and less skilled. Inevitably this will reduce the relative demand in Canada and the United States for semi-skilled and low-skilled workers. This tectonic shift in the labour market is obviously not a phenomenon that is caused by NAFTA. Nor is it one that can be arrested by rejecting NAFTA.

However, unless NAFTA turns out to be much ado about nothing, the agreement will accelerate the labour market changes that are already in evidence. Many of you will be aware of the study by the Economic

Council of Canada, *Good Jobs, Bad Jobs.*[2] That study documented the adverse shift in the distribution of income that had taken place in Canada. Similar studies have revealed comparable trends in the United States.

The background report to the study showed that the adverse shift in income distribution was sharpest in Ontario—the region most affected by the liberalization of trade. In essence, the study showed that the middle income segment had declined in relative terms from 30.6 percent of the wage earning population in 1967 to 22.4 percent in 1986. This shrinking middle was about equally divided between those who entered the upper income group and those who fell into the lower income group.

The fact that the polarization trend should be more pronounced in Ontario than in other regions is significant. Certainly immigration and changes in technology played a role in this polarization. It is difficult, however, to believe that the impact of trade liberalization was not also at work. During this same period, effective rates of protection declined from more than 20 percent to roughly 12 to 13 percent.

Evidence on income polarization in Canada is consistent with the findings of Edward Leamer. Leamer's econometric work, as many of you know, has found that NAFTA will depress the real incomes of lower-skilled American workers while at the same time raising the real incomes of higher skilled Americans.[3] Changes in tax policy have tended to reinforce rather than offset this increase in labour market based inequality.

---

2   *Good Jobs, Bad Jobs* (Ottawa: Economic Council of Canada, 1991); *Employment in the Service Economy* (Ottawa: Economic Council of Canada, 1991).

3   Leamer's findings are discussed in Rau Hinojosa-Ojeda and Sherman Robinson, "Labor Issues in a North American Free Trade Area," in Nora Lustig et al., eds., *North American Free Trade* (Washington: Brookings Institution, 1992).

Labour standards

The incorporation of Mexico into a trade agreement with the United States and Canada has sometimes been compared to the incorporation of Portugal and Greece into the European Community. The comparison is not convincing. Portugal and Greece were functioning democracies when they joined the EC. Both countries had ratified the relevant ILO Conventions on freedom of association and both were in nominal and substantive compliance with those conventions. Moreover, the process of integration into the EC was associated with the extension of European-wide standards enforceable through the European Court of Justice. This is especially true of health and safety standards, which can be adopted by a "qualified majority" and are not subject to veto by a single member state.

To describe Mexico as a functioning democracy is to do violence to the term. Mexico's statutory labour standards and its nominal attachment to ILO Conventions are of little significance in the real world of the *maquiladora* zones. It is not a shortage of resources that leads to lax enforcement. It is a shortage of political will. There are, quite obviously, reasons why wage levels in Mexico will be lower than levels in Canada or the United States. There are not legitimate reasons, however, why health and safety standards in a Mexican plant should be lower. There are not legitimate reasons why accident and fatality rates should be dramatically higher.

What is required is not an agreement to supply technical resources to Mexico and certainly not the pathetic Memorandum of Understanding entered into between the Mexican and Canadian labour departments last year. What is required is a means of enforcing labour standards and labour rights through appeal to an authority beyond the control of the Mexican state. In the absence of such an enforceability mechanism, NAFTA will be fundamentally flawed and its ratification should not be undertaken.

The Federal and Provincial Liberal Parties and NAFTA

Alan S. Alexandroff

IN HIS CLOSING REMARKS at the Aylmer Conference, held in November 1991, Jean Chrétien, leader of the Liberal party, sought to turn the corner on the party's struggles, and leave behind the humiliating election defeat of 1988. As Chrétien declared, "At this conference, we have learned that the old concepts of right and left do not apply to the world of today and tomorrow. What is important are policies that contribute to the well-being of our citizens."

Chrétien was trying to damp down the debate on economic nationalism between and among several factions of the Liberal party. He hoped to end the obsession that the party had with the Tory agenda on free trade and the Free Trade Agreement. In his most famous line, he declared, "Protection is not left wing or right wing; it is simply passé. Liberalization is not a right-wing or left-wing issue; it is simply a fact of life."

This did not mean that Chrétien and the Liberal party were prepared to leave the politics of trade behind. Far from it. The Liberal leader declared to the caucus and then to the Canadian people that no trade deal, neither the FTA nor the unratified NAFTA, would merit a crusade.

There would be no commitment at this time to tear up the deal, as Canadian nationalists demanded. Instead, there was only a commitment to renegotiate both the FTA and NAFTA, assuming that NAFTA would be ratified.

In a more recent speech entitled, significantly, "The Liberal Approach to Economic Growth," which was delivered at the Empire Club in Toronto on February 11, 1993, Chrétien set out Liberal policy on the trade agreement by asserting that a new Liberal government would seek the following changes to both the FTA and NAFTA: a subsidies code, an anti-dumping code, a more effective dispute resolution mechanism, agreed upon labour standards, agreed upon environmental standards, and the same energy protection as Mexico enjoyed (in other words, no more accords between the U.S. and Canada on the sharing of resources). What was not policy reflected a political calculation at the highest levels of the party—that it would not have to deal with NAFTA because of a new American administration. Remaining on the political agenda would be only a bilateral discussion with the Americans over the Free Trade Agreement.

The current Liberal position on the free trade agreements represents the gloss covering the struggle within the party to define its relationship to economic nationalism in an age of globalization. While the "renegotiation position" unites the party tactically, at least for electoral purposes, the struggle continues over the fashioning of a policy that will incorporate positive Canadian identity and deal with Canada's relationship with the world.

It is this broader and deeper struggle that I would like to examine. The struggle to fashion Liberal economic policy in the light of the demand for economic nationalism has existed within the party for quite some time. Within the various groups, and at the cutting edge, are individuals who disagree, such as Lloyd Axworthy, Paul Martin, Jr., and Roy MacLaren.

The fact that the cutting edge of the economic nationalism debate is over Liberal trade policy should not come as a surprise. The dispute is as much as anything over Canada's relationships, first to the United States and then to the rest of the world. In addition, the debate is over the role of the federal government in sponsoring and supporting the development of the Canadian economy.

Under John Turner, the Liberal party reached out to the economic nationalists in a most dramatic way. Today, there is still a lingering hope among traditional economic nationalists such as Tony Clark, Maude Barlow, and others, that the party will embrace a more traditional economic nationalist position in the fight over NAFTA. The emergence, however, of Mel Hurtig's nationalist party is an indication that the Liberals are no longer willing to embrace traditional nationalist ideals.

Lloyd Axworthy continues to represent the traditional economic nationalist position in the current debate over globalization and trade. His efforts to stake out a new trade policy for Liberals draws on traditional nationalist attitudes, but he has also attempted to revise nationalist prescriptions to meet a transformed and transforming global economy. His agenda is grounded in a general economic aversion to the United States. For Axworthy and other economic nationalists, North American trade agreements are dangerous because they feed into a trade arrangement dominated by the United States, and they are driven by forces that inhibit government action to aid the most vulnerable in our society. What is more, they threaten domination by multinational corporations espousing laissez-faire principles. Thus, "globalism can become a code word used to shape a right-wing agenda," which is what Axworthy said at the McGill Law School, among other places, in January 1992, in a speech entitled "Globalism and Liberalism Equals Confident Internationalism."

For Axworthy, the world marketplace is impersonal and inflexible. As he sees it, globalism will undermine cherished values and democratic responsibility such as an equitable sharing of economic and social benefits and of social burdens and social difficulties. Unbridled globalism means that individual men and women are powerless to affect the forces and decisions that affect them. Axworthy believes that the Tories, in their determination to support market forces, have condemned Canada to wither away as a nation state. With such an approach, there is no need to serve the public interest, either domestically or internationally.

As Axworthy suggests, Liberals have always striven to adjust, moderate, and ameliorate market forces to serve public interest goals. In the battle between economic and political forces, then, Axworthy strongly defends politics and government over economics and the market. Thus, the objective of Liberal trade policy must be to avoid the trap of continentalism, and the creation of trading blocs that would keep Canada tied to the domination of the United States. To do this, he favours multilateralism and the GATT, notwithstanding the limited hopes for progress within that particular arena.

Looking toward new links with other countries within the Western Hemisphere, but also nations of the post-1992 European Community, and even Eastern Europe and the Commonwealth of Independent States, Axworthy believes that Canada can develop special joint ventures with countries such as Australia and New Zealand, and even should strive to maximize its Pacific Rim opportunities. He envisions a new architecture of international economic institutions in which Canada will be in a position to offer leadership.

Axworthy, in fact, harkens back to concepts that are best described, in Canadian terms, as "Pearsonian." His image of Canada in the world is that of a middle power that fashions its options from "high politics," in other words, diplomacy and negotiations. This approach creatively calls on Canada to construct global arrangements through supernational bodies where the economic dominance of the United States can somehow be balanced by political and diplomatic accords fashioned by governments. These institutions will, among other things, according to Axworthy, cope with and hold accountable the transformations that are going on in the realms of capital, communications, technology, and corporate structure.

For Axworthy, politics dominates economics, and the measure of economic power is the non-military one described by Joe Nye as "soft power." A country like Canada, with sophisticated communication skills, generally strong resources, a good record in multilateral organizations, and a history of promoting international ideals such as disarmament, has no choice but to protect human rights and to develop closer North-South relations. It must become, in effect, a user of soft power. The bottom line for Axworthy on the specifics of the trade deal is that it creates a straight-jacket for public policy in what Axworthy views as the ability of the various levels of the government of Canada to take the lead in building a bold new domestic architecture.

The struggle over the meaning of economic nationalism within the Liberal party, however, entered a new and distinct phase with the leadership race of 1989 and 1990. There, Paul Martin, Jr., from Montreal, made a bid to identify economic nationalism with new ideas of economic growth. His views suggested a major break from previous policy within the Liberal party. Martin, long connected to the party, sought to identify economic nationalism with the growth agenda, derived from more neo-Liberal thinking, which placed markets and economics as front and centre in the arena of economic growth. The currency of power was not soft power, but economic and industrial power. He was a party loyalist, he had spent his formative years in business, and he understood that Canada was a small country and had no choice but to maintain an open stance toward the world.

That being said, Martin was convinced that Canada and Canadian business could achieve success. Well before the phrase "It's the Economy, Stupid" was popularized by Bill Clinton's presidential campaign staff, Martin strove to use it to capture the Liberal party agenda. On the leadership trail, Martin focused on economic strategies, described a "nationalism without walls," and pointed to success stories in Taiwan, Korea, and Austria, among other countries. He pointed to the concerted efforts in Quebec to raise economic growth through a "Quebec Inc." strategy, and declared that the objective of the Liberal party should be a "Canada Inc." strategy. Economic nationalism would lead to a partnership between government and Canadian business and strengthen Canadian multinationals to create jobs and assure the wealth and the future of Canadians. The efforts of all parts of the country would be required, however, to break down provincial barriers and encourage the co-operative effort of business in all parts of the country.

This is not to say that Martin accepted the FTA and the current NAFTA with all its implications. He had his own list of problems with the FTA. He did not worry as much as Axworthy about domination by the United States, but he believed that the key to Canadian success was in new economic strategies.

Since 1989-90 and in various roles that Martin has played since his election to Parliament, he has tried to serve as a bridge between the more traditional nationalist elements, such as Axworthy and others, and the economic wing of the party, now centred around Roy MacLaren. Because Martin is tolerant towards the economic nationalist tradition, he understands the concern in the party over domination by the United

States and the need for Canada to play an independent role in a global economy that is increasingly turning into economic blocs.

Martin recently urged Ottawa to seek alliances with American labour, the environmental lobby and other interest groups to avoid massive American-dominated trading blocs. He advised Canada to forge strategic links with other governments and interest groups that want to establish an international body similar to the European Community Commission to oversee matters of hemispheric trade. With this talk, Martin has struck a responsive chord in supporters of an international liberalism focused on political mechanisms to balance American dominance and Canadian weakness. The influence of Martin has reached well into the caucus, and he offers a bridge to others who stress the primacy of economic policy.

The most articulate economic voice within the Liberal party today is Roy MacLaren. MacLaren is a Toronto businessman and currently the Liberal trade critic. He starts with the assumption, like Martin, that Canada is a relatively small economy that must be open to the world and to the forces of globalization. He accepts the nationalist fear that the FTA and NAFTA distort trade in a continentalist fashion. He also accepts the reality that even before the FTA and NAFTA, many sectors between the two countries were becoming integrated economies. Rather than reacting with despair and rather than abrogating the FTA, however, he believes Canada should expand its trade and economic links beyond the United States and Mexico and into the European Community, the Pacific Rim, and then further into Latin America.

MacLaren has emphasized a growth agenda by making it explicit that a Canadian global policy relies on competitive economic policy. For MacLaren, Canadian success must be built on a domestic agenda aimed at orienting Canada's economy toward global competition. MacLaren has advocated broad transitional adjustment, more effective fiscal and monetary policy, and the removal of provincial barriers as just some examples of strategy that would lead toward economic success. The public policy that he supports advocates the encouragement of Canadian multinational organizations, which would penetrate foreign markets with the help of state support in the form of joint ventures, licensing agreements, direct foreign investment, and other mechanisms of this sort.

According to MacLaren, Canada's independence can be preserved through economic power and economic growth. A truly global, outward oriented economy will bring influence to Canada based on its wealth and not its political abilities.

Unlike Paul Martin, Roy MacLaren envisions a rule-based regime (as opposed to a bureaucratic, political regime) as the institutional basis for opposing U.S. domination and advancing Canadian globalization. While MacLaren agrees that Canada should extend free trade to Japan, to Europe, and other nations, its free trade regime should be built on a trading model based on a core set of rules and procedures. Stressing the objective of making Canada the first truly open, global economy in North America, and warning against trading blocs, MacLaren believes that regional economic integration can be part of a larger movement toward global integration.

In conclusion, if the Liberal party is fortunate, the issues of NAFTA and NAFTA ratification will be dealt with by the current Conservative government. Whether or not the immediate trade debate is resolved, the struggle for consensus on economic nationalism will go on within the Liberal party. If the party forms the next government, the debate could create a truly serious policy division for them. Even if the Liberals lose the election, the struggle is vital to the remaking of the party itself. It continues to be a formative influence on the direction of economic growth strategies within Canada, and in the longer term, in the political and economic outcome for the country as well.

Export Financing in the Context of NAFTA: The Practicalities of Commercial Bank Policy for International Trade

Michel Villeneuve

Scope of international banking

BEFORE I TALK MORE SPECIFICALLY about financing Canadian exports to Mexico and the United States, I would like to place in perspective international banking activities in the modern world. The good old days where banks and government agencies were eager to provide financing to Less Developed Countries (LDCs) are gone. At that time, it was easy to structure loans on a non-recourse basis in support of exports and projects. With the debt problem and radical political changes in many countries, banks have become more cautious when assessing risk. Moreover, the numerous reschedulings have caused the banks to take decisions on a collegial basis, as the Paris Club, rather than individually.

Banks today focus more and more on asset quality. Canadian monetary authorities have also given a clear message to Canadian banks regarding the importance of asset quality for a healthy banking system. In fact, the superintendent of financial institutions has introduced a loan provision policy in which banks are required to take a provision of up to 45 percent of loans extended to any of 42 designated countries. Mexico was removed from this list in July 1992. Taking a conservative approach, the Canadian Imperial Bank of Commerce has built provisions for 100 percent of the LDC portfolio. In addition to responding to pressure from the government, bankers recognize their responsibilities in making prudent use of the funds entrusted to them by shareholders, and more importantly by depositors.

As one might expect, the role of our international division has changed substantially over the years. This segment of our business is not viewed any more as a revenue generator *per se*, for we are not after large transactions to build up our total assets or to boost our revenues. Our mandate is to support our clients in their international endeavours.

Relationship banking is thus at the centre of our considerations. With globalization of the markets, our clients turn more and more to exports and have greater need for a banker with international connections, a banker who understands the mechanisms of foreign trade well and is able to structure transactions so as to provide the credit required by the buyer while limiting financial risks to the exporter. In that sense, "international" is considered as a core business and the executive officers of the bank are very receptive to the special requirements of export finance. The CIBC has always demonstrated a genuine interest in supporting exporters and is proud to have received an Export Canada Award from the Canadian government.

NAFTA

We view NAFTA as a great opportunity for Mexico to attain continuous and steady growth and reach the investment grade level. The CIBC is also of the opinion that NAFTA, while not a perfect agreement, is beneficial to Canadian enterprises which will have direct access to a consumers' market of 350 million.

In view of the NAFTA negotiations and the return of Mexico to international financial markets, our office in Mexico has acquired a higher profile with the addition of a trade finance specialist. Our strategy for Mexico is to emphasize trade-finance activities and investment bank products. Wood Gundy, our investment banking arm, is monitoring Mexico closely with regular visits; the results are already there, with three sales-equity transactions concluded over the past eight months for a total amount of $100 million.

Mexico's banking system

One cannot talk about export finance to Mexico without looking at its banking system. There are 18 banks in Mexico and five are reported to have about 80 percent of total banking assets. Most banks have been privatized, but many privatizations have proved costly for the new owners, with a weighted average price to book value of three to one; as of September 1992, 15 of the 18 commercial banks belonged to financial groups which are also active in brokerage, insurance, leasing, and factoring. In this post-privatization era, there are two major issues facing the Mexican banks: past due loans relative to stockholders equity and issuance of new capital.

Capital is required to comply with the Bank for International Settlements guidelines and to contribute to expansion of market share. Up to now, only two foreign banks have taken an equity participation in Mexican banks, which is viewed as an expensive avenue. At the moment, we have lines of credit with the main banks and have an overall country limit sufficient to meet our client needs.

Export financing

Export financing activities may be divided into two parts, short and medium term. Short term means transactions with a credit period of less than one year. We find in this category raw materials and consumer goods, and payment terms with Mexico call generally for a letter of credit. Exporters may request us to confirm the Letters of Credit (L/Cs) or to discount their deferred payment or to refinance the Mexican bank. The latter requires that we present to the applicable bank a term sheet outlining various conditions for refinancing. As banks are more and more active in this market, rates and conditions must be very competitive. For larger transactions, we may use the 90 percent insurance coverage provided by the Export Development Corporation (EDC).

In these transactions, government and commercial bank risk shall be considered. For private risk, the exporter must insure the account receivable with the Export Development Corporation, which is willing to cover good private risks for a reasonable period, normally less than 180 days. With a proper assignment of such insurance, the CIBC will be in a position to offer financing, either under an invoice financing facility or under a general line of credit.

Medium term

"Medium term" refers to a credit period of two to ten years, and for capital goods and services. Amounts involved are normally in excess of $100,000, but as we will see later, the new bundling program of the EDC allows for even smaller amounts. The main players in this business segment are export credit agencies. In Canada, the Export Development Corporation makes direct loans to foreign buyers instead of providing guarantees to banks as other Export Credit Agencies (ECAs) do. EDC itself funds loans for up to 85 percent of the value of Canadian goods exported. The role of Canadian banks is to act in a complementary manner, either in bringing the financing to the 100 percent level or in financing non-Canadian costs.

The EDC has currently signed lines of credit with nine Mexican banks for a total value of $240 million, plus three lines of credit with government agencies, like PEMEX, representing $650 million. Total exposure for medium term transactions is $1 billion, which makes Mexico one of the most important markets for the EDC. Interest in Mexico by Canadian exporters is high, as proved by an impressive $2 billion pipeline of potential transactions. Of course, a great proportion of those are at an early stage and may never materialize.

EDC lines offer terms from 3 to 8½ years, and all the lines are guaranteed by the Mexican government. With the privatizations, the EDC is looking at the possibility of offering financing on the basis of commercial bank risk; it may take one or two years. The EDC has recently launched a bundling program under the lines of credit that allows for accommodation of transactions as low as $50,000, while offering a more competitive interest rates structure.

In our complementary role, the CIBC tends to limit transactions to a five-year horizon. We also have the ability to structure multi-country sourcing involving two or three ECAs. Our office in London, England, is very active in the export credit guarantee department and has recently assembled a multimillion dollar transaction in Mexico. CIBC also has a trade finance group located in New York that may offer financing under the Export-Import Bank Guarantee Program. Medium-term financing may be structured by means of supplier credit, with promissory notes being sold on the secondary market to banks or forfeiting houses.

Financing of exports to the United States

Let us now turn to financing of exports to the United States. This market benefits from a sophisticated and extensive financial system, and there is little need for an export financing structure. Furthermore, Canadian exporters tend to consider the U.S. market like a domestic market, and therefore the usual term of credit is simply an open account.

The CIBC will agree to grant a line of credit on U.S. receivables, providing they represent first class risk, or providing they are insured with the EDC or another acceptable insurer. Although Canadian bankers are quite at ease with such American commercial risks, there is some concern about their security below the border. Even though there is a free trade zone, the legal environment remains different.

Conclusion

As we move toward implementation of NAFTA, the need for efficient export financing mechanisms becomes greater and the financial market is responding with genuine interest. The Canadian Imperial Bank of Commerce, for example, is considering itself now as a North American bank, rather than just a Canadian institution. We have established a North American Large Corporate Division, and the officer responsible for this inner-countries division is located in New York. New structures are being formed to adapt the banking business to North America as a prime market.

Should Free Traders Support NAFTA?

Andrew Coyne

I AM GOING TO ASSUME from the outset that free trade is, in fact, a good thing. The question then is whether or not a NAFTA-type arrangement will advance or retard the cause of international trade liberalization. Obviously, we need a criterion to judge that, for, although better than might have been expected, the NAFTA is less than a perfect example of a trade agreement. My criterion is going to be, is it a net gain, or is it a net loss, from the status quo, the status quo being the bilateral Canada-U.S. Free Trade Agreement.

NAFTA was certainly intended to be a free trade agreement, but vast sectors of the economy were left more or less untouched. We grandfathered virtually every existing restriction in services, particularly in transportation and telecommunications. Two-thirds of the assets of Canada remain under investment review. Agriculture was also largely exempted. Cultural industries were exempted. Provinces had all kinds of exemptions written in for them. Neither did we provide for the mobility of labour, nor, quite distressingly, did we create a subsidies code. Moreover, we did not jettison anti-dumping laws. Beer was not on the table, and as my sometimes colleague Bill Watson and I have argued in a different context, beer should always be on the table!

Selective trade liberalization has its costs and its distortions. The Auto Pact, for example, has been of great benefit to the automobile industry of North America. It has not produced significant benefits for Canada as a whole, firstly because of an exaggerated reliance on the province of Ontario in this one industry, and secondly because the vast exports of auto parts, and autos themselves coming from the Auto Pact, meant that everybody is paying higher exchange rates than they would otherwise be paying. On balance, the Auto Pact is good for the country, but in a fairly narrow sense.

It would be hard today to argue that trade between Canada and the United States is more distorted than it was prior to the FTA. In fact, we have evened out many distortions between different sectors. Contrary to the impression we often get, it did not give either party any new powers of protection. Anything the Americans can do to Canada now, they could do before the FTA was signed. Other things that they could not do before the FTA, they cannot do now. On balance then, the FTA has been pro free trade. With the possible exception of the auto industry, where they confined the business exclusively to existing members and basically shut out the offshore industries, it did not raise any significant new barriers to the outside world.

The second part of my discussion concerns the issue of trade diversion as it relates to the FTA and to NAFTA. In 1989, there was apprehension that the FTA and other regional trade blocs were creating a fortress North America and a fortress Europe. This obviously remains a hot topic and for several reasons.

One reason, in the most simple terms, is that the lower cost that one can get from continent-wide rationalization of industry increases the effective rate of protection of existing tariffs. This seems to be a rather inefficient method for imposing trade barriers, and it is going to be one of the attending costs of increasing efficiency.

Second, and more important, is the issue of trade diversion versus trade creation. If all we are doing is removing trade barriers against one country, and not against others, we gain very little. Diverting trade that would otherwise take place between Canada and France to flow between Canada and the United States, not on the basis of real cost differences, but on the basis of selective tariff preferences, is not much of an accomplishment. On the other hand, much of the trade that exists between Canada and the United States cannot be diverted. Simply by reasons of geography, transport costs and similar tastes, the United States is going to be our largest trading partner no matter what the trading regime.

As NAFTA expands to Mexico, and further south, we can see that this trade diversion argument figures more prominently when we consider Chile, for example. As transportation and communication costs decrease, however, and as the material content of traded goods declines, this argument will have less force. The trade diversion analysis also suffers from being too static. We must look at the dynamic effects of selective trade liberalization.

A third way in which regional trade blocs are said to damage international trade liberalization is through the effect on the multilateral trade talks in the GATT Round, which have been accorded less attention and importance. But the fact that we need the GATT less increases our bargaining power. We have also witnessed a certain degree of "cross liberalization" between the two pacts. The new multilateral trade organization that is being talked about as part of the Uruguay Round borrows a lot from the existing examples of the dispute settlement mechanisms of the FTA. We may indeed get some progress on defining subsidies out of the Uruguay Round that will be helpful to us in a bilateral context. All things considered, I would argue (in a non-rigorous way) that the FTA produced a net gain for free traders.

Now we come to NAFTA. Within the context of regional trade blocs versus the rest of the world, the key part of NAFTA appears to be the accession clause, and it affects some of the negative arguments in an interesting way. Regarding the route to trade liberalization, it is open to question whether a unilateral approach should be preferred to a multilateral effort. Some have argued that through external restraints we will be able to achieve free trade that we would not be able to get through persuasion and compromise. By turning negotiations into a kind of an arms talks setting, however, you send the message that something of benefit is sacrificed by getting rid of tariffs. I believe this can be potentially harmful in the long run to the persuasiveness of the free trade case.

As David Henderson, the chief economist of the Organization of Economic Cooperation and Development (OECD) says, this kind of bargaining gives rise to an opportunistic, mercantilist approach to trade liberalization. Each country attempts to give up as little as possible in exchange for another country's liberalization. And by negotiating bilateral free trade treaties, you lock in trade liberalization in a way that cannot be altered later. This could be beneficial, but it could also cause parties to be hesitant about entering into free trade for fear of facing trade barriers later.

On the other hand, free trade, in a multilateral context through the GATT, has so far exhibited a very mixed record. The pact has succeeded in lowering average levels of tariffs and in trying to civilize trade relations between countries, but it has also been a slow process. Under the most sacred principle of most favoured nation, it has even prevented trade wars from breaking out, but it also tends to mean that trade liberalization progresses at the speed of the slowest nation.

I wish to propose that an alternative exists. NAFTA opens an alternative in what I will call "progressive bilateralism." This is a bridge between the bilateral approach of the Canada-United States Free Trade Agreement and full-blown multilateral trade liberalization.

It is significantly easier to drop all trade barriers between one or two, or even a few, countries than it is to negotiate a few trade barrier reductions at a time with every country. The homely analogy I like to draw is that if you are shovelling your sidewalk or your driveway, which is easier to do? Take a small amount off of the top all over, or shovel right down to the ground a few feet at a time? The bilateral approach has its benefits.

Second, as witnessed already with prospects from the accession clause in NAFTA, a dynamic of competitive trade liberalization is created. One of the reasons why Mexico entered into the talks was to gain advantages that Canada attained after negotiating a bilateral trade agreement with the United States. Certainly, once the U.S. and Mexico started talks, Canada was very conscious of the "hub and spoke" dynamic, and did not wish to leave the United States with exclusive access to all three markets. Now we see Chile and other countries not wanting to be isolated from access to those markets by Mexico. It is a beggar thy neighbour motivation, but the effects of it over time are likely to be benign, and in fact, positive.

I should mention, parenthetically, that this was an idea suggested by Congressman Jack Kemp and Senator Phil Gramm of the United

States, which was to retaliate against countries that were not providing access to U.S. exports, rather than using the traditional mechanism of slapping a tariff on their exports. Since a tariff penalizes one's own consumers, they argue that the United States should drop its trade barriers against countries in competition with the offending nation and thereby reward American consumers while simultaneously punishing the offender. Thus, the accession clause could be the major benefit from NAFTA when compared with the FTA.

There are, however, some NAFTA negatives that should be considered. First, it is certainly irksome to see the raising of the rules of origin on certain sectors, which transpired during the negotiations, particularly in automobiles and apparel. Offsetting this, they did good work in altering the rules as much as possible. In the auto example, they more clearly defined what was meant by "content," or the "rules of origin," and in apparel by compromise in other areas.

Rules of origin are certainly worrisome, not only in terms of throwing up barriers to offshore producers, but also in impeding cross-border trade on the continent, if the rule of origin is so onerous that the producer simply decides to use the offshore components and pay the tariff.

Second, we have something still very much in flux, negotiations on environment and labour standard side agreements. Whatever the result, it is extremely difficult to decipher exactly what the Clinton administration intends from day to day. We even find contradictions within the same speeches. For example, last Thursday, Mr. Kantor, the U.S. trade representative, stated: "The commissions would have no supernational powers and would not invade the sovereignty of any nation, especially ours." Later in the same speech, however, he continued: "They would have real teeth; a meaningful advance of their objectives are concrete and contain serious commitment." I do not know what this means, and I am not sure if Mr. Kantor knows what this means.

Nevertheless, we were recently assured that President Clinton is not a protectionist, and that he appointed Mr. Kantor, who is not a protectionist, and is not a radical free trader. I must say that I am immensely hostile to including environmental concerns in trade agreements, particularly if enforcement leads to trade sanctions.

In closing, the weight of evidence indicates that free traders should support NAFTA. The concerns raised here have largely been addressed, and are outweighed by the prospect of positive gains from trade liberalization. However, the environmental side agreement has the potential to be a real Pandora's box if the United States Congress becomes involved. The agreement would be open to all kinds of loose interpretations, which would provide ample opportunity for trade harassment, even beyond what we are already seeing through the anti-dump examples. I would hope that the side agreement is ineffectual and merely symbolic. At the present moment, and on balance, free traders should support NAFTA.

Section III
What's in it for the United States?

The Phantom Campaign Issue: U.S. Presidents and Trade Policy

Gil Troy

THE UNITED STATES JUST COMPLETED a presidential campaign supposedly focused on "The Economy, Stupid." In the midst of that campaign, George Bush signed an agreement creating a $6 trillion trading
forum. If academics could create history rather than report it, this
agreement would have inspired a wide-ranging public debate. In fact,
NAFTA was virtually ignored. It merited barely two mentions in three
presidential debates—one of which was a digression from Ross Perot.

This silence about NAFTA is particularly striking in light of the
obsession with trade throughout American history. Free trade was
central to the American Revolution. It is no coincidence that the Declaration of Independence and *The Wealth of Nations* were published the
same year. American revolutionaries saw free trade as a path to salva-
tion.[1]

---

1   Bernard Bailyn, "1776: A Year of Challenge—A World Transformed,"
     Journal of Law and Economics 19 (Oct. 1976), pp. 437-466; Drew R.

Yet, in an imperfect world, protectionism was often necessary. The Constitution empowered the new government to be protectionist in Article I, Section 8. Throughout the 19th century, struggles between free trade and protectionism dominated American politics. But even as Americans shouted about the 1828 "Tariff of Abominations," some realized that trade symbolized many different concerns. "The tariff is the occasion, rather than the real cause of the present unhappy state of things," John C. Calhoun admitted in 1830.[2] As proof, Henry Clay's 1832 adjustments to the hated tariff led to the Nullification Crisis—a harbinger of Civil War and conflicts about states' rights and slavery, not tariffs.

Still, trade could prove politically treacherous. Politicians had to balance conflicting regional and national needs. There remains "but one question which can by any possibility defeat your election," Democratic Senator Robert J. Walker warned James Knox Polk in 1844, "It is the tariff."[3] By the Civil War, free trade unified a liberal Democratic party that was committed to laissez faire and sceptical about centralized government, just as protectionism appealed to the Republican party, which was trying to harness government in the service of free labour and fledgling industry.

The two camps became polarized. Trade policy no longer simply distinguished between Republicans and Democrats but between good and evil. In the hands of Republican orators, the Democratic commitment to "free trade" could appear as unsavoury as free love. In 1880, the Democratic nominee Winfield Scott Hancock tried to dismiss the tariff as a "local question." Republicans ridiculed the clueless "General Went-off Halfcock" and doubted "whether any ten-year-old boy could be found" who was so "ignoran[t] of his ignorance."[4] In 1887, the first

---

McCoy, *The Elusive Republic* (Chapel Hill, N.C.: University of North Carolina Press, 1980), pp. 76, 86, 88.

2   Quoted in William W. Freehling, *The Road to Disunion: Secessionists at Bay*, 1776-1854 (New York: Oxford University Press, 1990), p. 27

3   R[obert] J. Walker to James K. Polk, 30 May 1844, pp. 1-2, James K. Polk Papers, Library of Congress, Washington, D.C.

4   In fact, Hancock was right, attitudes toward the tariff were often

Democratic president since the Civil War, Grover Cleveland, bravely tried to reduce the tariff, calling it an unjust tax gouging American workers,

> crippling our national energies, suspending our country's development, preventing involvement in productive enterprise, threatening financial disturbance, and inviting schemes of public plunder.

The 1888 Democratic platform was equally hysterical, and concluded by casting the trade debate as the central campaign issue:

> Upon this great issue of tariff reform, so closely concerning every phase of our national life ...the Democratic party submits its principles and professions to the intelligent suffrage of the people.[5]

The Republicans countered just as vehemently. Their 1888 platform championed "the American system of protection," charging that Cleveland and the Democrats "serve the interests of Europe; we will support the interests of America." This "is not a contest between schedules," Republican nominee Benjamin Harrison thundered, "but between wide-apart principles."[6]

During that campaign, the protectionist William McKinley reported that "the demand for tariff literature is phenomenal." Protectionists

---

determined by regional economic needs. Still, and especially during a campaign, the broader symbol obscured minor variations and incidental concerns like the truth. Herbert J. Clancy, *The Presidential Election of 1880* (Chicago: Loyola, 1958), pp. 218-221; Thomas Nast, "A Financial Mistake," *Harper's Weekly*, 9 Oct. 1880, p. 45; "Hancock as a 'Self-Made' Statesman," *New York Evening Mail*, 18 Oct. 1880, Clipping, Scrapbook, 15:22, James A. Garfield Papers, Library of Congress, Washington, D.C.

5   "President Cleveland's Third Annual Message to Congress, Washington, December 6, 1887," "Democratic Platform, 1888" both in Arthur M. Schlesinger and Fred L. Israel, eds., *History of American Presidential Elections*, 1789-1968, 4 vols. (New York: Chelsea House, 1971), 2:1663, 1664-1655.

6   "Republican Platform, 1888," "Acceptance Letter of Benjamin Harrison, September 11, 1888," in Schlesinger and Israel, eds., *History of American Presidential Elections*, 2:1656-1657, 1691

ridiculed Democratic free trade sentiments by training parrots to mimic "the tariff is a tax, the tariff is a tax" in parades. A mischievous poet sang in *The Nation*:

> Protection, O Protection, the joyful sound proclaim
> Till each remotest nation has heard the Tariff's name....[7]

Clearly, trade was a powerful symbol to 19th-century Americans. Free trade triggered a beautiful series of associations in line with freedom of speech, freedom of religion, and other fundamental American liberties. Similarly "Protection," with its aura of general defensiveness, did not merely shelter particular industries but safeguarded the American way of life from the foreign threat of the moment, be it England, France, or, as the 1888 Republican platform perceived, Europe in general.

Furthermore, this was not an abstract issue. With no income tax throughout the 19th century (except during the Civil War), tariffs and excise duties were the main sources of federal operating expenses. Huge sums of money as well as the fate of particular industries were at stake. In arguing about the tariff, Americans were quibbling about pork—and nothing is more appealing than dressing your selfish needs in grandiose language harking back to the revolution and constitution. Also, the constant need to adjust rate schedules kept the issue fresh.

Finally, the very duality of the issue, the polar positions the two parties espoused, allowed the tariff to assume all kinds of symbolic meaning. The black-and-white tariff issue became a vehicle for articulating conflicting visions of the future and for exorcising various fears. Free trade became a rallying cry for Americans anxious to limit government power and corporate influence, just as protectionism became the identifying mark for sophisticated Americans embracing a new industrial order.[8]

---

7   H. Wayne Morgan, *From Hayes to McKinley: National Party Politics, 1877-1896* (Syracuse, N.Y.: Syracuse University Press, 1969), p. 309.

8   Morton Keller, *Affairs of State: Public Life in Late Nineteenth Century America* (Cambridge: Harvard University Press, 1977), pp. 194, 376, 380, 383-384.

Nevertheless, a century later, trade in general and NAFTA in particular functioned as the "phantom" campaign issue, often lurking but rarely apparent.[9] The three most unconventional and demagogic candidates in 1992, Pat Buchanan, Jerry Brown, and Ross Perot, tried to exploit the issue. Driving a Mercedes, wearing a Rolex, and having a wife partial to Hermes scarves did not stop Buchanan from offering an old-time, protectionist, Japan-bashing, America-First campaign, especially after George Bush's stomach-turning trade mission to Tokyo. As the Michigan nominating caucuses approached, Jerry Brown traded in his funky New Hampshire turtlenecks for a United Auto Workers' satin jacket and began denouncing free trade. Perot, as evidenced by his free association in the second debate, tried to pump up interest in the issue as well. The moderator Jim Lehrer asked Perot about CAFE auto emission standards. Perot responded:

> Well, everybody's nibbling around the edges. Let's go to the center of the bull's-eye, the core problem. And believe me, everybody on the factory floor all over this country knows it. You implement that NAFTA, the Mexican trade agreement, where they pay people a dollar an hour, have no health care, no retirement, no pollution controls, et cetera, et cetera, and you're going to hear a giant sucking sound of jobs being pulled out of this country right at a time when we need the tax base to pay the debt ....

"I take, it, then, from your answer," Lehrer chuckled, "you do not have a position on whether or not enforcing the CAFE standards will cost jobs in the auto industry."[10]

Ross Perot's literary equivalent was *America: What Went Wrong?* by two *Philadelphia Inquirer* reporters, Donald L. Bartlett and James B. Steele. First published in March 1992, by October the runaway best seller was in its 11th printing. Chapter 2, entitled "Losing Out To Mexico,"

---

9   The underlying methodological problem here, which is beyond the scope of this paper, is just what makes a political issue "hot." It is a bit easier to see what guarantees that an issue will not take off, as NAFTA failed to do.

10   "Presidential Debate," 19 Oct. 1992, East Lansing, MI. Transcript by News Transcripts, Inc., Washington, D.C., p. 10

told about Mollie James, who invested 33 years working for a company that manufactured electrical components. Then a wealthy Bel Air capitalist funded by "Michael Milken's junk bond machine" bought the company. The plant moved to Matamoros, a border town across the Rio Grande, along a veritable "highway of Fortune 500 companies." Mollie James, at 58 years old, is out of a job.[11] Bartlett and Steele, Perot, Brown, Buchanan, and others were trying to push Americans' buttons with fears of greedy capitalsts and sleazy foreigners. These attempts make the silence all the more deafening.

Still, a closer look reveals some very good reasons for NAFTA's failure as a popular issue. There were, in fact, 2,000 reasons why it was ignored, the page count of the agreement itself. The issue was flattened under the document's sheer bulk.

NAFTA is not just detailed, but complicated. It is not easily "sound-bited" (to use another Perotism) or reduced to the black-and-white issue of a century ago. George Bush declared himself for "free and fair trade" and Bill Clinton wanted "more trade but on fair terms." Bush signed and embraced NAFTA, while Clinton said "on balance it does more good than harm, if we can get some protection for the environment so that the Mexicans have to follow their own environmental standards, their own labour law standards ..." The differences thus appeared minor not major, questions of nuance not principle. In fact, rather than bundling a series of issues and serving as a major symbol, NAFTA was folded into Bush's critique of Clinton's "pattern" of "trying to have it both ways on all these issues." As the president insisted: "You can't do that," and the governor responded, "His whole deal is you've gotta be for it or against it, you can't make it better," the question of trade disappeared.[12]

Neither of the two likely winners, Bill Clinton and George Bush, would repudiate a free trade agreement. The one principle Bush seemed

---

11   Donald L. Bartlett and James B. Steele, *America: What Went Wrong?* (Kansas City: Andrews and McMeel, 1992), pp. 33, 35.

12   "Presidential Debate," 15 Oct. 1992, Richmond, VA. Transcript by News Transcripts, Inc., Washington, D.C., p. 2; "Presidential Debate," 19 Oct. 1992, pp. 11-12.

devoted to throughout his career was a free market that included free trade, while Clinton was trying to reassure Americans and their allies that he was mature enough to manage foreign policy, that some continuity could be expected. Furthermore, in what was still Ronald Reagan's America, it was difficult to fight something as American-as-apple-pie-sounding as a "free trade" agreement without a good phantom.

In the 1988 Democratic primary campaign, Congressman Richard Gephardt temporarily revived his sagging fortunes by running with trade because he found the right phantom. His most effective campaign commercial pictured auto workers diligently assembling a car. "They work their hearts out every day trying to turn out a good product at a decent price," Gephardt intoned. "Then the Korean government slaps on nine separate taxes and tariffs. And when that government's done, a $10,000 Chrysler K car costs $48,000." Gephardt's speeches cleverly focused on the Japanese rather than the Koreans, tarring the greater "yellow peril" with the same brush. "In Japan and many other modern industrial nations, government and industry and labour have produced a new model of co-operative enterprise," Gephardt said. "We're eating their economic dust." The congressman warned that, without protectionism, "America could become a modern-day Great Britain."[13]

Gephardt's ploy worked—albeit fleetingly. In a primary campaign, it makes sense to focus on particular constituent groups; in the general campaign, one needs to appeal more broadly and appear more statesmanlike. Also, every day, Americans could see the impact of Japanese success on their lives. Trade with Japan is a convenient vehicle wherein modern American fears of decline meet traditional fears of conspiracy. The United States has been successively, and sometimes simultaneously, a Protestant country founded in fear of Catholics, a democratic country fearing monarchists, a former colony fearing Great Britain, a fledgling society fearing French Jacobins, a capitalistic economy fearing Communists, and now a Western "free trader" fearing wily Oriental

---

13 Sidney Blumenthal, *Pledging Allegiance: The Last Campaign of the Cold War* (New York: Harper Collins, 1990), pp. 164-165.

protectionists.[14] Against such a harrowing parade of phantoms, Mexico and Canada just don't stack up. North America is not a category of analysis in American political discourse, let alone American political demonology. Mexico is perceived as too weak and Canada—dare I say it—too nice.

Thus shelved, discussion about the North American Free Trade Agreement is consigned to a few eggheads within the Beltway, some interested congressmen, the occasional displaced manufacturer, a handful of outraged union locals, and conferences like this one, over the border. This disinterest seems bad for democracy. The United States was deprived of a healthy and vigorous debate over a revolutionary agreement. But that very inattention gives the new president a lot of room to manoeuvre and the opportunity to do what he does best—what Democrats (now that he's their leader) call consensus building, what Republicans call weaseling, and what the distinguished former vice-president of the United States of America called "pulling a Clinton."

---

14 On the theme of conspiracy in American history, see the authoritative collection edited by David Brion Davis, *The Fear of Conspiracy: Images of Un-American Subversion from the Revolution to the Past* (Ithaca: Cornell University Press, 1971), which includes excerpts from Bernard Bailyn "A Note on Conspiracy" and Richard Hofstadter, "The Paranoid Style in American Politics."

What President Clinton's Trade Policy Should Be Toward Mexico and Why

Susan Kaufman Purcell

WHEN IT BECAME CLEAR that Bill Clinton would win the November 1992 presidential election, many supporters of the NAFTA, who had argued that its passage depended on a Bush victory, changed their position. They began claiming instead that a Clinton administration would have an improved chance of pushing the NAFTA through Congress since a Democratic president (avoiding the gridlock that characterized the Bush administration) would work better with a Democratic Congress.

It is difficult to determine today whether they were correct. Now we have a Democratic president and an unprecedented turnover in Congress. One hundred and ten new U.S. senators and representatives were elected with Clinton, perhaps reflecting the public's demand for new faces. Before 1992, the re-election odds for a congressional incumbent were nearly 98 percent. It was widely believed that this resulted from an excess of special interest and political action committee (PAC) power. Adding to the public's dissatisfaction was the Congressional check-writing scandal.

The representatives elected for the first time in 1992 are overwhelmingly Democratic. Many are women, members of minority groups, and from poor urban areas. Moreover, more than half campaigned against NAFTA because they believed that their constituents could not successfully compete with Mexican labour, which is paid as little as one-tenth the wages of U.S. labour. It seems fair to conclude, therefore, that this new Congress is more critical of NAFTA than of its predecessor.

Despite President Clinton's strong support for NAFTA during his campaign, he has sent mixed signals since his inauguration. There is no consistency in Clinton's political appointments. A strong pro-free trade group is headed by Lloyd Bentsen, Secretary of the Treasury, and Robert Rubin, Assistant to the President for Economic Policy and Director of the Economic Security Council. Clinton's other appointees appear to hold very different views on free trade. Robert Reich, Secretary of Labour, is known to tolerate the anti-free trade views of organized labour, and Laura Tyson, Chairwoman of the Council of Economic Advisors, is on record as an advocate of managed or fair trade.

Clinton's speeches also contain conflicting messages. While the president spoke in favour of free trade during his meeting with President Salinas of Mexico in January 1993, he subsequently delivered a speech that strongly implied support of managed trade. In addition, he delivered a protectionist-sounding speech to Boeing aircraft workers in Seattle that attacked the European airbus subsidy and then may have reversed his position on the subsidy shortly thereafter. In short, the early record shows an executive that is playing both sides of the free trade issue and a congress that is more anti-NAFTA than its predecessor.

Nonetheless, my impression is that President Clinton's own position on NAFTA has become more positive. Clinton, aware of global economic integration and the increasing percentage of the U.S. gross national product that depends on international trade, has become a strong proponent of U.S. competitiveness. He understands the advantage that the single European market gives to the Europeans. He is also aware of how Japan's economic involvement in Southeast Asia has improved competitiveness. NAFTA, he sees, has the potential to provide North America with a more competitive and productive economy.

As president, Clinton understands more clearly that Mexico is of great importance to U.S. national interests. Mexico, a developing country, needs a growing economy and political stability in order to deter a potential flood of emigrants crossing its 2,000 mile border into the United States. Even though their economy is improving, thousands of Mexicans continue to enter the United States illegally.

The White House also sees NAFTA as the best way to lock in economic reforms that began in Mexico in the mid-1980s; Mexico has abandoned an inward-looking and protectionist economic development strategy, and has revised its hostile views towards multinational corporations. In addition to welcoming foreign investment and soliciting foreign capital, Mexico has lowered its tariffs and eliminated many non-tariff barriers. To ensure continuation of Mexico's reforms and to secure continued economic growth, Mexico must be a partner in the North American Free Trade Agreement.

President Clinton has not yet spoken about the political and social consequences that Mexico will face without an agreement. My own contention is that those concerned about political stability, democracy, and environmental protection in Mexico should argue that the chances for progress in these areas and resources available to support it are greater with NAFTA. Mexico currently contributes about one percent of its GDP to environmental protection. With NAFTA, there is room for more. President Clinton has not publicly made this argument, but the administration is aware of it.

President Clinton's support of NAFTA has caused him political difficulties with constituents of the party that elected him, particularly with organized labour and environmental groups. As he has learned, it can be disadvantageous to have a Democratic president and a Democratic congress. A president is sensitive to the interests of his core supporters and is vulnerable to pressure from them. President Clinton's mixed messages, when combined with his need to accommodate his supporters, have encouraged demands to change NAFTA to fit their needs.

Not NAFTA but the new budget is the first priority of the Clinton administration. NAFTA must pass through the same committees, the House Ways and Means and the Senate Finance Committees, as must the budget. NAFTA may be disadvantaged if the debate over Clinton's budget proves difficult and lengthy.

Parallel agreements on the environment and labour pose another problem. How much enforcement authority will their trilateral commissions have? Sovereignty is a sensitive issue in Mexico. Although Mexicans and Canadians object, extreme environmental groups want the trilateral commissions to have law-making and enforcement capabilities. American environmental groups fail to recognize that Mexico and Canada would have the same right to influence U.S. laws and enforcement.

Mickey Kantor, the U.S. Trade Representative, stated recently that the trilateral commissions would not have law enforcement capabilities. Reversing a Clinton campaign position, he stated that their role would be to investigate, publicize violations and make recommendations. The legal systems of the three countries would then act on these recommendations.

The administration's new approach is to convince the Mexicans to strengthen their own laws and enforcement capabilities. Environmentalists presume, incorrectly, that Americans want a clean environment while Mexicans do not. Mexicans know they face severe environmental problems, and grassroots environmental organizations in Mexico stimulate additional concern.

In my opinion, President Clinton's position on NAFTA has evolved in the right direction. While this is encouraging, final judgement will depend on whether the president will continue to support reasonable parallel agreements and whether his pro-NAFTA lobbying effort in Congress is successful.

In the past few months, I have altered my position. Like President Bush, I thought the labour and environmental issues would take care of themselves once NAFTA was passed. I believed it was important to get the agreement approved, and that it would be easier to do so without the parallel agreements. I am convinced now that it is possible to elicit additional and faster positive changes in Mexico by pressing for parallel agreements, as long as they are not extreme.

My greatest concern is that domestic interest groups believe that Mexico—wanting NAFTA without regard to cost—will agree to anything. There is a limit (hard to define) beyond which Mexico cannot be pushed. If the president can restrain American interest groups, he may obtain a more effective NAFTA than was originally negotiated by President Bush.

Winners and Losers
from NAFTA

Robert M. Dunn, Jr.

THE PURPOSE OF THIS PAPER is to discuss potential winners and losers from NAFTA within the United States, and to argue that many of the winners and losers will be identical in Canada.

NAFTA appears to be more controversial in the United States than in Canada, and it is far from certain that NAFTA would pass the U.S. Congress, particularly the House of Representatives, if put to a vote now. It would probably pass the Senate fairly easily because of the power of agricultural interests, there being two senators per state in that body. In the House of Representatives, however, where populous states are far more powerful, NAFTA will encounter problems.

There is an instructive contrast between political acceptability in the United States of the U.S.-Canada trade pact in the late 1980s, and American feelings toward NAFTA today. When the U.S.-Canada deal was proposed, a few individual industries were unhappy and complained, as did a few individual labour unions. But there was no broad opposition to the FTA on the part of labour, capital, or owners of land.

Opposition was relatively muted in both countries because the United States and Canada have extremely similar relative factor endowments. Using an economist's phrase, we are Heckscher-Ohlin twins. We have about the same ratios of capital to labour, and we also have similar average educational levels. As a result, free trade between the United States and Canada, although it will affect some individual industries, does not have broad income distribution effects from one factor of production to another. This is because U.S.-Canada trade is not primarily based on differences in relative factor endowments, there being no striking differences. Lack of broad income distribution impacts of the U.S.-Canada pact within the United States made it easy for that arrangement to be accepted by Congress, and made it relatively uncontroversial.

The U.S.-Canada deal, like most regional arrangements, is really an arrangement between "similars." It is much easier to negotiate a free trade agreement among countries that are broadly similar, as was the case with the original EEC as well as with the U.S.-Canada FTA, than it is to complete a deal among countries that are very different in their relative factor endowments. NAFTA, of course, is an entirely different situation because the United States and Mexico (and also Canada and Mexico), have very different relative factor endowments. The United States and Canada are relatively abundant in capital, land, and human capital (highly skilled professional, technical labour), while Mexico is relatively abundant in unskilled and semi-skilled labour, and in tropical land.

What this means is that the trade that will grow up under NAFTA will be primarily Heckscher-Ohlin based, which is to say that it will be based on these large differences in relative factor endowments. Mexico will export tropical products, but far more importantly, unskilled and semi-skilled labour-intensive products, to the United States and Canada. The United States and Canada will export to Mexico capital and human capital-intensive products, and some products that require temperate climate land, particularly mechanized field crops.

What Heckscher and Ohlin explained in the 1920s, and what Wolfgang Stolper and Paul Samuelson expanded upon in the 1940s, was the fact that such trade produces large income distribution effects.[1] In each

---

1   Eli Heckscher, "The Effect of International Trade on the Distribution of Income" can be found in H. Ellis and L. Metzler, eds., *Readings in the Theory of International Trade* (Philadelphia, Blakiston, 1949), and Bertil Ohlin,

country the relatively abundant factor or factors of production win, i.e., they have higher incomes, but the relatively scarce factors lose, i.e., they receive lower incomes. It is not hard to figure out why this happens.

If the United States exports capital and human capital-intensive goods to Mexico, and imports from Mexico unskilled and semi-skilled labour-intensive products, a marked shift in factor markets occurs. The demand for unskilled, and semi-skilled labour, declines in the United States, producing lower wage rates for such people. Simultaneously, an increase in the demand for high-skilled professional technical labour, capital, and temperate climate land produces higher incomes for U.S. residents who own those factors of production. The same effects could be expected in Canada.

Under extreme and unlikely assumptions, it can be proved that the wage rate in the United States would ultimately equal the wage rate in Mexico. This is not going to happen because the assumptions do not hold, but the trend in relative factor incomes is quite clear. This means that, despite the complaints of my colleagues in the economics profession, the AFL-CIO is neither irrational nor short-sighted in opposing the NAFTA pact. Those unions represent primarily unskilled and semi-skilled labour who would be hurt by NAFTA. Total gross domestic product in the United States will go up, but union members will come out on the losing end of this pact. The AFL-CIO's job is not to represent broad national interests, but to advance the interests of its membership, which means opposing NAFTA.

There is a paradox here. Among the largest losers from this pact will be Mexican and other Latin American people currently employed in the United States. Who are the people who work in the garment factories of California, New York, and elsewhere? Primarily Latin Americans living in the United States, legally or otherwise. Many Americans of Latin American extraction will be on the losing end of this arrangement, as

---

Interregional and International Trade (Cambridge, Mass.: Harvard University Press, 1933). Wolfgang Stolper and Paul Samuelson, "Protection and Real Wages," *Review of Economic Studies*, Vol. 9, 1941, pp. 58-73. Paul Samuelson, "International Trade and the Equalization of Factor Prices," *Economic Journal*, June 1948.

will other U.S. minority groups who are disproportionate in the un-skilled and semi-skilled sector of the labour force. Robert Mundell pointed out in the 1950s that there is a very close parallel between the income distribution effects of free trade that is Heckscher-Ohlin based, and the distributional effects of free factor mobility.[2] If labour can move freely between nations, there will be an arbitraging together of wage rates. Free trade produces the same outcome. There is a close parallel between what happens with Heckscher-Ohlin free trade and what happens with free international factor mobility.

A painful paradox results from this process. In the United States and in Canada, NAFTA would increase total incomes but would also make the distribution of income within the United States and Canada more unequal. The people who would gain from NAFTA are over-whelmingly those whose incomes are already above average: owners of human capital, temperate climate land, and other capital. Losers from NAFTA would be overwhelmingly those whose incomes are already below average, namely unskilled and semi-skilled labour.

This movement toward a more unequal distribution of income as a result of NAFTA will add to a rather striking trend in this direction that has been underway in the United States for two decades. Real, or inflation-adjusted, wage rates for unskilled and semi-skilled labour (those referred to as "non-supervisory production workers" in the statistics) rose slowly but steadily for 20 years before 1973. That time series peaked in 1973 and then the real wages of unskilled and semi-skilled declined.

These hourly wages have fallen by about 13 percent since 1973. On a weekly basis, such wages have fallen about 19 percent, the difference being the impact of more part-time work.[3] Average per capita dispos-able income has risen by about twenty-five percent in the United States over this period. If, over two decades, real disposable income per capita

---

2   Robert Mundell, "International Trade and Factor Mobility," *American Economic Review*, June 1957, pp. 321-325.

3   *Economic Report of the President*, 1992, p. 396; and *Economic Report of the President*, 1991, p. 336.

in the United States rises by about one quarter, while hourly wages of the unskilled and semi-skilled workers go down by about 12 percent and weekly wages fall by 19 percent, it is pretty obvious that the distribution of income has become more unequal. The evidence for this conclusion is overwhelming.

This trend cannot be attributed to any single administration or any single policy. It occurred during the end of the Nixon presidency, and during the presidencies of Ford, Carter, Reagan, and Bush. There are many basic forces within the U.S. economy that are producing this outcome, one of them being a large increase in U.S. imports of labour-intensive manufactured goods from the newly industrialized countries of Asia. This trade places downward pressure on employment opportunities for less skilled U.S. citizens.

The United States has already experienced a clear trend toward a more unequal distribution of income, and NAFTA will arguably increase this trend. Is there a way to avoid this result? Is there a way for the United States (and Canada) to obtain the increases in real income total that will come from NAFTA without accepting the unpleasant distributional effects? Yes, there is, and it grows out of what is known as the compensation or bribery principle. Whenever a government policy increases total output but redistributes income, it can avoid undesirable distributional effects by taxing away some of the benefits to the winners and using the funds to compensate the losers. The most obvious way to do this would be to increase the earned income tax credit program for low wage workers in the United States. Such an increase has been proposed by the Clinton administration but has not been publicly tied to NAFTA. These distributional effects of NAFTA can be avoided by increasing what is basically a negative income tax for low wage workers in the United States.

Why have most of the economists who have talked about NAFTA said so little about this issue, because economists love comparative advantage. It was reportedly Paul Samuelson who said that there are very few things that economists know with certainty that are not trivial, one exception being comparative advantage. It is not trivial and it is true. The truth of comparative advantage can be seen in the theory and in history and experience. Trade does increase total outputs and incomes.

Since economists are so enamoured of Ricardo's theory of 1817, they tend to dismiss any argument that interferes with it.[4]

One of the most widely cited defences of NAFTA is a book by Gary Hufbauer and Jeffrey Schott, *NAFTA: An Assessment*. It was widely reviewed a few months ago. The conclusion of this volume that NAFTA will generate in the neighbourhood of 170,000 additional jobs in the United States has some major problems.[5] Basically, they use one argument to overwhelm Heckscher-Ohlin, and that argument turns out to be quite doubtful.

Hufbauer and Schott maintain that Mexico will improve its economic prospects so substantially as a result of NAFTA that there will be an investment inflow of $12 billion per year that will finance a $12 billion annual current account deficit for Mexico, $9 billion of which will accrue to the United States as an improvement in the U.S. current account. Basically, what they are saying is that the Heckscher-Ohlin effects, which were discussed above, will be overwhelmed by an improved U.S. trade balance of $9 billion a year, which is a mirror image of Mexico's predicted $9 billion current account deficit with the United States. The $9 billion a year improvement in the U.S. trade account is then used to predict a net job gain of 170,000 for the United States.

There are at least two problems with the Hufbauer-Schott conclusions.First, most of the $12 billion in capital inflows to Mexico is going to come from the United States. They must assume that these funds that American firms invest in Mexico would otherwise have been unemployed. They must assume that Mexico can get an extra $12 billion a year, much of it from the United States, without serious job losses in the U.S. resulting from decreased U.S. investment. That seems highly unlikely.

A more serious problem is that the capital flows to which they attribute such importance are inherently a temporary stock adjustment

---

4   David Ricardo, *Principles of Political Economy and Taxation*, (Homewood, Ill, Ricard D. Irwin, 1963), first published in 1817.

5   Gary Hufbauer and Jeffrey Schott, *NAFTA: An Assessment* (Washington, Institute for International Economics, 1993), p. 14.

or portfolio balancing process, while the Heckscher-Ohlin trade pattern is permanent, that is, this trade goes on year after year. As a result of NAFTA, firms will arguably reallocate some fixed percentage of their assets towards Mexico, and it will take them a few years to do this.

Once these firms have reallocated their capital stock to the new market circumstances with NAFTA, these capital flows will largely cease, or at least decline very sharply. If the capital flows cease, then Mexico must sharply reduce its current account deficit, and the current account surplus of the United States will decline. The 170,000 jobs that Hufbauer and Schott have envisioned will then be lost. The Heckscher-Ohlin trade that occurs between the United States and Mexico is not a stock adjustment process, it is permanent. It will continue, with its income distribution effects, while the job creation predicted by Hufbauer and Schott is likely to be temporary.

In light of this prospective problem of income distribution in the United States (and in Canada), from NAFTA, why have economists been so overwhelmingly in favour of the agreement? First, economists do love comparative advantage. It is not trivial, and it is true, which is not the case for most of the things that the profession argues about.

Second, NAFTA is seen as a vehicle for reducing the flow of illegal emigrants from Mexico to the United States. NAFTA will, of course, produce the exact opposite distributional effects in Mexico as it will in the United States. Wages in Mexico will go up, returns to capital and human capital in Mexico will go down. If wage rates for unskilled and semi-skilled labour in Mexico rise, while they are falling in the United States, the forces pulling people across the border from Mexico to the United States will decline. It is thought that NAFTA really will reduce the U.S. problem of illegal immigration. Also, NAFTA contains a number of provisions other than free trade in merchandise that the United States wants very badly. One of them is improved protection for U.S. intellectual property rights. Getting better protection for U.S. patents and copyrights is seen as important, and NAFTA will help. NAFTA also provides for much better access to Mexican markets for U.S. banking, insurance, and other service sector firms than has previously been available. In addition, the United States will have more secured access to Mexican gas and oil, as well as the possibility of U.S. drilling firms bidding on Pemex contracts.

There are a number of things in the agreement that the United States wants. Most important, NAFTA was seen by the Bush Administration as a strong impetus for the development of Mexico, and as support for the best administration in Mexico City that the United States has seen in living memory. There has been fear in earlier decades that Mexico might descend into economic and political chaos, producing huge problems for the United States, particularly in border regions. In the latter part of the 1980s, there has been an administration in Mexico City that is very good, not only by historic standards but also by absolute standards. Sound economic policies are being strongly enforced, and there is much less corruption in Mexico than has existed before.

The United States concluded that it should encourage this change, and help to see to it that Mexico will continue to operate under sound policies. NAFTA is seen as a way of strongly encouraging the success of the new Mexican policies. It is hoped that Mexico can become the first Latin American version of an Asian "tiger." NAFTA is seen as a way of preventing Mexico from reverting to the bad old days and the bad old policies.

Nevertheless, the problems of income distribution continue and must be dealt with. It is not a foregone conclusion that NAFTA will gain acceptance in the United States Congress. It is highly controversial, particularly in the House of Representatives.

Since the pact has been signed, and since much is dependent on it, it should be adopted, but with strong efforts in the area of job retraining, and with changes in the earned income tax credit program for low wage workers. Compensation is needed for people who are virtually certain to come out on the losing end of this agreement. They are unskilled and semi-skilled workers in the United States and, arguably, their counterparts in Canada.

NAFTA and Water: Dare We Talk About Water Markets?

James L. Huffman

I WAS IN VANCOUVER, BRITISH COLUMBIA, about a year ago at a conference sponsored by the Canadian Water Resources Association, and I talked about water there, and water marketing in particular. I felt some need to leave the country very quickly. A few months later I went to Calgary, Alberta, to another meeting, and I had some trouble getting into the country. Canada was more welcoming this morning, although I had my voter precinct card, which demonstrated to the official at hand my citizenship in the United States. And I promised to leave.

I am at the Heritage Foundation for the moment, but I grew up in the West, and my permanent place of employment is in Oregon. I grew up in Montana, the American West is my home, and therefore I am very familiar with water problems. Water problems have dominated politics in the arid West of the United States for more than a century, and will continue to do so for the foreseeable future, so I am not unaware of the controversial nature of water politics. I was taken a bit by surprise, however, when I visited Vancouver, and found what a heated issue it is in Canada. Canada is a country that is well-endowed with water—just about beyond comparison on the globe.

I wish to outline some ideas that I have about water and free trade. My interpretation of NAFTA is that it clearly excludes water. I think that there is no "secret agenda" to have water slip through the cracks. Nobody in the United States, to my knowledge, has any notion that the agreement involves water. In my opinion this is unfortunate, which I take it is not a popular idea with Canadians. I come to my view with the idea that water is like any scarce resource. It plays an important role in our lives, and for that reason ought to be used efficiently and allocated with great care. I believe that we can get a lot more out of our water, for whatever purpose, if we rely a little more on markets and a little less on centralized, governmental planning.

The history of water in the United States demonstrates in spades that government does not do well in allocating this commodity. In some ways, concern about water is not particular to Canada. It has been a preoccupation of arid western states of the United States for 100 years. States have fought over water and adopted laws prohibiting its export. Because the United States federal system is, in a sense, a free trade agreement, the Supreme Court has ruled that prohibitions are unconstitutional, but that has not kept the states from doing their best to keep their water at home. They do this even when it seems to be against their best economic interests.

As I said, I come from the state of Montana, which seems to be a very arid state. But it has an abundant water supply, since the headwaters of the Missouri and Yellowstone rivers are there, and these rivers flow almost unimpeded across the state. Yet Montanans are desperate to keep their water within the state, for reasons that are a bit of a puzzle, given the condition of the economy.

I think that water, with relation to NAFTA, is tied to broader concerns. Although environmental issues have been raised by American environmentalists, largely in relation to Mexico's participation in NAFTA, a free trade arrangement on water would affect all three countries. It is generally assumed in U.S. debates over water marketing that one of the reasons we cannot enter into widespread water marketing is because it would be detrimental to environmental uses—instream uses, wildlife habitat, pollution control, et cetera. I think that the evidence is not very supportive of that position. What we have accomplished in the United States by making it difficult to reallocate water through market transfers is a lot of environmental catastrophe.

If we think about the way water has been allocated among the nations of North America, we realize it has been accomplished almost wholly through the process of diplomacy and international agreements of one sort or another. To generalize broadly, the United States has always entered into these negotiations with Canada and Mexico from a position of power, both from a political and an economic point of view. Canadians have benefitted in many respects from geography. They have been able to threaten American political power (with re-orienting the flow of certain rivers), and have come out with reasonable agreements. Mexico, on the other hand, at the bottom end of the Colorado and Rio Grande, has not fared quite as well with regard to geography.

But those kinds of factors are not the ones upon which we ought to be allocating water. Questions of who has political power or economic power, or what the geography happens to be, should be set aside. Rather, we ought to allocate water with an interest to making the best use of it from the point of view of the people who inhabit the three countries. Overall, there is a scarcity of water on the continent. It is not evenly distributed. Canada happens to have more than its share, if one wants to draw some broad ecological conclusions that somehow North America is entitled to this water. But even for Canadians it does not seem to be in the long-term interests of this country to be hesitant or even to get anxious about water marketing and water transfers. I argue that water ought to be traded, in the long-run, like any other goods or services that concern NAFTA.

In getting from where we are to where we want to be, the heart of the problem is institutional—the same that affects trade in other goods and services—except that water is a little more complicated because of its physical nature. If we are going to have markets, we need something in the form of property rights so that the tradable goods have clearly defined ownership that may be transferred. People must know what they are dealing with in these markets, and that is a little more difficult with water, but certainly possible. Water in the United States has been largely allocated by private means, different in the east and west, but in both cases a private rights system, with various kinds of public regulation superimposed.

In order to achieve water marketing across international boundaries, we have the added complication of what I would describe as "hydrologic nationalism," that is, nations feeling some protective interest in their water without regard necessarily to the impact on people who live in the affected nation. Basically I believe that the allocation of water can be accomplished through market transfers with modest institutional changes on a national level. In the United States, the principal obstacle to water marketing has been the limitations on water rights transfers. Water rights are largely defined in private terms, but most of the states have severe restrictions on transferring rights.

Some of these restrictions on transfers are important, of course, because water is different from many other forms of property in the sense that it is reusable—one person's return flow is the next person's water rights. It is important when transferring rights to take into account those relationships. But those restrictions are certainly things that we have both the technology and the social and institutional knowledge to overcome—if we have the will to do it.

When we start talking about transferring water across international boundaries—unless we assume that the nations have the water rights and will do the transferring, then we need some kind of system that permits the transfer. That is a more formidable restriction or challenge, although not insurmountable.

There is an enlightening old case in the United States Supreme Court at the turn of the century, recounted by the notable jurist, Oliver Wendall Holmes. It involved a river, actually a small stream that runs from the state of Montana into Wyoming called the Stinking Water. I do not know why, but one might imagine. Both states have basically the same system of water rights: the first person who gets there and puts it to use has the right to use it—senior rights have the priority. A junior right-holder lived in Montana and a senior right-holder in Wyoming. The person in Montana refused to let the water go by to the senior right-holder in Wyoming. The Wyoming claimant went into the courts of Montana and demanded that the state uphold his rights. The Supreme Court in Montana said, "Forget it. We don't care about you folks in Wyoming." In the United States Supreme Court, where the case ended up, Oliver Wendall Holmes said that if Montana had thought for a moment, they would have decided differently, because the Stinking

Water River empties into the Big Horn River, which in turn runs back into Montana. And so the situation would be reversed.

That might be a persuasive argument with respect to transfers across international boundaries, but only if the flow is equal in both directions. That is not always the case, certainly not between Mexico and the United States. There is some parity, I suppose, in the way waters flow between Canada and the United States. So we cannot simply use the self-interest of the people to get Canada and the United States to agree to protect the rights of water holders. We need something more than that.

I have written a paper, recently published in the *Proceedings* of the Canadian Water Resources Meeting in Vancouver, in which I have outlined what I describe as a "North American Water Marketing Federation," an international organization to be created expressly for the purpose of facilitating the allocation of water across international boundaries in North America. One might say this sounds like a grand engineering scheme, if we talk of reallocating water from Canada to Mexico; but of course no grand scheme is required to effectively reallocate water—from the upper basins of the Colorado and the Missouri, between the United States and Canada, and in the lower ends of basins between the United States and Mexico. There are great economic benefits to be accomplished in both directions with no environmental threat.

Why should Canadians be more willing to take advantage of the enormous resource in water that their country possesses? A proposal that the City of Santa Barbara, California, had with British Columbia to acquire a municipal water supply is relevant. Theirs was a relatively small order, but Santa Barbara gave up the idea very quickly when it found that the politics of water in Canada made it a very uncertain proposition. What did Santa Barbara do? They built a desalinization plant, costing them about $2,000 an acre-foot for water. The initiative must be looked at as a lost opportunity for Canada. Desalinization, with all the energy that is needed to do it, is not the most desirable method of obtaining water, from an environmental standpoint as well as an economic one.

I would agree that, yes, NAFTA has excluded the subject of water for political reasons, but I also would urge Canadians and Americans, and the citizens of Mexico, to think long and hard on the issue. In the long run, it is in everybody's interest to facilitate the transfer of water, including the interest of environmentalists.

Intellectual Property Rights in NAFTA: Implications for International Trade

Carlos A. Primo Braga[1]

L ET ME BEGIN BY POSING a question that is probably on the minds of
many who are not familiar with the latest developments in the area
of intellectual property rights. Why are intellectual property rights
being discussed at a conference focusing on the North American Free
Trade Agreement (NAFTA)? Or alternatively, why is a trade economist
addressing an issue that was, until recently, in the realm of lawyers?
Part of the answer is that knowledge has become a major determinant
of international competitiveness and as a consequence the economic
importance of intellectual property protection has increased significantly. Moreover, the ongoing internationalization of economic rela-

---

1   The findings, interpretations, and conclusions presented in this note are the
    author's own and they should not be construed as the World Bank's official
    position on these matters.

tions has increased the relevance of intellectual property rights for trade and investment flows. One should also note that political expediency has played an important role in forging links between trade and intellectual property rights.

Intellectual property rights are, by definition, territorial, involving acts of sovereign nations. As international trade and foreign direct investment in knowledge-intensive products increase, frictions among nations with different intellectual property regimes tend to escalate. Over the past ten years (under the leadership of the United States), there has been a kind of "marriage of convenience" between intellectual property rights and trade law.[2] The United States began to use trade instruments to advance its intellectual property rights initiatives.

The lack of protection of intellectual property rights works, to a certain extent, as a non-tariff barrier from the point of view of a country with higher standards of protection. In this sense, the fact that intellectual property rights have become a common theme in trade negotiations is not surprising.

This note compares the results of intellectual property rights negotiations in the context of multilateral and "minilateral" (regional) trade negotiations. The minilateral perspective focuses on NAFTA, relying on the text released in September 1992. The multilateral perspective, in turn, reflects the TRIPs (Trade Related Aspects of Intellectual Property Rights, Including Trade in Counterfeit Goods) draft agreement released in December 1991 by the General Agreement on Tariffs and Trade (GATT) Secretariat in the context of the Uruguay Round.

At this stage, we have no idea when or how the Uruguay Round negotiations will be completed. In the case of NAFTA, the text has already been initialed by the governments, but will have to attain congressional/parliamentary approval in all countries involved. So my remarks must be taken with a grain of salt, for I am reminded of an old Arab saying: "He who foretells the future is wrong, even when he happens to be right."

---

2   This term was originally used by R. Michael Gadbaw, "Intellectual Property and International Trade: Merger or Marriage of Convenience?" *Vanderbilt Journal of Transnational Law*, 22 (2/1989): 223-242.

The road to the TRIPs negotiations

At the multilateral level, efforts by the United States to safeguard its intellectual property rights through trade negotiations go back to the 1970s. During the Tokyo Round, the United States supported the negotiation of an anti-counterfeiting code. Despite its efforts at that time, it could not gather enough support from other contracting parties to advance this proposal. When the Uruguay Round started in 1986, the issue of counterfeiting trade was again brought to the negotiating table. By that time, most developing and developed countries were willing to discuss the question. Ironically, the United States had expanded its negotiating objectives towards a much broader agenda centered on the issue of minimum standards of intellectual property rights protection.

Why bring intellectual property rights to the GATT? After all, there is a specialized agency of the United Nations, the World Intellectual Property Organization (WIPO), that deals with exactly these issues. Why did not the United States pursue its objectives under WIPO's jurisdiction? The answer seems to be associated with the perception that the WIPO had no enforcement powers, not to mention the view that the agency was controlled by developing countries. By bringing intellectual property rights to the GATT, the United States was seeking to legitimize the "marriage of convenience" that its Trade Act of 1984 had already established.

Antecedents to the NAFTA negotiations

What was the status of intellectual property rights protection in Canada and Mexico by the mid-1980s? There were some major areas of friction between the United States and its neighbors at that point. With respect to patents (more specifically pharmaceutical products), for example, Canada had "liberal" compulsory licensing rules and gave preferential treatment—a longer patent term—to products researched at home. Another contentious issue was the protection of "cultural industries" (e.g., motion pictures, TV, video, music, recording and publishing industries), a practice that in theory can discriminate against foreign copyright holders. Because of these frictions, intellectual property rights were left out of the Canada-United States Free Trade Area (CUSFTA) signed in 1988 (the only major exception was the issue of copyright protection for retransmission of audio-visual programs).

Mexico, in turn, had a system of intellectual property rights characterized by low levels of protection and weak enforcement. The duration of patent protection was limited to fourteen years. Patents for pharmaceutical products were not available. Compulsory licensing language was vague and importation did not satisfy patent working requirements. And copyright protection for computer software, although available since 1984, was not enforced.

In the early 1990s both countries reformed their intellectual property regimes and increased their levels of protection. Why did this happen? There is a temptation to associate these changes with the NAFTA negotiations. It was common knowledge that NAFTA would face strong opposition from knowledge-intensive industries in the United States if the negotiations did not address the perceived shortcomings of the Canadian and Mexican intellectual property regimes. In this context, the reforms could be rationalized as strategic movements designed to smooth the negotiating process. This theory, however, is debatable at best. After all, Canada did resist changes in its intellectual property system in the context of the previous CUSFTA negotiations.

I would argue that a shift in priorities at the domestic level, more than external pressures, fostered reform in both countries. In the case of Canada, the local research-and-development based industries prevailed over the generic drug industry in shaping the intellectual property rights agenda in the early 1990s. In the case of Mexico, as you are aware, the whole economic regime changed 180 degrees beginning in 1986.

With regard to intellectual property rights, for example, under the direct guidance of President Salinas, a new "industrial property" law was introduced in 1991. The Salinas administration adopted a strategy of "convergence" with the United States not only because of NAFTA, but also because the old intellectual property regime did not match Mexico's new attitudes towards foreign direct investment and trade.

Analyzing intellectual property rights regimes

All of this leads inevitably to the question, what makes a system of intellectual property rights a good system (particularly, from the point of view of a developing country)? As an economist, I must confess that I do not have a good answer. Lawyers might prepare normative guidelines focusing on the substance of the law, on administrative and enforcement practices. An economist, in turn, will balance the benefits and costs of intellectual property rights protection.[3] The typical benefits will be stimulus to research and development, both domestically and internationally; disclosure of new knowledge; higher productivity and attraction of foreign direct investment (at least in theory); a better environment for technological transfers; and increased capital formation in high tech areas.

An economist will also check the costs. These include administrative and enforcement costs and net royalty payments under the assumption that the country is a net importer of knowledge. Another cost is the economic displacement of "pirates." We must be careful in using this term, for after all, copying may not be illegal, given the territorial character of property rights. The opportunity costs of additional investments in research and development should also be taken into account. I would suggest that once you add to these calculations the possibility of trade retaliation, which is a reality nowadays, most newly industrialized economies will be better off by reforming their outdated laws. This is because when you add trade retaliation to the other costs and benefits, the net welfare impact of the reform tends to become positive. Most of the benefits of changing an intellectual property rights regime, however, will come in the future, but costs are current. As a consequence, developing countries tend to resist change.

If we turn now to a lawyer's perspective, typical questions asked in the context of an evaluation are: how broad is the scope of protection (i.e., what is protected); what is the strength and duration of protection; what are the requirements for protection; and what are the legal remedies for infringement? In other words, the focus of analysis shifts from

---

3   For a detailed analysis of this theme see C. A. Primo Braga, "The Developing Country Case For and Against Intellectual Property Protection," in W. E. Siebeck, ed., *Strengthening Protection of Intellectual Property in Developing Countries: A Survey of the Literature*, World Bank Discussion Paper No. 112 (Washington, D.C.: The World Bank, 1990).

the overall welfare impact of the intellectual property regime (the main concern of economists) to the mechanics of the system itself. Against this background, what can we say about the intellectual property rights chapter of NAFTA and how does it compare with the TRIPs draft agreement?

NAFTA and TRIPs: the main differences

In general terms, NAFTA has received a much more positive evaluation from the intellectual property community in the United States than is the case for the TRIPs. This should not constitute a surprise. The TRIPs draft agreement was negotiated among approximately one hundred countries with very diverse regimes of protection and levels of development. Accordingly, it had to accommodate quite different views with respect to the role that intellectual property protection plays in the development process. Chapter 17 of the NAFTA text, in turn, was the outcome of negotiations among countries that had already significantly harmonized their systems prior to the negotiations.

Before addressing the main differences between these agreements, it is interesting to review their many similarities (the focus of the analysis here concentrates on patents and copyrights). TRIPs and NAFTA provide broad patent coverage, encompassing almost all fields of technology. Biotechnology remains the only area in which potential major inventions (in the context of higher-life forms) continue to be excluded from patentability. Both agreements strongly support national treatment.

With respect to the duration of protection, the treaties adopt what is now becoming the international standard. According to the TRIPs agreement, patents should last for 20 years from the date of filing. In the United States, the duration of a patent is 17 years from the date the patent is granted. On average it takes three years between filing and the patent grant, but from a legal perspective the TRIPs standard, if adopted, will probably require a change in the United States law. The NAFTA agreement, in turn, makes appropriate accommodation for the United States practice, by specifying either 20 years from filing or 17 from the patent grant as acceptable standards. With respect to copyrights, TRIPs and NAFTA adopt the Berne convention standard for the duration of protection (generally, the lifetime of the author plus 50 years) and protect computer programs as literary works.

It is also worth noting that both agreements adopt strict guidelines for the implementation of compulsory licensing and recognize importation as satisfying patent working requirements. Moreover, they both support strong enforcement measures and establish dispute settlement mechanisms.

There are, however, some basic differences between the TRIPs and the NAFTA agreements. The main ones are the long transitional period offered to developing countries in the context of TRIPs and the issue of pipeline protection. Developing countries will have as much as ten years from entry into force of TRIPs to introduce patent protection for pharmaceutical and agrochemical products. It is important to note that this does not mean that only pharmaceutical products patented after 2005 (assuming that the agreement enters into force in 1995) will receive protection in countries that currently do not provide patents in this area. Actually, products patented (for example, in the United States) after the TRIPs agreement comes into force will be protected for the rest of their patent terms in the countries that observed the transitional period. Under the timetable mentioned above, for example, a product patented in 1995 in the United States would still be eligible for protection for an additional ten years in a developing country that adopts the transitional procedure. TRIPs, however, offer no pipeline protection—i.e., products patented before the agreement comes into force are not entitled to any protection in countries that did not provide protection in this area.

In contrast, the intellectual property rights provisions of NAFTA will have immediate implementation once the agreement is approved. Moreover, NAFTA provides for pipeline protection as of July 1, 1991. These differences explain to a large extent the more favorable evaluation that NAFTA has received from industries that rely on patent protection.

Turning now to copyrights, both agreements—as already noted—provide for substantive protection. The main weakness of the TRIPs agreement, from the United States perspective, is its inability to impose national treatment on the use of copyright-related policies (e.g., levies applied by some countries to blank tapes and that are not shared with United States copyright holders). At the NAFTA level, a similar concern exists with respect to Canada since the cultural exemption clause (from

CUSFTA) was maintained in the new agreement. The United States, however, has reserved the right to revoke comparable concessions if actions by Canada, under the cultural exemption clause, discriminate against U.S. interests. In other words, discrimination under NAFTA may foster "retaliation."

Against this background, I predict that NAFTA's intellectual property rights chapter will not face major opposition in any of the countries involved. Of course NAFTA may "fail" in other areas. The TRIPs text in its current format, in turn, will face strong opposition from the main intellectual property rights lobbies in the United States.

Intellectual property rights and their trade implications will continue to be "high profile" issues in the years to come. TRIPs is the main development in this area since the Paris Convention in the late 19th century. It is ironic that while it delivers a much higher level of multilateral "harmonization" than was thought feasible a few years ago, the effort may not be sufficient to appease knowledge-intensive industries. The higher standards obtained under NAFTA, in turn, illustrate the appeal of minilateral arrangements as mechanisms to promote "deep integration" among trading partners. The importance of a healthy multilateral trade regime, with a TRIPs component, however, should not be belittled.

Section IV
What's in it for the
Business Community?

The Economics of NAFTA: A Canadian Business Perspective

Thomas d'Aquino

Introduction

NAFTA IS A FORWARD-LOOKING TRADE ARRANGEMENT that improves Canada's ability to compete in the global marketplace. It builds upon the Canada-United States Free Trade Agreement (FTA) to forge stronger trading links with Mexico and, eventually, other Latin American countries. NAFTA will create a market of more than 360 million consumers with an income of more than Cdn $7 trillion.

Trade creates wealth for Canadians. Exports account for about 30 percent of Canada's gross domestic product and provide one in three private sector jobs. Imports provide Canadians with a wide variety of goods and services and raise our standard of living.

Benefits of NAFTA

The following are among the positive features of NAFTA:

- Clearer and more predictable rules of origin;
- An extension of existing Canadian duty drawback provisions;
- An improved mechanism for consultation and dispute settlement;

- A strengthened "sideswipe" exemption from United States safeguards;
- Further liberalization of Canadian access to United States and Mexican government procurement markets;
- More stringent obligations regarding energy regulation, which should improve Canadian security of access to the United States;
- The inclusion of land transport and specialty air services in the agreement;
- A commitment, by all three countries, to implement the NAFTA in a manner consistent with environmental protection and the promotion of sustainable development;
- The addition of an intellectual property chapter; and
- Higher content requirements for North American auto assembly and parts producers.

Key areas of Canadian sensitivity are well-protected, including Auto Pact safeguards, our supply management system for poultry and dairy products, our cultural sector, the freedom of our governments to act in the area of social services, and our capacity to screen foreign investment.

The threat of hub-and-spoke

A hub-and-spoke trading system gives the United States a preferential position at the hub, with bilateral spoke agreements with each of the other countries that wish to establish trading relationships.[1] In contrast, NAFTA puts both Canada and the United States in the position of having free and equal access to Mexico's market. This will help Canada position itself as an attractive location for investors wishing to service the North American market.

---

1   Ronald J. Wonnacott, *U.S. Hub-and-Spoke Bilaterals and the Multilateral Trading System*, C.D. Howe Institute Commentary, No. 23, October 1990, p. 1.

Expected impact

Mexico stands to reap the biggest gains from NAFTA. For Canada, the impact will be small. Two-way Canada-Mexico merchandise trade, about $3.5 billion per year, represents less than 2 percent of total Canadian trade. A quadrupling of Canada's annual exports to Mexico would amount to about two weeks' worth of our current exports to the United States. Nevertheless, a number of Canadian industries and sectors stand to benefit from NAFTA. These include telecommunications, aerospace, agri-food, financial services, energy, information technologies, urban transit/rail equipment, environmental technology, mining technology/services, industrial machinery/equipment, and professional services. The Canadian industries best positioned are those that: 1) produce capital goods, 2) are based on advanced technology, and/or 3) focus on higher value-added products and services within their respective sectors.

A few Canadian industries will be disadvantaged. The proposed new NAFTA rules on the use of imported fabrics are a step backward for Canadian apparel manufacturers, compared to the rules of the existing Canada-United States FTA.[2] On the credit side, most Mexican goods (73 percent) already enter the Canadian market duty-free, or else face very low tariff barriers. In 1990, the average rate of duty on all imports from Mexico was about 2.7 percent.[3] Thus there is little prospect of a large job-displacing surge of imports from Mexico once NAFTA is implemented.

NAFTA does not heighten import competition in Canada. It does, however, threaten investment diversion and diversion of United States purchases of goods and services from Canada to Mexico. This possibil-

---

2   The disadvantage to apparel manufacturers from the NAFTA's "triple transformation" requirement—which will limit their ability to use offshore fabrics and components—will be partially offset by the increase of export quotas for certain Canadian apparel products in the United States market.

3   Government of Canada, Department of Finance, *The North American Free Trade Agreement: An Economic Assessment from a Canadian Perspective,* November 1992, p. 25.

ity hinges on the ability of Canadian-based production to compete with Mexican production, and on the extent of overall competition between the two economies. At least two studies have questioned the degree of competition between the Canadian and Mexican economies and between industrial sectors in the two countries. One analysis concludes that the Canadian and Mexican economies are more complementary than competitive.[4] The Brown-Deardorff-Stern study goes even further by suggesting that Canadian exports to the United States would not be harmed by increased Mexican competition under NAFTA, but in fact would displace certain Mexican exports into the American market.[5] Both of these studies are static in nature and thus do not take into account the dynamism associated with a more integrated North American market. The general conclusion, however, is that NAFTA itself should not have a large impact on Canada's economy or business sector.

The business challenge

Too few of our manufacturers have made international business a top priority. Only 30 percent of Canadian manufacturers currently export. Industry associations have an important role to play in helping companies—particularly small and mid-sized enterprises (SMEs)—to become "export-ready." Currently, most associations lack the financial resources and institutional capacity to offer much tangible competitive assistance, including in areas linked to international business. The private sector would be better served by a smaller number of stronger, and more financially resilient, business associations, coupled with more effective co-operation among them.

---

4   Lorraine Eden and Maureen Appel Molot, "Comparative and Competitive Advantage in the North American Trade Bloc," *Canadian Business Economics*, Canadian Association of Business Economists, November 1992, p. 56.

5   Drusilla Brown, Alan Deardorff and Robert Stern, "A North American Free Trade Agreement: Analytical Issues and a Computational Assessment," paper presented at the Policy Forum on the North American Free Trade Area organized by the John Deutsch Institute for the Study of Economic Policy, Kingston, Ontario, October 1991, p. 12.

Mexico itself has recognized the benefits of, and adjusted its development strategy toward, greater reliance on market forces. The impact of market-oriented economic reforms and restructuring throughout Latin America promises to make the entire region a more dynamic part of the global economy well into the next century.

The Business Council on National Issues is confident that Canadian exporters and manufacturers will rise to meet the challenge. Free trade with the United States has been positive for many Canadian companies and industries, even though in some sectors it has accelerated the often painful but necessary process of industrial restructuring and adjustment. Overall, our merchandise trade surplus with the United States has grown since the late 1980s. And, as noted in a recent C.D. Howe Institute report and predicted by the Business Council prior to 1989, Canada's export performance since the FTA has been especially impressive in the high value-added industries on which our future prosperity increasingly will depend.[6]

NAFTA will bring Mexico into the free trade area created by the bilateral FTA in 1989. Canada—as compared to Mexico—has a skilled and educated labour force, a well-developed public infrastructure and economic system, an efficient and sound financial system, and a large number of internationally competitive companies. What remains is for these factors to be utilized to their fullest potential.

The low wage controversy

It is sometimes argued that Canadian wages will fall as Canada is forced to compete with Mexican wage rates. These concerns are misplaced. A recent study shows that although Mexican labour costs are only one-seventh as high as Canada's, Canadian workers are about 6.5 times more productive than their Mexican counterparts—thus largely offsetting the effect of much lower Mexican wage levels. Moreover, the cost of capital is lower in Canada, and capital productivity is higher. Canada thus has a strong competitive edge in the production of many high value-added

---

6   Daniel Schwanen, *Were the Optimists Wrong on Free Trade?* C.D. Howe Institute Commentary, October 1992.

and capital intensive goods.[7] Canada also has many competitive advantages over Mexico in a wide range of service industries that are becoming a more important part of international economic activity.

This is not to minimize Mexico's competitive potential. Particularly in the manufacturing centres located in the *maquiladora* zones in the northern part of the country, Mexican productivity is rising. To some extent, American and Canadian companies in such industries may shift parts of their operations now located offshore to northern Mexico.

The outlook is poor in Canada for relatively low-wage, low-skill industries, regardless of whether NAFTA comes into effect. Low wages are not a principal source of competitive advantage for the increasingly sophisticated and knowledge-intensive industries that are playing an ever larger role in all modern economies. If wages were the key driver of investment location decisions, then we would expect poorer regions of Canada and the United States to account for disproportionate shares of domestic business investment. In fact, relatively low wage regions of both Canada and the United States generally receive disproportionately small shares of business investment, including manufacturing investment.

Investment

Canada's position relative to the United States in terms of foreign direct investment flows has shifted from one of net outflows in the years prior to 1989 to net inflows since then. Foreign investors have gained confidence in Canada, in part because of our favourable access to the American market, accelerated by the FTA. We believe that NAFTA will not change this outlook.

An Ernst and Young study concludes that United States manufacturers invested in no fewer than 84 Canadian projects in 1991.[8] Canada

---

7   Government of Canada, Department of Finance, *The North American Free Trade Agreement: An Economic Assessment from a Canadian Perspective*, November 1992.

8   Ernst and Young, *The Ernst & Young International Business Database: U.S. Manufacturing Investment Abroad*, October 1992, p. 3.

was the number one spot for United States foreign direct investment in manufacturing—despite both a recession and the proposed NAFTA. Mexico ranked fifth, with 56 projects receiving the benefit of United States manufacturing investment. This undermines the claims that all manufacturing businesses are constantly in search of cheap labour havens in which to invest, and that investment in Canada will dry up because of proposed trade liberalization with Mexico.

To date, few Canadian companies have made direct foreign investments in Mexico—either in the *maquiladoras* or in other areas of the country. Much of the increase in outbound Canadian investment is likely to occur not in traditional manufacturing industries (most of which are not strong in Canada), but in resources (especially mining), financial services, and other service sectors.

Mexican labour standards

Many critics have claimed that NAFTA will unfairly exploit Mexican workers. Included in the agreement, however, is a commitment that no NAFTA country should lower health and safety standards to attract investment. NAFTA should encourage Mexico gradually to raise its standards. Ultimately, the best way to upgrade Mexico's labour standards is to work toward a global and North American economic environment that allows it to create better paying jobs and prosperity through freer trade and an open market.

While it makes sense to argue that Mexico should raise its domestic employment standards as its economy grows richer, it does not follow that wages and working conditions should match those found in wealthy countries like Canada *as a condition for entering into a freer trading arrangement.* Imposing such a condition would be blatantly protectionist, would fail to acknowledge the reality that Mexico's per capita income is only one-tenth that of its North American trading partners, and—if applied on a global basis—would virtually preclude moving toward liberalized trade between developed countries and the more than 100 nations comprising the Third World.

The BCNI remains open, however, to the idea of a "side agreement" on labour standards. A North American Commission on Labour could emerge from the current side agreement talks. Such a body would have a mandate to address the issue of appropriate enforcement of labour standards. Its other principal tasks would include monitoring developments in the signatory countries, facilitating the exchange of information, and providing a mechanism to discuss issues and resolve disputes. We would strongly oppose including trade sanctions within a NAFTA labour standards side agreement.

NAFTA and the environment

NAFTA represents a significant advance in the fusion of trade and environmental policy for the following reasons:

- It is one of the first trade agreements to include a commitment by the parties to promote sustainable development, and to achieve the goals of the agreement in a manner consistent with environmental protection and conservation.
- Each NAFTA country retains the right to set strong environmental standards, including standards that are more stringent than the international norm.
- There is a commitment by all three countries not to lower environmental standards in a bid to attract or retain investment.
- Mechanisms are provided in NAFTA to pursue "upward" harmonization of environmental standards.
- Mechanisms are also proposed to resolve trade disputes related to environmental matters; these include rules allowing for resort to expert scientific and technical advice.
- NAFTA provides for co-operation, assistance, and training to enhance enforcement of environmental standards, particularly in Mexico.
- The trade liberalizing effects of NAFTA will spur investment and technology development in Mexico, thus increasing the resources available to pursue environmental goals.

Still, concern has been expressed that the agreement should do more. Some fear that low standards or lax enforcement could give Mexico-based production an "unfair" cost advantage within the context of NAFTA—the so-called "environmental dumping" issue.

The business community believes that the establishment of a new North American Commission on the Environment (NACE) could play a useful role in settling such issues. We are firmly opposed, however, to the use of trade sanctions to deal with instances of alleged "persistent" failure by one of the parties to enforce environmental (or labour) standards—a proposal that we understand the United States has introduced into the side agreement negotiations. Given the differences in the size of the markets, and the demonstrated penchant of American companies and unions to use trade litigation to achieve protectionist ends, allowing use of trade sanctions as part of a NAFTA side agreement on the environment would expose Canadian exporters to greater risk of costly harassment and potential penalty in the United States market. Acceptance of the use of trade sanctions would also run counter to principles of national sovereignty.

Dispute settlement provisions and trade remedy laws

Chapter 19 of the Canada-United States FTA provides for binational dispute settlement panels to serve as final appeal bodies in dumping and subsidy/countervail disputes between Canada and the United States. Panels are charged with ensuring that domestic trade authorities considering Anti-dumping/Countervailing Duties (AD/CVD) cases have applied national trade laws and procedures appropriately and fairly. In practice, these panels have worked well for Canada.

Some commentators fear, however, that minor changes in the dispute settlement provisions of NAFTA as compared to the FTA may cause binational panels established under the new agreement to be less inclined to overturn the decisions reached by domestic trade authorities, and may apply a narrower standard of review in examining cases once NAFTA is operational. If the United States implementing legislation points to any substantive change in the role and mandate of dispute settlement panels relative to our experience with the existing FTA, Canada must be prepared to act strongly to protect its interests.

Looking to the future, we remain convinced that Canada should continue to press vigorously, within the framework of NAFTA, for the development of new trading rules in the critical areas of dumping, subsidies/countervail, and safeguards. The failure to agree to a substitute set of trade remedy laws was a disappointment at the time of the FTA, and it remains a source of disappointment to Canadian business as we evaluate the results of NAFTA negotiations.

In particular, much of the Canadian business community would be supportive of replacing existing national anti-dumping laws with a common set of competition/anti-trust standards that would apply to trade within North America. Reaching an agreement on subsidies must be a top priority for Canadian trade policy. The subsidy agreement likely to emerge at the conclusion of the GATT Uruguay Round may well provide an excellent basis for developing a more far-reaching North American understanding on trade-distorting subsidies.

A long term perspective

International trade agreements are not cast in stone. The GATT, to take one example, began as a bare-bones agreement signed by 23 countries in 1947-48. Today, there are 105 GATT contracting parties. We believe that NAFTA should be seen in this light. Through the agreement's accession clause, it is virtually certain that other countries in the hemisphere will become signatories before the end of the decade. NAFTA's rules and institutional mechanisms can be changed or elaborated in the future based on the evolving goals and priorities of the signatories. It is also conceivable that the scope of the agreement itself could be widened to encompass a larger sphere of economic activity.

The fall of communism, in concert with the emergence of a more integrated and globalized marketplace, has encouraged many countries to pursue new, and to deepen existing, regional economic and trade arrangements. In Latin America, five trade alliances have been created to date. These include the *Mercosur*, the Andean Group, the Organization of Central American States, the Caribcan, and Caricom. Looking at developments in the Western Hemisphere and globally, it seems to us that the choice for Canada is clear. Either we adopt an open trade policy toward our own hemisphere, or we will be left outside of a future trade arrangement that may eventually stretch from Alaska to the southern tip of South America.

The business community of Canada has long supported broadly based world trade liberalization on the basis of the GATT principles of national treatment, non-discrimination, and transparency. At the same time, we have been at the forefront in advocating a multi-tiered approach to Canadian trade liberalization through our support for the FTA, a successful Uruguay Round, and now NAFTA. However, we recognize that NAFTA will lead to improvements in global welfare only as long as it creates trade and does not become an inward-looking regional scheme characterized by increasing barriers to the trade and investment of non-member countries.[9]

The best strategy for Canada is to continue its multifaceted approach to trade liberalization, and aggressively to pursue markets and strategic linkages outside North America as well as within it. For instance, we have raised the idea of creating new institutional arrangements between Canada and Japan—or, more broadly, between Canada and Pacific Rim countries.[10] Most important, we believe that business managers and government policy makers in Canada must adopt an outward-looking approach and vision, one that recognizes that the entire globe is fast becoming the relevant arena for pursuing Canada's long-term economic interests.

---

9   "Building Blocks or Stumbling Blocks?" *The Economist*, October 31, 1992, p. 69.

10   Business Council on National Issues, *Beckoning Opportunities: Towards a Stronger Canada-Japan Economic Relationship*, Ottawa/Osaka, May 1991.

The Economic Policies of Subnational Governments in North America: The Potential Impact on NAFTA

Earl H. Fry

NAFTA and Federalism

IF THE NORTH AMERICAN FREE TRADE AGREEMENT (NAFTA) is successfully ratified by the national legislatures in Canada, the United States, and Mexico, it will create within 15 years a free trade area extending from the Yukon to the Yucatan, with a population base of 370 million people, a combined annual gross domestic product of U.S. $6.7 trillion, and three-way merchandise trade exceeding U.S. $270 billion per year.[1] It will also unite economically three federal systems in which authority

---

1   NAFTA must be ratified by both chambers in the Canadian Parliament and the U.S. Congress, and by the Senate in Mexico.

to govern is divided constitutionally between the national government and state and provincial governments. Indeed, businesses which hope to take advantage of NAFTA must contend with a governmental laby- rinth consisting of three national governments, 91 state and provincial governments, two federal districts, six major territorial governments, and tens of thousands of county and local governments. In what ways will these federal systems facilitate business and economic co-operation across the continent, and in what ways will they hinder it? These questions will constitute the major focus of this paper.

Most nations around the world maintain unitary political systems, which means that authority is concentrated at the national level, with regional governments being dependent on decisions rendered by the general government. In contrast, federal systems divide authority among the general and regional governments, with each possessing certain assigned powers and functions and each exercising within its own sphere of competence a high degree of autonomy. A confederacy, different still, places most decision-making authority in the hands of the regional governments. This means that the general government will be largely dependent on these regional units.

The United States of America was once a confederacy, with its first constitution, the Articles of Confederation, providing for a very weak general government. By 1787, the country was evolving into a Disunited States, with some of the 13 constituent units beginning to go their own separate ways. Delegates from every state finally gathered in Philadel- phia that summer and decided to tear up the Articles of Confederation and replace it with America's current constitution. This new document provided for the establishment of a federation with an effective execu- tive, legislative, and judicial authority at the national level. On the other hand, the constituent state units were to be given equal representation in the Senate, and reserved powers were to remain in the hands of the state governments. Nevertheless, during the 20th century and especially since the first election of Franklin D. Roosevelt in 1932, the pendulum of power has certainly shifted in favour of Washington, D.C. Presently, governmental authority in the U.S. federation is much more centralized than in the Canadian federal system.

The Fathers of Confederation in Canada hoped to learn from America's catastrophic Civil War and decided to place the bulk of authority in the hands of the national government when Canada became a nation in 1867. They also stipulated that the reserved or residual powers would belong to the national government, exactly opposite to the wishes of those who framed the U.S. Constitution. Nevertheless, subsequent interpretations of the Constitution Acts of 1867 and 1982 by the Judicial Committee of the Privy Council, headquartered in London, and by Canada's federal courts, have resulted in a great deal of authority being exercised by the ten provincial governments.[2] Both the Meech Lake and Charlottetown accords of the late 1980s and early 1990s were intended to address some of the perceived problems in Canada's federal system, and without any doubt, Canada's system is now facing more onerous challenges than either its U.S. or Mexican counterparts.

Mexico's federal system was also intended to provide some discretionary authority for its 31 states and its federal district. However, the Mexican system is far more centralized than either of its northern neighbours, with Mexico City being the repository of almost all governmental authority. In addition, Mexican politics have been dominated for more than half a century by one political party, which has had a virtual stranglehold on power at both the national and state levels. This monopoly of power may be eroding somewhat because opposition parties now control a few state and municipal governments. If NAFTA is enacted and continental economic forces begin to take precedence over national and local political and economic forces, the nature of Mexico's federal system may change dramatically over the next two decades.

The origins of NAFTA

NAFTA would trilateralize the Canada-U.S. Free Trade Agreement (FTA) that went into effect in 1989 and will be fully implemented in 1998. Canada-U.S. bilateral economic linkages are the most extensive in the

---

2   Judicial Committee decisions ended in 1949 when Canada's Supreme Court became the court of last resort. However, amendments to Canada's constitution were ratified by the British Parliament up until the enactment of the Constitution Act of 1982.

world, with more than U.S. $200 billion in goods and services crossing the 49th parallel every year. Canada is the leading national market for U.S. exports and direct investment, and the number one source of foreign tourists who visit the United States annually. For their part, Canadians shipped 77.6 percent of their merchandise exports to the United States in 1992, with American buyers purchasing 25 percent of everything that Canada produces. During the last quarter of 1992, Canada's entire growth rate of 3.5 percent (on an annualized basis) was attributable to export activity.[3] These figures were compiled by Statistics Canada. Canadian companies with subsidiaries in the United States also provide job opportunities for 740,000 Americans, 123,000 more than Japanese-owned firms and 227,000 more than German-controlled enterprises. Americans also account for almost 90 percent of all the foreign tourists who visit Canada annually. More than three million jobs on each side of the border are attributable to bilateral trade, investment, and tourism linkages.[4]

Mexico entered the stage in June 1990, when President Carlos Salinas de Gortari and President George Bush agreed to commence Mexico-U.S. bilateral trade negotiations. Some U.S.-based critics of NAFTA claim that the United States has much more to lose than to win because Mexico is a developing country with an economy approximately the same size as Florida's, whereas the United States has the world's largest economy with a U.S. $5.9 trillion GDP in 1992. On the other hand, U.S. merchandise exports to Mexico increased by 328 percent between 1986 and 1992, the fastest export growth in any major market for the United States, and in the process created 560,000 new jobs.[5] Indeed, U.S. exports to Mexico in 1992 were within a few billion

---

3   *Wall Street Journal*, March 2, 1993, p. A2.

4   See Earl H. Fry, *Canada's Unity Crisis: Implications for U.S.-Canadian Economic Relations* (New York: Twentieth Century Fund, 1992), pp. 1-13.

5   *Survey of Current Business*, June 1988, p. 46, and January 1993, p. S17. Statistics for 1992 were extrapolated on an annual basis using data for the first 11 months of 1992. The job creation figures were based on 20,000 net new jobs for each U.S. $1 billion dollars in additional merchandise exports.

dollars of equaling U.S. exports to Japan. Moreover, U.S. direct investment in Mexico increased by almost 250 percent between 1986 and 1991, and Mexicans are the second leading source of foreign tourists for the United States.[6] Approximately 70 percent of Mexico's imports and exports are also directly linked to the U.S. marketplace.

If NAFTA goes into effect in 1994, it will be fully implemented within 15 years, with much of the accord to be phased in within a decade or less. For example, Mexico will eliminate immediately all tariffs on nearly 50 percent of the industrial goods it imports from the United States and Canada. NAFTA is an expansive free trade accord because it will not only eliminate tariffs but will also do away with many onerous barriers linked to the flow of services, investment, and agricultural commodities. Procurement restrictions for both government agencies and state-owned enterprises will be eased, intellectual property protected, standard technical specifications made fair and transparent, and trade dramatically liberalized in sectors as diverse as land transportation and telecommunications. Rules of origin will also be simplified, with 50 percent North American content sufficient for duty-free treatment for most products, although this increases to 60 percent for automotive parts and to 62.5 percent for automobiles and light trucks. The innovative dispute-settlement mechanism found in the FTA will also be transferred to NAFTA, a mechanism that can be highly effective, especially in the resolution of anti-dumping and countervailing duty cases.

NAFTA and the issues affecting subnational governments

The NAFTA will integrate trade relations between the world's largest, eighth largest, and fourteenth largest national economies.[7] It will also

---

6   *Ibid.*, August 1988, p. 48, and August 1992, p. 125. Cumulative U.S. direct investment in Mexico in 1991 was U.S. $11.6 billion. The U.S. Travel and Tourism Administration estimates that Canadians made 20 million visits and Mexicans made 7.5 million visits to the United States in 1992.

7   The Paris-based Organization for Economic Cooperation and Development (OECD) estimates that Spain passed Canada to become the

affect some of the most powerful political and economic subnational governments in the world. California alone ranks ahead of Canada in both population and GDP and controls 20 percent of the votes needed to select the president of the United States in the electoral college. Both California and New York rank among the ten largest economies in the world. Any one of ten states would, if independent, rank among the top 25 economies, any one of 33 states would rank among the top 50, and any one of the 50 states would rank among the top 75 national economies.[8] Ontario is an even more dominant force on the Canadian political and economic landscape, accounting for 36 percent of Canada's population, 34 percent of the seats in the House of Commons, and 41 percent of GDP. In contrast, California and New York together account for only 19 percent of the total population, 19 percent of the seats in the House of Representatives, and 22 percent of GDP.[9] As for Mexico, the Valley of Mexico, in which the Federal District is located, singlehandedly accounts for one-fifth of the nation's population and one-third of its manufacturing production.[10]

Many of these sub-national government units will welcome NAFTA, insisting that a regional free trade area will help their business communities to become more competitive both on a regional and global basis. Although still suffering significant merchandise trade deficits, the United States has emerged as both the world's largest importer and

---

seventh largest economy in 1992 as measured by GDP. However, on the basis of purchasing power parity, Canada remains substantially ahead of Spain.

8   See Earl H. Fry, "U.S. States in the International Economy," in Douglas M. Brown and Earl H. Fry, eds., *States and Provinces in the International Economy* (Berkeley: Institute of Governmental Studies Press, University of California, and Kingston: Institute of Intergovernmental Relations, Queen's University, 1993), p. 26. This book features articles by scholars in the United States and Canada who examine various dimensions of the international economic activities of state and provincial governments.

9   Fry, *Canada's Unity Crisis*, pp. 50-51.

10   *New York Times*, March 22, 1993, p. A2.

exporter, with merchandise trade topping $980 billion in 1992. The United States also enjoyed a U.S. $69 billion surplus in trade in services in 1992, a sector where many tariff and non-tariff barriers will be eliminated if NAFTA is enacted.[11] Canada has also increased both its exports and merchandise trade surplus with the United States since the creation of the FTA, and this pattern should continue for the foreseeable future, especially if the Canadian dollar remains at the level of about 80 cents to a U.S. dollar. Mexico has also been the fastest-growing economy in North America over the past four years and has witnessed a dramatic increase in trade volume with its two regional neighbours.

State and provincial governments are also better prepared than ever before to compete in the North American and global economies. In the past decade, state governments have almost tripled the number of overseas offices they sponsor for trade, investment, and tourism promotion purposes, to a total of more than 160 bureaus in 1993. In 1990, eight Canadian provinces operated more than 50 offices abroad, and provincial governments now spend far more proportionally than their U.S. counterparts on international trade and investment activities. Foreign direct investment is an integral part of the Canadian economy, with a larger percentage of foreign ownership in the business sector than in any other major advanced industrial society. Exports of goods and services also account for 30 percent of Canada's GDP, almost twice the level of Japan and three times the level of the United States. With international trade and investment being so vitally important to Canada's economic well-being, it should not be surprising that provincial governments are so actively involved in economic pursuits abroad.

Ottawa also consulted on a regular basis with the provincial governments during both the FTA and NAFTA negotiations. In Washington, on the other hand, only sporadic meetings were held between representatives of the National Governors' Association and the Office of the U.S. Trade Representative. In Mexico, there was apparently little

---

11 *Survey of Current Business*, January 1993, p. 14. Preliminary figures indicate U.S. imports and exports of services added up to U.S. $315 billion in 1992, almost one-third the level of merchandise trade.

contact between federal and state representatives, although the northern states in particular did meet occasionally with their counterparts in the U.S. Southwest, and also undoubtedly asked the Salinas government to focus on certain key trans-border issues.

Conversely, sub-national governments may also play obstructionist roles in both the ratification of NAFTA, and if unsuccessful there, in the implementation of the agreement. For example, provincial governments representing more than half of Canada's population have voiced their opposition to NAFTA (the governments of Ontario, British Columbia, and Saskatchewan). Several state and municipal governments in the United States have also voiced displeasure with the agreement in its present form.

If the Mulroney, Clinton, and Salinas governments are successful in overcoming domestic opposition to the trade agreement during the ratification process, they or their successors must then pay close attention to the role played by sub-national governments in the implementation phase. Under current conditions, Salinas will face the least opposition in this area because of the highly centralized nature of Mexico's federal system and the dominance at all levels of his Partido Revolucionario Institucional (PRI). In addition, another conservative political movement, the Partido de Acción Nacional (PAN), is generally supportive of NAFTA. On the other hand, the left-wing grouping of movements coalesced around Cuauhtemoc Cárdenas are opposed to NAFTA and may gain greater support at the state and municipal levels in a period of growing democratization and/or economic stagnation.

The commerce and supremacy clauses in the U.S. Constitution provide federal officials with the legal right to enforce NAFTA provisions at the state and local governmental levels, but politicians in Washington, D.C., generally loathe paying the political price of taking on these regional governments. As an illustration, neither the Congress nor the White House was willing in the early 1980s to order state governments to abandon their unitary taxation formulas, although bilateral treaties (and the accepted practice of the supremacy of treaty obligations over state laws) arguably gave federal officials the right to do so. Quite simply, the politicians were unwilling to face the wrath of government leaders and their constituents in states ranging from Florida to California.

If jurisdictional problems do arise in the U.S. federal system, they may be linked to government procurement and subsidy issues. NAFTA will open up many more government contracts to outside bidders, even though minimum thresholds, Buy America, and minority offsets may be maintained in most cases. In 1992, state and local governments spent much more in the non-defence sector than did Washington, D.C., and many lucrative opportunities will be available at the sub-national level for Canadian and Mexican contractors. For example, the U.S. federal government spent U.S. $7.4 billion in 1992 for non-defence durable goods, whereas state and local governments spent $37 billion; Washington spent $8.4 billion for non-durable goods, while the regional governments spent $58.5 billion; Washington expended $43.2 billion for services (exclusive of employee compensation), compared with $22.4 billion for sub-national governments; and the federal government allocated $11.1 billion for structures, compared with $93.2 billion expended by the non-central governments.[12] Almost all state and many large municipal governments also provide some financial assistance to businesses as inducements to locate or expand operations at the local level or to engage in export activity. In the case of New York City, it also provides incentives just to keep major businesses from shifting operations to other parts of the country.[13] In many instances, these practices may be subject to countervailing duties and may lead to a confrontation between Washington, D.C., and some of the state capitals.

The potential for confrontation may be even greater in Canada, where sectors under provincial jurisdiction are carefully mapped out in Section 92 of the Constitution Act of 1867. Areas of particular concern would include the procurement practices of non-central governments and Crown corporations; public pension plan preferences; export, man-

---

12   *Ibid.*, p. 13.

13   New York City and the state of New York have recently agreed to provide CBS Inc. with U.S. $37.5 million in city and state tax incentives and $12.2 million in subsidized power. In return, CBS has pledged to remain in New York City for at least 15 years and to invest at least $300 million in a variety of projects. See the *Wall Street Journal*, March 12, 1993, p. B8.

ufacturing, energy, transportation, and regional subsidies; and selected activities of agricultural marketing boards.

Concluding observations

Most studies indicate that once NAFTA is fully implemented, all three North American nations will benefit economically and the North American business community will be better prepared to compete against enterprises headquartered across the Atlantic and the Pacific.[14] Nevertheless, the costs and benefits of NAFTA will be distributed unevenly across regions and business sectors. Some manufacturing, service, and agricultural concerns will simply not be able to compete, leading to significant job losses. Many large businesses are also in the process of creating North American divisions and may no longer see the need to maintain extensive facilities in all three of the North American countries.[15] Some regions within the same nation-state may also benefit much more than other regions. For example, more than 40 percent of U.S. exports to Mexico are funnelled through just one state, Texas. Several states and provinces along the two borders are also located near major population centres in the other country, providing both new market opportunities and new competition.

---

14   In particular, consult Gary Clyde Hufbauer and Jeffrey J. Schott, *North American Free Trade: Issues and Recommendations* (Washington, D.C.: Institute for International Economics, 1992), as well as the study completed by the U.S. International Trade Commission. Hufbauer and Schott estimate that 175,000 net new jobs would be created in the United States by 1995, but that job gains would be negligible or might even turn into a slight net loss after 15 to 20 years. See the *New York Times*, February 22, 1993, pp. C1 and C2.

15   This conclusion is borne out by a survey of selected Fortune 500 corporations that was administered by the Americas Society. See Stephen Blank, Stephen Krajewski, and Earl H. Fry, "Toward a New 'Architecture' of North America: NAFTA's Impact on Corporate Restructuring," a paper prepared for the annual convention of the International Studies Association, Acapulco, March 27, 1993.

On the whole, state, provincial, and municipal governments in North America are gearing up for freer trade, although some support the multilateral route through the GATT more than the regional route through NAFTA. They generally understand that the world economy is becoming more complex and more interdependent, and that protecting and enhancing the interests of their constituents requires active involvement both continentally and globally. The Canadian government has done the best job of keeping its non-central counterparts abreast of NAFTA developments and of inviting input from these governments. The record of the U.S. government is not nearly as good, and Mexico City simply does not have a tradition of vigorous two-way give-and-take consultations with its states.

If NAFTA is to be as effective as envisioned, non-central governments in the three federal systems must become energetic supporters and not reluctant partners. Many more business-related laws in the United States and Canada are being legislated and implemented at the state and provincial levels than at the national level. Many subnational governments also pursue policies that are blatantly protectionist or provide trade-distorting subsidies.[16] To avoid protectionist skirmishes and foot-dragging in the implementation of NAFTA's myriad provisions, intergovernmental co-operation will be needed both within and among the three nation-states. As the former governor of Arkansas and former chair of the National Governors' Association, President Clinton should clearly understand the need for extensive consultation and policy co-ordination with state and local government officials. President Salinas has definitely been an enlightened leader of Mexico and should also recognize the potential dividends in pursuing an active dialogue with elected representatives at the sub-national level. Unfortunately, in the rush to negotiate a NAFTA text and have it ratified before the end of 1993, too little attention has been paid by national officials to the role

---

16 The Canadian Manufacturers' Association estimates that subnational barriers or subsidies cost Canadian consumers more than Cdn $5 billion per year and adversely affect the competitiveness of Canadian-owned companies. See the *Financial Post*, April 17, 1991, p. 6.

of sub-national governments in both the formulation and implementation of the accord. Perhaps it is not too late to initiate intergovernmental discussions that will facilitate the successful phasing in of the North American Free Trade Agreement.

A Corporate Perspective on Environmental and Labour-Related Side Agreements

Colleen Morton

I WANT TO TALK ABOUT THE POLITICAL CLIMATE in Washington with respect to NAFTA. I will touch on the labour side, or parallel agreement and the import surge agreement, but I will focus on the environmental accord.

I was the executive director of the U.S.-Mexico Business Committee in Washington for the past two years, and in that capacity ran the major corporate "support group" for NAFTA. I did some lobbying and I was also the chairperson of the environmental working group of the U.S. Alliance for NAFTA, which is the large corporate umbrella organization. I am very sympathetic to many aims of environmentalists, both in the supplemental negotiations and elsewhere.

Let me begin with the political climate in Washington. NAFTA is extremely controversial in the United States, and it is more controversial in Washington among interest and pressure groups who focus on these kinds of issues, and within the Congress. There is a lot of public controversy, and not because of economics. In general, people are uninformed about trade economics, about comparative advantage, about anything having to do with exports and imports.

Moreover, Americans have a view of Mexico that is unfortunately very negative, although it varies from region to region. In Texas, you would find a much more positive image than you would discover in California. In California, the popular image of Mexico is created by illegal immigrants who swamp the school system and thwart the ability of social services to support them. In 1987-88, Americans also had an unrealistic image of Canada during the Canada-U.S. free trade negotiations, but it was basically a positive view that Canadians were all nice; they were practically part of the United States anyway, so why even talk about the issue? It would have been much better if we could have slid NAFTA through in the same fashion that we finessed the Canada-U.S. agreement.

Another reason for the negative image, why NAFTA is so controversial in the United States, is because it has become symbolic of everything Americans fear about being integrated into the global economy: fears about the deficiencies in their education system, of companies not being competitive, about moving jobs overseas, and about globalization in general. NAFTA has become a lightning rod for concerns of labour, interest, and environmental and consumer groups, who believe the United States is losing control of her economic destiny by linking up with a country that is so different. Of course, other factors that contribute to the fear of change are the recession and defence cutbacks, particularly in specific regions of the country. These contribute, for example, to the general xenophobia that one sees in California. Of the 50-member congressional delegation from California, well over half are strongly opposed to NAFTA, in spite of the fact that California may emerge as a major beneficiary.

With respect to political issues presently on the table, there are two that I particularly wish to address before approaching the environmental issue. One is the question of how much political capital President Clinton will be willing or able to spend in order to support NAFTA. In November or December of this year, he may not have sufficient political capital left to get the agreement through Congress.

We have lost our major champions for NAFTA in Congress, especially Lloyd Bentsen—which Clinton perhaps understood, but maybe not completely—when the senator became Secretary of the Treasury. Now the president must face Senator Daniel Patrick Moynihan, who is not a friend of Mexico, nor a friend of NAFTA. Not a team player, Moynihan has his own agenda, and he tends to pursue it regardless of political costs to the Democratic party. In the House of Representatives, we have a difficult situation as well. There are 110 new members, 80 of whom are already on record as being opposed to NAFTA. Dan Rostenkowski, chairman of the Ways and Means Committee, is under investigation for campaign violations and other alleged wrongdoing.

Congressman Rostenkowski is the most powerful person in the House, the one that President Clinton intended to rely upon to get his economic program through. If the chairman is indicted, he will have to give up his position on the Ways and Means to Sam Gibbons. Congressman Gibbons is an ideologically pure free trader, but does not have credibility. Known as a "wheeler and dealer," he lacks background on the tax issue, so he will be unable to use that leverage against other people in the House to cut the deals that need to be made. The likely replacement for Gibbons as chairman of the Trade Subcommittee of the House Ways and Means Committee is Bob Matsui from California, where NAFTA is not popular.

I am not overly optimistic about the prospects for NAFTA in Congress. Its chances are 50-50 for the present. But obviously critical to passage are parallel or side agreements. The side agreements, environmental, labour, and import surge (which has yet to be defined) are purely political constructs. They were created by President Clinton during an October 1992 campaign speech in Raleigh, North Carolina, where he alluded to what might or might not go into them. It was not clear at the time, nor is it yet known, how strongly he feels about the actual substance or content of the agreements. What is clear is that the president is committed to side agreements, and that these parallel agreements are essential to selling the deal to Congress.

The problem is that instead of having somewhat rational process in which all three parties come to the table with their concerns, we have a presidential candidate setting the agenda, and once he comes to power, having to fill in gaps. The substance is what all three governments have been frantically scurrying around for the past three months trying to define. That is also what corporate, environmental, and labour groups, and everybody else with an interest, have on their minds: What can we sell? What can we get? What can we put in here? What makes sense? What doesn't make sense? It is not a rational way to proceed, but I think we have finally begun to reach a consensus around a few key issues.

The environmental side agreement, I think, is the most important one because labour is in the process of being "bought off," to some extent, through pretty generous promises about adjustment assistance. Labour's real agenda is to obtain income maintenance within the adjustment assistance package, which is something that the Bush administration opposed because it is very expensive.

The four themes that will emerge in the environmental side agreement are enforcement, financing, standards and the responsibilities of a trilateral trade commission. Enforcement is basically a problem within Mexico, and they are bringing vast resources to bear on it, but there has to be a lot of investment, a lot of training in human capital, in order to bring up their enforcement capacity. Lack of enforcement has two effects that impact on U.S. interests. One concerns competitiveness, because if Mexican standards, even though they are as high as U.S. norms in many areas, are not being enforced, then conceivably the cost of production in Mexico could be lower. A second consideration where enforcement has an impact regards border areas (quality of life, standard of living, public health issues with respect to U.S. citizens)—the extent to which problems on the Mexican side of the border spill over into the United States.

The issue of competitiveness is, in a sense, trade-related, because it concerns the ability of companies to compete on a "level playing field." Environmentalists would like to see the use of countervailing duties in order to cajole Mexico into levels of enforcement like those of the United States. Environmental groups would also like to see in the supplemental side agreement a cross-national, supernational enforcement mechanism to ensure that in addition to creating a level playing field, NAFTA does not contribute to increased environmental degradation in Mexico.

The corporate community, however, does not think that the second priority is any of its business. Corporate business would say that Mexicans have their own environmental concerns, that they also want to protect their own health and their own environment, and they are taking steps to achieve these ends. NAFTA, promoting economic growth, will provide them with more resources and more opportunities to do it. We do not see the necessity for having cross-border, supernational enforcement capacity in the supplemental agreements in order to force Mexico to raise its standards to some arbitrary level.

The competitiveness issue is certainly alive for some parts of the corporate community, but business does not support the idea of countervailing duties. It will, however, ask the Trade Commission to take action to increase and improve enforcement levels in Mexico over a period of time. The corporate community is aware that it takes a very long period of time to bring in enforcement of standards, and to raise standards themselves to a level that the United States has achieved over the past 20 years. Business shares some of the concerns that the environmentalists have, but for different reasons. We are approaching the same issue from different angles, with different perspectives.

Let me turn now to the financing issue. Within this category there are four sub-issues: border infrastructure, how to finance enforcement, Trade Commission activities, and technology transfer (or how to finance the technology transfer so that Mexico will actually have the know-how it needs to upgrade its environmental performance).

Proposals that have been put on the table for financing border infrastructure are basically of two varieties. One is to tax the profits of corporations that are engaged in trade, investment or services across borders, and to utilize those taxes to pay for the needed border environmental infrastructure. The second proposal is to create a new fund: a North American development bank, or a NAFTA fund, or a border infrastructure fund.

Obviously, the corporate community is strongly opposed to the tax, the main reason being that NAFTA is designed to get rid of cross-border impediments. A tax such as the one Congressman Richard Gephardt has proposed would not only affect products and services that are currently taxed, but also tax all goods and services that are currently tariff free. That would be a major step backward, and it makes absolutely no sense from the point of view of economics or trade policy.

This is like saying that we are a little sceptical about the idea of a North American development bank at this point because no one really knows exactly what the problem is. Nobody has done research necessary to quantify what it is exactly that we need on the border. So let's just throw some money at the problem, get it out of the way, and go on from there. The question is, exactly how much money must be thrown at the problem? Nobody is really dealing with the substantive issue. Before I left the Mexico-U.S. Business Committee, I commissioned a study on the border infrastructure financing problem: what is the need, what are the gaps, and why isn't the money flowing to where its supposed to be?

Let me turn now to standards (again a problem because of the competitiveness issue), from the point of view of harmonization, both internally and across borders. Within the United States, under NAFTA, states do not have commerce clause rights. For instance, if Mexico decided to come to the North American Trade Commission and say, "California has established a trade barrier against avocados, and we know it is a trade barrier because it is ten times more rigorous to meet than Arizona's avocado policy," California lacks the legal standing to defend itself under NAFTA. Any president would go out of his way to invite California to present its case, but legally, under NAFTA, states do not have any right to defend themselves, to defend their standards. The United States must decide whether to take up the case. It may ignore the arguments of California.

I think, therefore, that states are just waking up to the fact that they need to pay attention to what is going on in the side agreements. It is also likely that there will be a lot of pressure for upward harmonization of standards. Does the United States really want to adopt the entire Canadian environmental law? Canadian environmental law is not necessarily applicable to all of the situations and circumstances in the United States. Why should we expect Mexico to adopt our law, and why should Canada expect us to adopt your law? Harmonization in general is a very serious question, one which the commission will need to address, and one which the side agreements will probably end up addressing in one fashion or another.

Standards are also a problem with respect to dispute resolution because of the rights of states or provinces, because of the question of the burden of proof and because of the question of the "relevance standard," which is that standards should be based on objective science, or should be, at least, science-based. NAFTA does not identify which scientific standard to use, and in many cases there are conflicting scientific standards, for example, what level of toxicity is acceptable in shellfish? There will be countless disputes, which should be very lucrative for trade and environmental lawyers.

The final topic I want to explore is the commission itself. The Trade Commission is presently an empty vessel waiting to be filled by somebody with imagination who wants a job. It is very likely that the commission will wind up preparing many reports. The corporate community can live with that; in fact, we would like it to compile a lot of reports, particularly on how governments are co-operating. They have already produced a whole range of bilateral, and one or two trilateral, agreements on environmental issues, and environmental commitments to co-operate. Are they honouring these commitments? Maybe the commission should do reports on levels of compliance with those agreements. The commission should also undertake reports on the overall level and consistency of enforcement over time. If the commission finds a pattern of non-enforcement in a particular sector, that would be a matter for consultation among the three parties.

The Trade Commission will also have to deal with a very serious issue: that of investment diversion and the lowering of standards. This is a question of state, not federal, jurisdiction. In Canada, Mexico, and the U.S., states or provinces acting independently will frequently provide "enforcement holidays" to companies invited in. Does a holiday, even for a relatively short period of time, constitute a conscious decision to lower investment standards on the part of the nation in order to attract investment? If it is, it violates NAFTA. This is something that the commission will probably have to take under advisement.

The commission will also have to do many other things, in terms of technology transfer, training, consultations and reviews, and identifying projects for infrastructure financing. There are many ways the commission may act without getting into the supernational enforcement area, which the corporate community believes would be disastrous from the point of view of implementing the agreement, from the point of view of sovereignty, and from the point of view of equity.

Macro-Based International Competitiveness with Free Trade

Rodrigue Tremblay

Introduction

THE RULES OF THE GENERAL AGREEMENT on Tariffs and Trade (GATT) and especially the rules of the Free Trade Agreement between Canada and the United States (FTA), which came into effect on January 1, 1989, make it ever more difficult for countries to pursue explicit micro-economic policies to raise productivity and promote growth industries. Tariffs and quotas cannot be relied upon to change the industrial structure within the FTA, and this will be also the case with the North American Free Trade Agreement (NAFTA), while their use is very conditional at best within GATT. On the other hand other micro-tools of industrial policies, such as direct subsidies through sector-specific or through industry-specific industries, can be subjected to countervailing or anti-dumping duties and are therefore also less likely to be used in the future.

If explicit micro-based industrial policies are bound to be less relied upon in the future, this will not preclude the reliance on implicit industrial strategies, which can be disguised under military and government procurements or under environmental regulations. However, the emphasis of public policy to reinforce the industrial structure may have to be more general and macro-based regarding fiscal, labour and immigration, monetary, exchange rate, and general investment and industrial policies.

Moreover, economists researching the impact of trade policy shifts, such as the joining of a regional free trade area, have tended to adapt the problems to the methodology at hand. Ever since H. Johnson (1958) estimated the (small and favourable) static welfare effects of the United Kingdom joining the European Economic Community, economists have found it more convenient to stress the static welfare gains and losses arising from trade liberalization, rather than the more elusive but potentially more important dynamic effects accompanying the move to freer trade. The tool of predilection has been the applied general equilibrium model, which was initially used by Johansen (1960), and adapted to the U.S. by Shoven and Whalley (1972) and to Canada by Boadway and Treddenick (1978). These models measure the effects that changes in relative prices resulting from alterations to the trade environment cause to production, real income and employment, after labour and capital have had time to adjust and move from the declining sectors to the expanding sectors. Efficiency gains resulting from better resource allocation normally lead to welfare gains, albeit often relatively small, depending on the assumptions of each model. The smaller welfare gains came from the "perfect competition and constant returns to scale" version, estimated by Hamilton and Whalley (1985) at 0.6 percent for Canada and Brown and Stern (1987) at 0.3 percent for Canada, with the implementation of the FTA. The larger welfare gains arose from the "imperfect competition and increasing returns (declining average cost functions)" version of the model, with Harris and Cox (1985) placing the Canadian FTA welfare gains to Canada at 8.9 percent, and with Brown and Stern (1989a) establishing the same gains for Canada at 1.1 percent.

Essentially, the models showing net welfare gains place the emphasis on industrial rationalization and better resource allocation, while those arriving at negative net welfare results stress the worsening of a country's terms of trade when its relatively higher tariffs are removed.

Therefore, if efficiency gains from trade liberalization are estimated to be relatively small and sometimes negative, one may ask why such trade policy shifts attract so much attention. The answer lies in the competitiveness requirements that accompany the opening of an economy and increased competition. With free trade, consumers and buyers in general cannot be relied upon to subsidize inefficiencies and higher costs. Cost containment measures become a prerequisite for the economy that must adjust to freer trade. If these cost containment measures (such as technological and productivity improvements through new investments and lower real wage bills) are successfully applied, the adjustment to freer trade will be the intra-firm and the intra-industry type and the overall productivity of the economy will improve. However, if the cost containment measures are insufficient or non-existent, the adjustment to freer trade will be of the inter-industry type, and it is not impossible then not only that structural unemployment will rise, but also that the overall productivity of the economy could decline, and a lower rate of economic growth could result.

Unfortunately, the Canadian government did not pay much attention to competitiveness and the real exchange rate during the process of industrial adjustment to North American free trade after 1989. On the contrary, an Advisory Council on Adjustment created by the federal government to "examine the possibilities for Canadians to gain maximum advantage from the Canada-U.S. Trade Agreement," essentially concluded that only minor adjustments to existing policies were required (*Adjusting to Win*, 1989). Another indication of complacency can be found in the fact that Canada has no joint ministry of industry and international trade as in the United Kingdom or Japan. In Ottawa, the Department of International Trade is an adjunct to the Department of Foreign Affairs, and diplomats run economic affairs, not industrialists. Indeed, after such a fundamental shift in trade policy as the Free Trade Agreement, one would have expected that the priority would have been placed on reinforcing competitiveness by encouraging industrial investments, productivity gains, wage restraints, and other intra-industrial policies. Such policies above all would have contributed to avoiding the dislocations that inter-industry adjustments and massive plant closures were bound to create, with the concomitant rise in structural Canadian unemployment.[1] Partly because of this neglect of macro-based general industrial policies, Canada has fallen back in industrial competitiveness since the advent of free trade, and as a consequence, seems to have suffered some degree of disindustrialization and a rise in structural unemployment.

Macro-based international competitiveness

In a general sense and in the long run, international competitiveness is the ability of an economy to use its resources (labour, capital, and land) so that its producers can compete with those of other countries. Competitiveness does not evolve only from relative cost efficiency, but also relates to the design, quality, and delivery of tradable products and services. The more narrow concept of international competitiveness relates primarily to relative cost and price competitiveness, and it is used to explain how domestic producers fare in terms of profitability and of market shares, internally and internationally, and how the industrial structure evolves.

If a country is to reap the benefits derived from the dynamic effects of free trade, the competitiveness of its manufacturing and tradable services sectors must improve, or at least not regress. Indeed, increased competitiveness of the tradable goods sectors means faster capital accumulation and faster productivity growth, and therefore, faster economic growth. In order for free trade to provide net economic benefits, it must improve the dynamic outlook for economic growth (Tremblay, 1991).

Since the export sector expands with free trade, while the import-competing sector and the non-tradable goods sector are bound to contract, at least in relative terms, new investments (plant and equipment) and capital transfers to the export sector must be encouraged. And since

---

1 For a good discussion of the distinction between macro-economic industrial policies, sectoral industrial policies, and micro-economic and firm-specific industrial policies, see M.N. Jovanovic, *International Economic Integration* (London and New York: Routledge, 1992).

large segments of Canada's industries, especially in the import-competing sector, are foreign controlled, North American free trade has always presented the threat that U.S. firms would repatriate capital to overcome the tariff wall. Such a movement of capital would tend however to depreciate the Canadian dollar and encourage the expansion of the export-oriented industries, while cushioning the impact of tariff reductions on the import-competing sector.

If free trade is to result in a relative expansion of the tradable goods sector, its profitability must improve. And for the cost-competitiveness of the tradable goods sector to improve, the domestic terms of trade must move in favour of that sector. For a small price-taker country, this means in effect that the real exchange rate (e_R) must suffer a real depreciation with a rise of the price of tradable goods relative to the price of non-tradable goods $\left(\dfrac{P_T}{P_N}\right)$.

Indeed, there are two ways to use the real exchange rate as a measure of competitiveness. First, it is a measure of the competitiveness of home goods *vis-à-vis* foreign goods. Second, it is a measure of the competitiveness of the tradable goods domestic industries *vis-à-vis* the non-tradable goods domestic industries. The latter measure conveys the idea that the entire economy must adjust to free trade and increased competition, and not just the foreign sector.

$$e_R = E \cdot \frac{P^*}{P} = \frac{P_T}{P_N} \tag{1.0}$$

where: E is the nominal exchange rate of foreign currency in units of the domestic currency; P^* is the index of foreign prices and P the index of domestic prices, while P_T is the index of tradable goods prices and P_N is the index of non-tradable goods prices.

When only the foreign sector is considered, the equilibrium real exchange rate is the level that generates a current account surplus or deficit equal to net long-term capital flows. When the entire economy is considered, a sustained real depreciation tends to lower real wages and increase profits and employment in the tradable sector. A sustained real appreciation has the reverse effect on real wages and on the profits and employment in the export and import-competing industries. In the latter case, resources and workers are displaced from the tradable sector, even though they should remain in that sector if the exchange rate were at its long-run equilibrium.

Because of the openness of its economy and the relative large size of its tradable goods sector, Canada's most important single price is the exchange rate. And because average Canadian tariffs on imported goods were twice as high as their U.S. equivalent in 1989 (11.2 percent vs. 6.5 percent), it could have been expected that a stable or slightly depreciating exchange rate was called for, if Canadian industry were to adjust to the increased competition from imports and to the increased opportunities in the U.S. market.[2]

The real appreciation of the exchange rate for the manufacturing sector, which is deemed to comprise essentially tradable goods, can be measured by assuming that industrial prices are determined as a mark-up of unit labour costs. Industrial prices in the U.S. (P^*) can thus be expressed as the ratio of U.S. industrial wages and the average or marginal productivity of labour $\left(\dfrac{W^*}{PROD^*}\right)$, and similarly for Canada, except that unit labour costs in the manufacturing sector must be expressed in the U.S. dollar for the purpose of comparison, hence, $\left(\dfrac{1}{E} \cdot \dfrac{W}{PROD}\right)$. And therefore

$$e_R = \frac{\left(\dfrac{W^*}{PROD^*}\right)}{\left(\dfrac{W}{E \cdot PROD}\right)} \tag{2.0}$$

---

2   According to the concept of net effective protection (Gordon, 1971), the country with the highest tariffs should see its currency depreciate with the advent of free trade. See R. Tremblay, "Compétitivité canadienne et libre-échange nord-américain les trois premieres années de l'ALE," *L'Actualité Economique*, Spring 1993.

For a given period, the change in the relative competitiveness of the manufacturing sector or the real appreciation or depreciation can be expressed as follows:

$$\Delta e_R = \Delta W^* - \Delta PROD^* + \Delta E - \Delta W + \Delta PROD \qquad (3.0)$$

A real appreciation or a loss of competitiveness in Canadian industry occurs when U.S. manufacturing productivity grows faster than Canadian productivity, or when industrial wages in Canada grow faster in U.S. dollars than U.S. industrial wages.[3] As S. Arndt (1990) has well stressed, however, the real exchange rate is not determined primarily in the tradable goods sector, where trade flows maintain equilibrium, but in the non-tradable goods sector where the price must adjust to clear the markets. As a consequence, there is more than the nominal exchange involved here. Indeed, competitiveness policies or general industrial policies cannot be directed solely towards the tradable goods sector, but must also be oriented towards non-tradable goods. If competitiveness is to improve, this requires more supply-oriented and fewer demand-oriented policies. In practice, this means lower budgetary deficits at both the federal and provincial levels, and more incentives for investments in the tradable industries. It also means less reliance on monetary policy and more on fiscal policy to combat inflation.

Canadian industrial competitiveness, 1987-91

Table 1 provides a summary of the evolution of industrial wages and productivity in Canada and in the United States, as well as the trend of unit labour costs in each country. Since movements in costs take time to influence output and employment decisions, in fact between one and a half to two years, the relative cost history of the Canadian manufactur-

---

3   Changes in relative taxation levels could also be taken into consideration, but can be assumed to be minor if the period considered is short, as is the case here.

Table 1: Index of Productivity, Wages and Unit Labour Costs in Canada and in the United States, 1982-1991 (Manufacturing Sector)

	CANADA Unit labour costs in Can $ (1)	CANADA Hourly wages (2)	CANADA Output per hour (3)	U.S.A. Hourly wages (4)	U.S.A. Output per hour (5)	CANADA Unit labour costs in U.S. $ (6)	U.S.A. Unit labour costs in U.S. $ (7)	Ratio (6)/(7) (8)	Bilateral exchange rate $\left(\dfrac{\$\,CAN}{\$\,US}\right)$ (9)
1982	100	100	100	100	100	100	100	100	81.3
1983	98.9	106.1	107.3	102.5	102.9	99.0	99.6	99.4	80.3
1984	95.5	111.1	116.4	105.7	105.6	91.0	100.1	90.9	75.6
1985	97.6	116.8	119.8	111.0	108.0	88.2	102.8	85.8	71.5
1986	102.9	121.3	117.9	115.4	122.6	91.4	105.5	89.2	72.4
1987	106.0	125.0	119.0	118.0	117.2	97.8	100.7	97.1	76.9
1988	110.4	130.1	119.6	122.6	122.0	109.1	100.5	108.6	83.8
1989	115.1	138.4	120.2	127.5	123.5	120.0	104.0	115.4	86.3
1990	121.6	148.1	121.8	134.3	125.7	128.7	106.9	120.4	86.2
1991	127.6	155.9	122.1	140.1	127.4	138.6	109.8	126.2	86.5

Sources: U.S. Department of Labor, *Monthly Labour Review*, January 1993; Bank of Canada, *Bank of Canada Review*.

ing sectors is considered over the two years preceding the FTA and the three years following the FTA, i.e., the five years 1987-91.

Until 1987, Canadian manufacturers enjoyed a cost comparative advantage over their American counterparts. After 1987, however, the Canadian manufacturing sector was hit on three fronts. First, industrial wages in national currencies increased about 25 percent faster in Canada than in the United States during the five years 1987-91 (24.7 percent vs. 18.7 percent). Second, productivity growth in Canada was three times slower than in the United States (2.6 percent vs. 8.7 percent) for the same period. As a consequence of these two factors, unit labour costs in the manufacturing sector in national currencies increased twice as fast in Canada as in the United States from 1987 to 1991 inclusive (20.4 percent vs. 9.1 percent). Third, the bilateral nominal exchange rate between the U.S. and Canadian dollars responding more to capital inflows and tight Canadian monetary policy than to relative production costs, resulted in a nominal appreciation of the Canadian dollar of 21.2 percent between 1987 and 1991 inclusively.

As a consequence, the drop in Canadian manufacturing competitiveness was even more pronounced when expressed on a U.S. dollar basis. This loss of competitiveness of the Canadian manufacturing sector was equal to 30 percent during the crucial 1987-1991 period preceding and following the FTA. This was the result of an increase of Canadian manufacturing unit labour costs in U.S. currency of 41.7 percent from 1987 to 1991, while U.S. comparable costs increased only by 9.1 percent.

The structural impact of Canada's loss of international competitiveness

Impact on the trade balance

Canada's loss of manufacturing competitiveness from 1987 to 1991, and the beginning of a Canada-U.S. phasing out of initial tariffs on January 1, 1989, were bound to affect the structure of each country's balance of payments and industrial structures. Since Canada is ten times smaller than its American counterpart, one could expect that Canadian relative structural adjustment would be ten times larger (Table 2).

Table 2: Canada-U.S. Bilateral and Global Balances of Payments, 1982-1991 (Millions of Canadian Dollars)

Year	Canadian merchandise exports to the U.S.	Canadian merchandise imports from the U.S.	Canada-U.S. bilateral merchandise trade balance	Canada's trade balance with the rest of the world (excluding the U.S.)	Bilateral exchange rate $\left(\dfrac{\$\,U.S.}{\$\,CAN}\right)$	Canadian dollars index against G-10 currencies 1981=100	Canada's current account balance
1982	58,097	47,072	11,025	6,629	1.2288	99.33	2,004
1983	66,388	52,721	13,667	3,790	1.2444	100.27	2,102
1984	84,816	65,893	18,923	914	1.3217	96.66	1,686
1985	93,793	73,406	20,386	-3,994	1.3983	92.05	-3,095
1986	93,326	76,427	16,899	-6,955	1.3805	86.30	-11,394
1987	96,605	78,985	17,620	-6,399	1.2993	88.19	-11,601
1988	102,642	88,794	13,848	-4,931	1.1925	93.93	-15,483
1989	105,657	94,026	11,631	-5,212	1.1585	98.81	-22,886
1990	110,475	93,727	16,748	-6,828	1.1599	99.26	-25,709
1991	107,617	93,733	13,884	-8,103	1.1555	100.83	-29,249
Changes							
87-91	11,291	14,748	-3,736	-1,704	-0.144	12.64	-17,648
89-91	1,960	-293	2,253	-2,891	+0.004	2.02	-6,363

Source: *Bank of Canada Review.*

Regarding the bilateral Canada-U.S. balance of payments, the advent of freer trade was only one influence among many on trade and capital flows (including relative competitiveness and the 1990-91 recession), but should have been expected to have resulted in both a trade creation effect and a trade diversion effect. For the first three years of the FTA, as compared to a 1988 base, Canada's merchandise exports to the U.S. did increase in nominal terms by 4.8 percent, while merchandise imports from the U.S. expanded by 5.6 percent, with the net result that the net bilateral trade hardly changed (0.2 percent). However, if one considers the five years between 1987 and 1991, when Canada's manufacturing competitiveness was under pressure, Canada's merchandise exports to the U.S. increased by 15.3 percent, but Canadian merchandise imports from the U.S. increased even faster at 22.6 percent, contracting Canada's trade surplus with the U.S. by 17.8 percent. The big jump in Canada's imports from the U.S. from 1987 to 1989 occurred when Canadian manufacturing competitiveness was dropping the fastest (21.9 percent in two years). Therefore, one has to notice that the competitiveness of the Canadian manufacturing sector was dropping sharply before the implementation of the FTA.

Canada's trade balance with the rest of the world started to deteriorate seriously in 1985, in parallel with the current account. In 1984, for instance, Canada had a trade surplus with the rest of the world. In 1991, it had a Cdn $8.1 billion trade deficit. Similarly, Canada had an overall current account surplus in 1985 (Cdn $1.7 billion), but registered a whopping Cdn $29.2 billion deficit in 1991. This could be partly due to the appreciation of the Canadian dollar against the G-10 currencies starting in 1984, while the appreciation of the Canadian dollar vis-à vis the U.S. dollar only began in 1987.

In conclusion, Canada's bilateral trade balance has deteriorated *vis-à-vis* the U.S. since 1987 (Cdn -$3,015 million), but this deterioration started earlier with the rest of the world in 1985, and was much more pronounced. The advent of the FTA in 1989 did not markedly influence Canada's bilateral trade balance with the U.S., since exports had increased by 4.8 percent by 1991, but imports had also increased by 5.6 percent, leaving the merchandise trade balance surplus at Cdn $13,884 million in 1991 just as it was in 1988 (Cdn $13,848 million). It is likely that the 1990-91 recession in Canada and in the U.S., and the Canadian dollar appreciation were much more influential in shaping Canada's external trade balance with the U.S. than the partial implementation of the FTA in 1989.

Impact on the structure of Canadian employment

Was the FTA instrumental in shifting the Canadian industrial structure of output and employment during the 1989-91 period? Table 3 illustrates how severe the contraction of employment in the Canadian manufacturing sector has been during the 1988-91 period. Since the advent of the FTA, Canada has lost 18 percent of its manufacturing jobs (347.8 thousand), while the rest of the economy experienced net job losses of only 2.9 percent or 296.4 thousand jobs. In other words, Canada's tradable goods industries have been much more negatively affected by the 1990-91 recession, by the advent of the FTA, and by the real appreciation of the Canadian dollar.

We have used a simple model of demand for tradable output and employment (Tremblay, 1993) in order to approximate the relative contribution of relative price and income changes to the fluctuations of manufacturing employment in Canada. Movements in the Canadian real exchange rate for the manufacturing sector have a delayed impact six quarters later. Historically, a ten percent real appreciation of the Canadian dollar has resulted in a 1.4 percent contraction of manufacturing employment. And since Canada experienced a 30 percent real appreciation of its currency in the 1987-91 period, a net loss of 80,644 manufacturing jobs can be traced to that single factor.

The 1990-91 recession in Canada and in the U.S. contributed to downsizing the Canadian manufacturing sector. Income effects can attribute a net loss of 12,080 Canadian manufacturing jobs to the U.S. recession and a net loss of 126,221 Canadian manufacturing jobs to the Canadian recession, which was longer and more severe than the American one. This would indicate that the brunt of Canada's job loss in the manufacturing sector is directly the result of the 1990-91 recession. However, the real appreciation of the Canadian dollar can explain about one quarter of the loss of Canadian manufacturing jobs during the 1989-91 period. If one goes back further to 1987 to encompass the 1987-1991 period, as much as one third of Canada's loss of manufactur-

Table 3: The Structure of Employment in Canada 1986-1991

Thousands: Annual Averages

Year	Total employment (1)	Manufacturing employment (2)	Service sector employment (3)	Goods producing sector employment (4)	Ratio (2)/(1) in percentages
1986	9,173.2	1,738.4	6,844.2	2,329.0	19.0
1987	9,896.3	1,891.3	7,336.6	2,559.7	19.1
1988	10,107.8	1,920.1	7,485.0	2,622.8	19.0
1989	10,342.4	1,935.9	7,678.0	2,664.5	18.7
1990	10,154.2	1,786.7	7,673.5	2,480.7	17.6
1991	9,463.6	1,572.3	7,288.2	2,175.5	16.6
Changes					
1988-1991	-644.2	-347.8	-196.8	-447.3	54.0

Source: Statistics Canada, *Employment, Earnings and Hours*, no. 72-002.

ing jobs can be traced back to the real appreciation of the Canadian dollar.

This leaves about 85,000 jobs having been lost on average because of real shocks such as the partial implementation of the FTA on January 1, 1989, and the introduction of the Goods and Services Tax (GST) on January 1, 1991. Since the GST was much more comprehensive and general than the partial reduction of tariffs and quotas related to the FTA, it can be assumed that the FTA itself did not play a large direct role in the reduction of Canadian manufacturing employment. However, because the macro-economic environment was so negative in Canada when the FTA was implemented, it is likely that American-controlled installations in Canada were downsized or closed at a much faster rate than one could have expected. Further detailed research would be required to know if this was in fact the case.

If there is no hysteresis in the contraction of Canadian manufacturing employment, a return of the Canadian dollar to its long-term equilibrium value would re-establish the viability of the Canadian manufacturing sector. If there is hysteresis, however, an overshooting of the real depreciation of the Canadian dollar would be required to correct the damage that the previous overvaluation has done to the Canadian industrial structure.

Conclusion

The move towards free trade and an export-led growth strategy for Canada does not concern trade policy alone, but requires that all economic policies must be re-assessed as to their contribution to the macro-competitiveness of the economy. Indeed, the real exchange rate of the currency occupies a central role in reallocating resources towards more productive uses. The real exchange rate is not only a measure of the competitiveness of home goods *vis-à-vis* foreign goods. It is above all a measure of the competitiveness of the tradable goods domestic sector *vis-à-vis* the non-tradable goods domestic sector. For the transition towards free trade to be a success, all economic policies have to be co-ordinated in order to increase the competitiveness of the tradable goods industries and facilitate their rationalization and reorganization. This does not seem to have been done in Canada before or after the implementation of the FTA on January 1, 1989. As a consequence, the loss of Canadian manufacturing jobs was much more severe than was necessary to adapt to the Canada-U.S. free trade area.

References

Adjusting to Win, Government of Canada, March 1989, 171 pages.

Boadway, R. and J. Treddenick (1978), "A General Equilibrium Computation of the Effects of the Canadian Tariff Structure," *Canadian Journal of Economics*, pp. 424-446.

Brown, D. K. and R. M. Stern (1987), "A Modelling Perspective," in R. M. Stern, P. H. Tresize and J. Whalley (eds.), *Perspectives on a U.S. Canadian Free Trade Agreement*, The Brookings Institution.

Brown, D. K. and R. M. Stern (1989), "Computable General Equilibrium Estimates of the Gains from U.S.-Canadian Trade Liberalization," in D. Greenaway, T. H. Hyclak and R. J. Thornton (eds.), *Economic Aspects of Regional Trading Arrangements*, London, Harvester Wheat Sheaf.

Brown, D. K. and R. M. Stern (1989), "Some Conceptual Issues in the Modelling and Computational Analysis of the Canada-U.S. Free Trade Agreement," *The North American Journal of Economics and Finance*, pp. 1-20.

Gordon W. Max (1971), *The Theory of Protection*, Clarendon, Oxford.

Hamilton, B. and J. Whalley (1985), "Geographically Discriminatory Trade Arrangements", *Review of Economics and Statistics*, pp. 446-455.

Harris, R. G. and D. Cox (1985), "Summary of a Project on the General Equilibrium Evaluation of Canadian Trade Policy," in J. Whalley (ed.), *Canada-U.S. Free Trade*, Vol. 11, Research Studies, Royal Commission an the Economic Union and Development projects for Canada, University of Toronto Press, Toronto.

Johansen L. (1960) *A Multi-Sectorial Study of Economic Growth*, Amsterdam, North-Holland.

Johnson, H. (1958), "The Gains from Freer Trade with Europe: An Estimate," Manchester School of Economic and Social Studies, pp. 247-55.

Shoven, J. B. and J. Whalley (1984), "Applied General Equilibrium Models of Taxation and International Trade," *Journal of Economic Literature*, pp. 1007-51.

Tremblay, R. (1990), "The Export-Import Effect and Economic Growth," *The North American Journal of Economics and Finance*, pp. 241-252.

Tremblay, R. (1993), "Compétitivité Canadienne et Libre-échange Nord-Américain: les trois premières années de l'ALÉ," *L'actualité Économique*, spring.

The Economics of NAFTA: How Much Zero-Sum?

William G. Watson[1]

THE QUESTION I WANT TO RAISE in this paper is "how much zero-sum?" I do not doubt that NAFTA will produce net benefits. Mexico's gains, which stand to be substantial, will not all come at the expense of its northern neighbours, while together the three countries' gains will not all come at the expense of other countries. On the other hand, though the upside probably is greater than the downside, there will be a downside. Some NAFTA gains will come at other people's expense. Other papers in this volume accentuate the positive. What I want to suggest is that we cannot eliminate the negative, though we may be able to compensate for it.

In judging whether NAFTA creates net benefits, economists generally accept the nationalist perspective that our customary methods of statistical aggregation impose on them. Thus, a number of economic

---

1   The last time Al Riggs and Tom Velk invited me to participate in a conference I spoke slightly less than 48 hours before being married. This time I spoke slightly more than 48 hours after our first child was born. I await their next conference with great anticipation.

studies confirm what the trade negotiators have been telling us: that the deal is win-win-win. It is curious that economists, of all people, should consent to a national formulation of the problem. Our discipline operates from the bottom up, emphasizing the importance of individuals. Thus, while each of the three countries as a whole may gain,[2] it seems certain that there will be losses to certain individuals and groups within each country. People who benefit from current trade and investment regimes are likely to be hurt by new regimes. Standard trade theory, with its Stolper-Samuelson theorem, tells us that. In fact, there may be even greater losses—together with greater net benefits—the better the agreement works, since as a rule more international specialization requires more adjustment.

I should emphasize that this is not an argument for not going ahead with the NAFTA—though it could be—but simply a plea that it is best to be up-front about the possibility of losses—especially in this country, after the rough political ride that the Canada-U.S. FTA has had.

Who loses? Trade creation

Economists distinguish between trade creation and trade diversion. Trade creation is generally regarded as the "good" change caused by the formation of customs unions or free trade areas. Canadians, Americans, and Mexicans who had been prevented from trading with each other by tariffs or quotas will find new markets in which to buy or sell. Even this "good" trade will cause harm, however. The trade theorem referred to above tells us that the relatively scarce factor of production in each country will lose, while relatively abundant factors will gain. In this case, capital and skilled labour are scarce in Mexico and abundant in Canada and the United States. Goods produced with these "factors of production" will therefore flow from north to south after tariffs are removed. Of course, as any Canadian or American trade unionist will tell you, Mexico's abundant factor is unskilled labour, which means goods produced with it will flow north after NAFTA, to the likely

---

2   Leamer, Edward (1992), "Wage Effects of a U.S.-Mexican Free Trade Agreement," National Bureau of Economic Research Working Paper 3991.

detriment of unskilled workers in Canada and the United States. Edward Leamer has "guesstimated" that the wages of unskilled American workers may fall by roughly $1,000 a year after NAFTA is fully in place.[3] That this will happen eventually anyway, as countries whose workforces come much cheaper than even Mexico's introduce market reforms and expand their exports, is unlikely to persuade such workers of the benefits of NAFTA, which—probably correctly—they see as hastening their economic demise.

It is true that a number of computer models of North American trade liberalization predict an increase in wage rates in all three countries as a result of economic specialization. On the other hand: these models generally do not differentiate among different types of labour; they often simply assume that there are potential economies of scale throughout manufacturing that can produce substantial productivity gains, at least some of which accrue to workers; and, for technical reasons, they often understate the degree of specialization, and therefore the disruption, that might result from NAFTA.[4] The contrary prediction, that some workers' wages probably will fall as a result of NAFTA—though many who claim it are neo-Marxists or worse—is in fact an impeccably neoclassical notion.

Who loses? Trade diversion

What economists regard as the "bad" change resulting from preferential trading arrangements they call "trade diversion." People in the three countries who had been buying goods or services from suppliers in fourth countries may decide after NAFTA to buy from their NAFTA partners. This is "bad" change because the fourth-country suppliers may actually be the most efficient producers of whatever is being

---

3   Assuming that that expression means anything.

4   Brown, Drusilla (1992), "The Impact of a North American Free Trade Area: Applied General Equilibrium Models" pp. 26-57 in Lustig, Nora, Barry P. Bosworth and Robert Z. Lawrence, eds. (1992), *North American Free Trade: Assessing the Impact* (Washington: Brookings Institution).

traded, but because their exports into the NAFTA region face tariffs while NAFTA partners trade with each other tariff-free, they end up being priced out of the NAFTA market. This distorts the worldwide allocation of resources: goods that would be produced most efficiently outside NAFTA end up being produced inside NAFTA.

Ron Wonnacott has argued recently that this may not be that big a problem.[5] His reasoning is that Canada and Mexico currently do most of their trade with the United States, so they do not have that many fourth-country imports to be diverted. And while the U.S. *does* trade mainly with the rest of the world, U.S. tariffs are generally low to begin with, so the preference it will give Canada and Mexico via the NAFTA is not that large. Though Wonnacott's reasoning is sound, there obviously will be some trade diversion as a result of NAFTA. Seventy-five of the products Canada currently imports from Mexico faced tariffs greater than 8.8 percent in 1989. Though they accounted for only $93 million of Mexico's exports to Canada, these 75 products competed with $16 billion of imports from countries other than Mexico. If Mexico makes further inroads into the Canadian market after these tariffs go, this may be at least partly at the expense of other countries' exporters. Canadians who worry that only Canadian producers will be displaced by Mexican firms should be reminded of this.[6]

In fact, while economists decry trade diversion, ordinary citizens often like it. Thus one argument that has been used to support NAFTA is that, since the investment and jobs that will be lost from Canada and the United States eventually will be going anyway, better to have them go to Mexico, which currently has a high propensity to consume American goods, rather than to Taiwan or Singapore or other places that do not trade as much with North America.

---

5   Wonnacott, Ronald (1993) forthcoming paper for the C. D. Howe Institute, Toronto.

6   In fact, the same 75 goods accounted for $37 billion of production in Canada. See Investment Canada (1991), "The Opportunities and Challenges of North American Free Trade: A Canadian Perspective" Working Paper 7, April 1991.

There are at least four things wrong with this argument. First, Mexicans may buy a lot in the United States but they buy hardly anything from Canada, so the argument is moot as far as we are concerned. Second, what Mexicans currently buy in the U.S. may not be a good indicator of what they will buy in future from the U.S. Because Mexican tariffs are higher than Canadian and American tariffs, NAFTA will give their trade a bigger North American tilt than will be true in the other two countries. But there is no reason to suppose that Mexican liberalization with Canada and the United States will not be followed by Mexican liberalization with fourth countries. Third, and much more important, as far as liberals are concerned,[7] trade diversion should always be regarded as a cost of a preferential trading arrangement, not a benefit. If the Taiwanese or Singaporeans can do a better job producing the goods than the Mexicans, the world is worse off if production goes to Mexico. People interested in the world's welfare should want Mexico to specialize in those things it is best at, not in what the North American tariff structure says it is best at. Finally, the argument is based on the incorrect assumption that the overall level of employment in Canada and the United States is determined by whom these countries trade with. It is not. It is determined by aggregate supply and demand. If exports to Mexico are lost, it does not follow that this produces a permanent decline either in aggregate exports or aggregate demand.

Who loses? Trade rediversion

Departing from this global perspective for a moment and adopting a nationalist outlook, we note that Canada currently benefits from trade diversion under the Canada-U.S. FTA. We do not pay duty—or at least will not pay duty when the FTA is fully in place—on shipments into the U.S. market. The rest of the world does.[8] Unfortunately, NAFTA gives Mexico the same privileged access to the U.S. market that we currently

---

7   And all economists should be liberals.

8   That's not quite true. The U.S. has preferential trade agreements with Israel and with several Caribbean countries.

have (albeit not such privileged access now that two countries have it). In 1989, Canada and Mexico competed in the U.S. market in 2,503 different commodities, accounting for $60 billion of Canadian trade and $20 billion of Mexican. Post-1989, Canada would have had an advantage in this trade. Under NAFTA, Mexico will enjoy the same tariff reductions by the end of the century or shortly thereafter. Thus, the trade diversion we could reasonably have expected to see as a result of the FTA will be somewhat reduced. On the other hand, these gains have not yet been fully realized, so perhaps losing them will not hurt so much. Moreover, Mexico's current trade disadvantage in the U.S. market is not great: American tariffs on Mexican goods are quite low on average, though there are a few cases in which tariffs remain high and quotas are quite restrictive.

Who loses? Altered investment patterns

Most computer models suggest NAFTA is likely to make investment in Mexico more attractive. Some of this investment will come from entirely new savings: better profit opportunities in Mexico will cause the world, Mexico included, to do a little more saving than it otherwise would have. Some of the investment will come from saving that might have financed investment outside of North America. And some of it undoubtedly will come from saving that, were it not for NAFTA, would have financed investment in Canada or the United States. In brief, some companies will move. Economic theory suggests that the firms that are most likely to move are those that make significant use of Mexico's most abundant factor of production, unskilled labour. That such investments would remain in Canada over the long term is very unlikely, given the large number of countries in the world that have lower labour costs than Canada, though once again knowledge of this is not likely to comfort workers whose jobs may disappear as a result of the capital moving.

Who loses? Sovereignty

This should not have been a serious concern last time round, though it was. It is true that the greater economic competition brought about by trade liberalization may induce governments to change policies, but it does so only by revealing the true cost of these policies. The FTA itself required no changes in the area of social policy. This is not the case with NAFTA, or at least it will not be if NAFTA is accompanied by side agreements on the environment and labour standards. Most Canadians presumably would not object if the side agreements affected only Mexican domestic policies. But because Mexico is unlikely to sign any agreement written in this asymmetric way, the side agreements will probably open up the possiblity of tripartite regulation of Canadian policies. Most Canadians, both supporters and opponents of the FTA, were opposed to this in 1988. It is hard to understand why they should accept it in 1993. It is even more puzzling that those Canadians who were most insistent on retaining Canadian sovereignty in 1988 are now most insistent on securing sovereignty-reducing side agreements.

Bottom line

There clearly are zero-sum aspects to NAFTA. Though most Canadians may gain (however slightly) from the agreement, and though the gainers' gains may well outweigh the losses suffered by those Canadians who do lose from it, there are likely to be losers. Such people have an obvious and understandable interest in opposing the agreement. In addition, a large number of groups in Canadian society have an overriding ideological interest in opposing NAFTA, despite the impressive gains it would bring to Mexico, at very little if any net cost to Canada. Unfortunately, for a variety of reasons these groups probably are more influential now than they were in 1988.

It would be surprising if a 2,000-page document representing the results of a year's negotiation among three closely connected countries did not contain error. Thus, some aspects of the agreement are easier to endorse than others. Yet NAFTA itself is, fundamentally, a profoundly liberalizing document. By North American standards, Spain and Portugal were not at a high level of economic development when they entered the European Community. But they were significantly more advanced than Mexico currently is. If NAFTA can be made to work for the overall benefit of all three of its member countries, this will demonstrate in the most convincing manner imaginable that it is possible for very different economies to benefit from free trade. No lesson could be more helpful to the continuing development of international institutions for the governance of trade.

For this reason—and I suspect no other—it makes sense to provide special assistance to people who will be hurt by NAFTA. In 1989, the Conservative government very sensibly decided that because it was both hard to tell exactly who lost their job because of trade and unfair to provide different assistance to people who were unemployed for different reasons—even assuming it were possible to tell who was unemployed for what reason—there should not be a special assistance program for victims of the FTA. These arguments are still persuasive. On the other hand, given the current politics of trade liberalization in Canada, it probably would be wise to set up a separate program with its own acronym, letterhead and bureaucracy to provide essentially the same assistance as would be available to workers who can make a plausible case that the reason they lost their job is greater competition from Mexico. If Paris was worth a mass, NAFTA, and the further liberalization it promises, may be worth an acronym.

Section V
What's in it for Mexico and the Hemisphere?

NAFTA's History and Future Prospects

The Honourable Michael H. Wilson, Minister of Industry, Science and Technology and Minister of Trade, Canada

LADIES AND GENTLEMEN, I AM DELIGHTED to be with you at this conference. It is ironic that the place that I have just come from was a meeting between the federal and provincial governments on interprovincial trade barriers.

I am the co-chair of a committee of federal and provincial ministers that has the objective of eliminating these trade barriers, and we have just taken an important step by using the same technique that we employ in international trade negotiation. You go in with a comprehensive agenda to ensure that everything gets put on the table. Nothing is agreed until everything is agreed.

We have found in recent years that the governments involved have always tried to eliminate provincial barriers on a step-by-step basis. While one province wants to see the elimination of a certain barrier, they do not want the elimination of another one involving other provinces, and vice versa. This time we were able to get an agreement from the provinces to put everything on the table, and to negotiate in a comprehensive way, as we did with the free trade agreement with the United States and, more recently, with NAFTA.

I am delighted to be here to talk about some important aspects of NAFTA, and also to answer your questions regarding this agreement.

But first, I would like to congratulate the hosts of this important seminar, McGill, for arranging the facilities, and also The Fraser Institute and my old alma mater, the University of Toronto.

Let's talk a little bit about NAFTA. This agreement took us about 14 months to conclude. From the day that we started in Toronto to the day of completion in Washington, D.C., it took 14, tough, slugging months to conclude negotiations. This compares to almost 2½ years of FTA negotiations with the United States.

There are some very important benefits that will accrue to Canada as a result of NAFTA. We have had some complaints from opponents of the free trade agreement, saying: "Why are we already putting forward the NAFTA implementing legislation at a time when the Americans and the Mexicans are not putting forward their legislation?" Let me be very clear here; the negotiations resulted in an agreement that I think is good for Canada.

We in Canada have been the first to put forward the formal legislation, but I should say to you that the Americans started their legislative process last September and the Mexicans have sent the agreement to their Senate. So we are all moving forward in the legislative process in different ways, because the process is different in each of the three countries.

In Canada, the level of interest in the agreement is high. We have had close to four months of parliamentary committee hearings in nine cities across the country, and have had about 120 different organizations, as well as individuals, make presentations on this agreement.

We introduced the bill in February because we wanted to make sure that people had an opportunity to examine it and to look at the specific elements of the implementing legislation. But also, we wanted to do this in a way that gives business a sense of what is in the legislation, so that they could make plans, at an early stage, in order to take advantage of the opportunities present in Mexico.

Concerning the level of interest that Canadian business has shown in the Mexican market, in 1990, there were about 1,000 business visitors to our embassy in Mexico City. In 1991, there were 2,000. In 1992, they more than doubled to 4,500. So this is growing in an exponential way, and I believe it indicates what business feels about opportunities in the Mexican market.

There are a number of questions that are being raised about the side agreements. Today, in Washington, we are opening the first stage of negotiations on these side agreements on labour and on the environment. Some have said that Canada should leave the legislation, not proceed with it, until we know what is in the agreements on labour and the environment. I reject that for a very simple reason. The agreement, as it stands, is a good agreement for Canada in itself.

All three governments have agreed not to reopen the agreement, and not to delay the implementation date of January 1, 1994. So it is important that we begin the parliamentary process.

We are encouraged that the Clinton administration has decided to pursue parallel agreements. You may recall that in February 1992, when the NAFTA negotiations were held in Montreal, I put forward a proposal to have parallel agreements on labour and on the environment. The Americans and the Mexicans rejected this at the time. It was not until a change in administration in the United States that we had an opportunity to reopen the question. When we concluded the negotiations last August, we knew we had an agreement that had more elements in it that took into account the environmental impacts of trade than any other trade agreement in existence today. I believe it will be seen as a base point for future trade negotiations. In September, the three countries agreed to create a North American Commission on the Environment. We have taken an active part in developing a mandate for that commission.

As I said, our negotiators are in Washington today, and we have some very clear objectives that I would like to share with you. One is to promote sustainable development. The second is to strengthen environmental co-operation, and particularly, strengthen co-operation in the enforcement of environmental laws and regulations. This has been an area where Mexico has been weak. Their regulations, their laws, are as good as Canada's or the United States', but their enforcement of them has been weak. This is an area in which we believe that we and the

United States can be of great assistance to them. This is one of our clear objectives.

Finally, we want to make sure that the proposal to have a North American Commission on the Environment moves ahead with a very effective mandate.

As for negotiations on the labour side agreements, we want to activate the part of the preamble in the North American Free Trade Agreement that says, "To improve working conditions and living standards in all three countries, and to protect, enhance, and enforce basic workers' rights."

We will be advocating the establishment of a trinational commission to cover labour matters in order to establish a set of common principles that we can follow and have a degree of dialogue and co-operation in seeking the achievement of the objectives that are set out in those principles.

Let me make an obvious point here that is never given much credit by our opponents. People are concerned about labour and environmental matters in Mexico. If we did not have a North American Free Trade Agreement, we would not have the opportunity or the basis for entering into these side agreements with Mexico. So it is important that we proceed on both fronts, with the negotiations on the parallel agreements as well as the implementation of NAFTA.

I believe that NAFTA is a pivotal part of our overall economic strategy. Trade is very important to Canada. One job in three, almost 30 percent of our economic activity, depends on trade. It is one of the key reasons why we have been an active part of the GATT, the General Agreement on Tariffs and Trade, and of all of the trade negotiations under the GATT since 1947.

But we also have to look at our regional opportunities, particularly in the United States. With 75 percent of our trade being conducted with the United States, it was important to move ahead with the Free Trade Agreement with the United States, and now to expand that to Mexico, because of the important opportunities we have with our next closest geographic trading partner.

Four years ago, after we completed the Free Trade Agreement with the United States, we had a pretty active election campaign. I believe that I was in this building, it may even have been this room, debating the Free Trade Agreement at the time of that election. I made an observation at that time that I thought the FTA would be good and that it would lead to an increase in our trade with the United States. Let me give you some numbers concerning this increase. Last year, our exports to the U.S. were up 13.5 percent compared to 1991, in a period when the U.S. economy was somewhat sluggish. We have been able to increase our market share in the United States because our exports since 1988 are up about 30 percent. Japan, the country that is supposed to be killing the United States with their export performance, is only up about 16 percent. Germany is up 7 percent, the United Kingdom is up about 13 percent. So we have been able to increase our market share, and that applies even on an industry-to-industry basis. Eighteen out of 22 Canadian industries that are measured by Statistics Canada have gained market share in the U.S. during this period of time.

Imports are also up, but the key point here is what has happened to the trade balance. Our trade surplus increased 27 percent from 1991 to 1992, and it is important to note that this trend continues. Our trade performance is up considerably. The surplus has risen another $900 million, driven primarily by a solid increase in our exports to the United States.

There are some very clear signals of benefit that have come from the Free Trade Agreement with the United States. It has had a positive effect on job creation. Last year, 118,000 jobs were created. I believe, and I'm not alone in saying this, that one of the driving forces in job creation in our economy today is our export performance.

So I say to our critics: "What is your point? Why don't you like the Free Trade Agreement with the United States?" We have seen a performance in our exports that has never been greater. Last month the export trend was up 12 straight months. NAFTA builds on this success.

We wanted to have an agreement that made Canada a more favourable place to invest for companies that are seeking to serve the North American market, and we succeeded in this. We also sought to maintain the benefits that we had in the Free Trade Agreement with the United States, and, if possible, to improve on those. There are a number of ways that we were able to make improvements on these benefits. Finally, we wanted to gain greater access to the Mexican market, a market of 85 million people. Of those 85 million people, there is a middle income market of about 25 million people, which for a country of 27 million people, such as Canada, is a pretty important market. We succeeded in gaining greater access to the Mexican market.

So the conclusion that I come to when I look at the reasons for being in the NAFTA negotiations are very clear. We should not stand on the sidelines for any trade negotiations. I never claim that any trade agreement or trade negotiation will produce economic miracles, but it will contribute to solid job-creating economic activity.

During the visits that I have had to Mexico over the past year and a half or so, I have seen a number of Canadian companies down there. I gave you the figures concerning the number of Canadians who are down there, but our exports to Mexico last year, without the free trade agreement involving Mexico, were up about 35 percent.

One of the real winners in any trade negotiation is the consumer. People forget about consumers. They always talk about special interests, but they never talk about consumers. Back in 1947, before we started any GATT negotiations, tariffs were about 40-45 percent on average. They are down now in Canada to less than 5 percent. On a worldwide basis, tariff rates are down to somewhere between 5 and 8 percent. The consumer gets the benefit of lower tariffs because they mean that prices decline. There is also a greater number of products to which the consumer has access. I can see that there are some very exciting times ahead for Canadians as our economy becomes more internationally oriented and takes advantage of the openings into other markets that these negotiations foster. I believe it is important to realize the opportunities that exist, and to recognize that these opportunities are there for the taking.

I have said that a free trade agreement will open the door, but someone has to walk through that door to take advantage of free trade opportunities. This is where the private sector, the business community, can show its initiative, its entrepreneurial bent, and take advantage of free trade.

We wrote a book called Mexico-Canada, *Partnering for Success*. This book explains how to take advantage of this market. It is a best seller, and we are now on our second printing. It sets out all the nuts and bolts aspects of how to get into the Mexican market, how to take advantage of it, what opportunities exist there, what the Mexicans are buying, and how well we are doing in selling in that market.

Let me conclude by thanking you again for the opportunity to be with you. This is the 25th anniversary of the North American Studies Program. Graduates from this program have been a very important part of our international success over the years. I am sure that, as we look back over the next 25 years, this will continue to be the case and that the opening up of trade opportunities through the GATT, the North American Free Trade Agreement, and the FTA with the United States will be important milestones in measuring the success that we have had.

Questions and Answers

Question:
What is the role of Canada in enforcing the implementation of labour and environmental laws?
Answer:
There is a distinction that must be drawn between assisting in the enforcement and sanctions to cause the enforcement of labour and environmental standards. I do not think that Mexico would take well to our imposing ourselves on their sovereignty in enforcing their labour or environmental laws, any more than we would take kindly to the United States coming in and telling us how we should enforce our laws. These trilateral agreements seek to assist all three countries in their own enforcement of their respective laws.

Question:
Section 301 of the U.S. Trade Act: this law enables the U.S. to retaliate against any practice of another country deemed to be unfair, unreasonable, or discriminatory. Does this allow the U.S. to impose countervailing tactics and reinforce or change laws whenever it deems fit?
Answer:
Both Canada and the United States have trade remedy laws. These laws are designed to provide protection for our own countries against the unfair trade practices of other countries. We don't want to eliminate our

trade remedy laws any more than the Americans want to eliminate theirs. What we want to see is a fair application of these laws. The dispute settlement mechanism provides a basis to judge whether we are all implementing these laws in a fair way, not in a way that responds to political or other pressures. This is one of the major achievements of the Free Trade Agreement with the United States, and this will be an important part of NAFTA.

Question:
Could you please clarify two statements made in your speech? One is that our tariffs are at an all-time low. One of the results of that is the GST and we, as consumers, are still paying. The other point concerns the increase of trade exports to the U.S. of 13.5 percent, which includes multinational corporations with headquarters in the United States, does it not? In that sense, it is a movement of the products and not really a movement of the money.

Answer:
Yes, the tariffs on the products that the United States or other countries sell to Canada are at an all-time low. What is the reason for the GST as it relates to international trade? With the previous manufacturing sales tax, there was a hidden tax on all of our exports, in other words, a tax on our production. Also, the way that the federal sales tax was applied on imports resulted in imports being taxed at a lower level than Canadian production. By changing from the manufacturing tax to the GST, we were able to eliminate the tax on production, the tax on our exports, and so make us more competitive in export markets.

Concerning the second point of your question, the movement in our exports includes exports that are produced by Canadian subsidiary companies. This is the case, but the production of these products creates jobs here in Canada. One of the things that is a very important part of our economy today is the competition between sister companies, companies owned by the same parent. We are going to have to face the fact that Canadian companies must be competitive. If we are able to compete, we can attract business into Canada that could otherwise take place in other countries.

Question:
In your talk, you made implicit reference to civil and human rights. Human rights abuses continue to increase in Mexico. How is it possible that Canada is turning a blind eye to cases of corruption and civil rights abuses when it is just about to sign a free trade agreement?

Answer:
I do not think that anybody is turning a blind eye. What the representatives of our government have said is that there has been an improvement in the human rights record of Mexico and an important effort on the part of the Salinas government to provide for tribunals and other ways of ensuring that these human rights abuses are exposed. It is quite clear that as the economic performance of a country improves, so does its record on human rights, and its record on labour standards and environmental standards.

Question:
What assurances does NAFTA offer that we, as Canadians, will benefit from this agreement? A half-million jobs have been lost and many of the employment increases were in low-paying service sector jobs. Is this the vision that we have of Canada for the 21st century?

Answer:
I can't provide you with specific assurances. You mentioned 500,000 jobs lost, the implication being that a large part of that is attributable to the Free Trade Agreement with the United States, which is a real leap of logic. We have endured a very tough international recession, and we have also been going through a tremendous amount of restructuring in all countries of the world. Canada is not immune to that.

It is important not to automatically draw the conclusion that the service sector is low paying. If you look at the 13.5 percent increase in exports to the United States, a lot of it is in high technology industries. According to the C.D. Howe Institute, one of the real winners in the Canadian economy is in value-added industries because this is where the tariffs have been reduced. We have been able to take advantage of this. Canada has increased its exports of high-technology products to the United States by 63 percent, whereas the United States has only increased its exports of high-technology products to Canada by 12 percent. This means we are gaining market share.

Question:
How do you see the North American commission on the environment helping the global environment within the three countries? We see many countries moving to Mexico to take advantage of these lax environmental norms.

Answer:
One of the provisions in NAFTA says that countries should not lower their environmental standards to attract new investment. If you get new investment based on low environmental standards, then in four to five years time, you will probably want to upgrade those standards. If companies have gone in at lower standards, it will cost them a lot more to upgrade than if they went in at higher standards in the first place.

Second, the costs of environmental equipment for most industries is only about 2 or 3 percent of total capital investment. This is an average figure.

As a country begins to increase its standard of living, it gets more industrialization, and, at first, a greater degree of environmental degradation. But as you further improve the standard of living, you come down the other side of the bell curve where you are able to enforce environmental protection, thereby decreasing the level of environmental degradation.

Question:
What are your opinions concerning the trend which seems to be emerging in the United States toward an increase of trade protectionism, as evidenced in the steel industry? Are you concerned about this trend? In general, what is your opinion of the trade policies of the Clinton administration?

Answer:
Protectionism in the United States is always a concern. There are many challenges including steel, live swine, beer, and softwood lumber. One of the most active parts of my job is to try to manage this relationship and these disputes to ensure that Canadian interests are upheld as firmly as possible when such protectionist actions occur.

At any one time, usually only about 5 percent of our trade with the United States is subject to this sort of harassment. We take actions too. Our actions create headlines in the United States; they are not much news in Canada. Their actions against us create headlines in Canada, but they do not hear about them in the United States. This is the nature of the way these issues are reported. Without the dispute settlement mechanism that we have, we would not see satisfactory results in these disputes.

Question:
For small business, doing warranty work, the tariff one has to pay is a kind of roulette. The customs brokers' fees are not in proportion to the cost of the good. In effect, there are administrative barriers for small businesses. These kinds of barriers put small businesses, working with limited capital, out of business. So this is not free trade, as they do not have free access to the American market.

Answer:
A free trade agreement is not total free trade. An FTA gets that name because there has been an effort made to eliminate tariffs and eliminate as many non-tariff barriers as possible. We are far more successful in the former because under the FTA, 80 percent of our tariffs are now zero. In the next five years, we will get all our tariffs down to zero. Non-tariff barriers have not been totally eliminated. We in Canada have them, the United States has them, and we will probably see some in Mexico as well. We try to minimize them, to the maximum extent possible.

The FTA was never meant to eliminate the border. There is assistance in helping people who are conducting business across the border. There are these elements of a border that are not going to be removed by a FTA. Therefore, to facilitate the movement of a product from Canada to the United States, and the reverse, there is a role for the customs broker to go through all of the requirements of exporting. I cannot control those fees and I do not believe that you want me to control those fees. If those fees get too high relative to the cost of doing business, I am sure there will be other companies coming in or other companies cutting those fees.

We are trying to resolve problems that we are aware of through the U.S.-Canada Trade Commission, which will become a trilateral commission (under NAFTA). This will be a continual effort to help facilitate cross-border trade.

Question:
What are the prospects of expanding the NAFTA to include South and Central American countries? When might this happen? What are the advantages for Canada? What obstacles do you see?

Answer:
I think that there will be a number of countries in Latin America who will want to join. Interest in NAFTA is not limited to Latin America, but this is where the main political draw is.

I have spoken to trade ministers from Colombia, Venezuela, Chile, and Argentina, and they are all very interested. I suspect that there will be substantial pressure on them to join because Mexico has better access to the United States and Canadian markets than those countries have. This will cost them investment, so they will put their policies in place as quickly as they can so that they can join NAFTA.

What are the opportunities for Canada? The Latin American market is a market that we have not really taken advantage of as Canadians. There are some tremendous opportunities. We are going to see the same sort of activity as we saw with Canadian business people going to Mexico.

What are the problems? We will find, as with Mexico, that those Latin American countries have greater access to Canada than we have to them. Eighty percent of Mexican exports came into Canada duty-free last year. We faced high duties, ranging up to 20 percent in Mexico. Mexican import licensing means if you don't get the import license, you cannot export, period, even if you have the right price. There are other non-tariff barriers. NAFTA puts us on a level playing field with Mexico.

There will always be pressure as you drop tariff barriers on certain companies. Never draw fast conclusions. People told me that the clothing industry would be ruined by the FTA. What has happened? Some clothing companies have been hurt, but Canadian exports to the United States have grown from $190 million in 1988 to more than $400 million last year.

Question:
Some say that the expansion of NAFTA into a NAFTA including other Latin American countries is catching Canada as off guard as the expansion of the FTA to include Mexico into a NAFTA did. Is it true that the

Canadian government did not see the Mexican initiative coming when it concluded the FTA? Or did the Canadian government know it all along?

Answer:

Mexico, up until now, has not been a big market for Canada. Canada's exports to Mexico stalled in the $500 to $600 million range for about five years. We didn't have the push inside Canada that there was with the United States, which had about $30 billion in exports to Mexico. The additional problem of illegal immigration of Mexicans to the United States caused additional pressure. As long as you have low standards of living in Mexico, there will always be illegal immigration to the U.S.

One of the objectives of the Americans was to address this illegal immigration by doing something to help Mexicans raise their standard of living. In part, we did not have that push. We were not the aggressive demandeurs for NAFTA.

When the opportunity for NAFTA presented itself, there were two reasons why we went into it. The first reason was defensive. If we are going to be part of an FTA with the United States, and they are going to expand it into Mexico, we had better be there. If someone is going to invest in North America, and they have the choice between Canada and the United States and one has access to the Mexican market and the other doesn't, where will they put their money? Obviously in the United States, with access to all three countries. We felt we had to be there at the table to protect Canada's interests. It is important that we be there both for defensive reasons and also for the second positive reason: to promote business opportunities.

NAFTA's Effects: A Mexican Analysis

Jorge Juraidini

THANK YOU FOR YOUR WARM WELCOME. It is indeed a pleasure to be at this university today and to speak with you about the North American Free Trade Agreement (NAFTA).

As you know, NAFTA, an agreement involving two developed nations and a major developing country, represents a significant step forward in creating a global trade system. It strikes another blow against protectionism and will strengthen the concept of open regionalism.

I know that some speak of a "fortress North America," but building a trade bloc was not Mexico's, nor I believe, our NAFTA partners' intent. And it has not been the result of the negotiations. Canadians and Mexicans have learned, often the hard way, that parochial thinking and parochial policies do not work. Barriers to trade and other forms of economic nationalism, like all protectionist policies, stifle opportunities for all concerned, particularly for those who adopt them.

All of you know that NAFTA is based on the FTA, which, despite the recession afflicting both countries in the last years, has played an important role in the evolution of Canada's foreign trade. Canadian exports have gone up by more than $17 billion since 1988, and since free trade came into effect, Canadian products have gained a share of the American market in almost every sector.

At its inception, opponents of free trade warned Canadians of, among other things, a dramatic drop in investments in Canada. All the money was supposed to start flowing to the United States. Well, since four years ago, direct foreign investment in Canada has increased by $17.8 billion, and in a recession! These figures speak for themselves. They show that Canadians have been able to take advantage of the opportunities that free trade offers them.

We believe that the FTA has made Canada stronger, more able to compete and prosper and more able to hang on to the social safety nets that so many people consider to be one of the finest aspects of Canadian life. And we consider that, for those very same reasons, Canada entered into negotiations with the United States and Mexico. The overall benefits of the North American Free Trade Agreement are just as clear:

- Canada and the U.S. will gain access to the Mexican market of 85 million people.
- Canada will improve the original Free Trade Agreement with the United States, and the three countries will ensure their positions as an attractive locations for investment.
- When NAFTA goes into effect on January 1, 1994, we will be part of the largest and richest free trade area in the world: 360 million people with a combined wealth of $7 trillion.

What are the implications of NAFTA for Canada? We feel they are very positive. They include barrier-free trade access to Mexico; a phase-out of tariffs for virtually all Canadian exports to Mexico over ten years; the elimination of Mexican import licensing requirements for goods; and opportunities to bid for major Mexican government procurement contracts. Canadian financial services companies will also be able to open subsidiaries, invest in, and acquire financial institutions in Mexico for securities and insurance.

Canada will also enjoy the benefits of a major liberalization and preferential access to the Mexican investment regime. It may take advantage of the liberalization of the Mexican services market, including land transport, speciality air sectors, professional services, and enhanced telecommunication (e.g. advanced data-processing services). NAFTA also includes an agreement between Canada and Mexico to maintain their relatively open international maritime shipping services.

FTA benefits plus improvements for Canada include the retention of the Auto Pact, and protection of cultural industries, social and health services. High health, safety, and environmental standards in Canada are preserved and can be strengthened. Canada's supply management import quotas for egg, dairy, and poultry products are not affected, and there are clearer North American content rules, including those for autos, thus reducing the risk of unilateral interpretations by customs officials (as, for instance, in the Honda case).

The impact of the new rules of origin for textiles and apparel is offset by increases in the quotas giving preferential access to the U.S. market for Canadian goods that do not meet the rules of origin. For example the export quota for Canada to the U.S. doubles for non-wool apparel, nearly triples for fabric and is four times the 1991 export levels for yarns.

Another beneficial provision of NAFTA is the extension of duty drawback for two years beyond the FTA expiration date in 1994. The old system will be replaced in 1996 by a permanent duty refund system that will reduce input costs for Canadian manufactures who still pay duties on goods into other NAFTA countries. The agreement also includes more stringent controls on the United States with respect to imposing border restrictions against imports from Canada, and an improved dispute settlement process.

All those advantages demonstrate for us that NAFTA will be an excellent agreement for Canada as well as for Mexico and the United States. On the other hand, with the globalization process that is taking place all over the world, we have to consider that competition is no longer the company across the street or across town. The competition could be any single company around the world. If you are not competitive, you stand to lose your traditional customers to a rival in Germany or in Korea.

The issue of competitiveness has not received as much attention in the debate over NAFTA as I think it should. Thus far, the debate has recently centred around labour and environmental issues. These are important matters worthy of discussion, but in my opinion they are not really the *core* of what NAFTA is all about, namely, how to help North America remain competitive into the 21st century.

When one looks at other countries or regions that are competitive, one tends to see that they have in common five basic conditions or elements (see below). We see this with Japan and its neighbours in the Pacific basin, and we see it with Europe. The driving force behind these economic regions is the search for a greater degree of competitiveness. It is my view that NAFTA will create those same five conditions of competitiveness here in North America. This is obviously of great importance to business in North America, which will create the jobs and the economic opportunities for the future. So let me take a few minutes to explain what those five important conditions are, and how NAFTA will create them.

I call the first condition certainty of rules. Business people must know that the "rules of the game" will be stable now and well into the future. This is the only way they can make wise and proper decisions on how best to allocate their resources. They must know the rules will be permanent, that there will be permanence and continuity in economic policy.

The second condition that is so important to competitiveness is economies of scale, the ability to lower average costs by serving a large market. NAFTA will create the largest regional market here in North America—360 million people and more than $7 trillion in regional production—and therefore allow North American firms to realize the advantages of lower average production costs. What's also important is that the definite timetables contained in NAFTA let you know exactly when tariffs will be eliminated, and thus how quickly a particular firm will be able to enter the larger market.

For example, we know that on the day NAFTA goes into effect, 40 percent of the exports from Canada will enter Mexico duty free. Tariffs on the remaining 60 percent will be phased out over a ten-year period, most within the first five years. These timetables will not change, and so you will be able to tell exactly when a particular market will be fully open. This is an important competitive element.

A third element that I think is essential in NAFTA pertains mostly to small and medium-sized firms who might not have the resources to take advantage of economies of scale. NAFTA offers these smaller businesses something called economies of scope, the ability to become very competitive by specializing in a given segment of the market and knowing that segment inside-out.

The best example of this is the market niche Mexico has served selling refrigerators to the United States. Did you know Mexico is the number one supplier of refrigerators to the U.S.? You might ask, how did this happen? Doesn't the United States have the largest refrigerator makers in the world? Isn't this like Mexico trying to sell hockey pucks to Canada? Let me tell you what Mexico did, because we are very proud of it. We do not compete head-to-head with the big refrigerator companies serving the entire market. We selected a particular market niche, selling small refrigerators to offices and college dormitories. This is a tremendous market. By specializing in this one niche, a small Mexican firm can react quickly and efficiently to changing tastes, technologies, and trends. This allows the firm to stay highly competitive.

NAFTA will create many niches like this throughout North America. The typical Mexican consumer is different from a typical consumer in Canada or the United States. Even within those countries, there are numerous niches based on income levels, taste, and culture. NAFTA will give firms that specialize in these niches a greater margin of competitiveness than they currently enjoy.

The fourth element, and perhaps the most important, is the ability to have a wide choice of technologies. This is where the lessons of Japan are the clearest. When people marvel at how competitive the Japanese are, they often mention the quality of the Japanese work-force and the attitude of Japanese management. All of that is true. But what is seldom mentioned is that 35 percent of Japan's exports are made through production sharing, in other words, taking advantage of a wide range of technologies. The idea behind this is simple. If a job is labour-intensive, a firm should have access to adequate labour. If, on the other hand, a job is capital-intensive, a firm should have access to capital.

Finally, the fifth condition for competitiveness is to have available a range of services at a reasonable cost. We have to recognize the importance of services to the modern economy—things like transportation, telecommunications, and financial services. In Mexico, these services still carry a very high cost, which puts us at a competitive disadvantage. But NAFTA will have a dramatic impact on lowering the cost of services because it achieves the most comprehensive opening of the services market of any trade agreement.

For instance, as I mentioned before, NAFTA opens land transportation throughout the entire region. Today, if we wanted to ship something from Monterrey to Montreal, the truck would leave Monterrey, sit at the border while the cargo would be re-loaded onto a Canadian or U.S. truck, then shipped through to Montreal. That Monterrey merchant is placed at a competitive disadvantage. If fact, you could almost fly goods more cheaply from Europe to Montreal. Under NAFTA, the truck will be able to go directly from Monterrey to Montreal.

Second, take the area of telecommunications. This is becoming more and more important in the production process of modern society—things like phones, faxes, and other information services. NAFTA opens the North American market in this area as well. This will make industries more competitive by providing reasonably priced and reliable communications.

Finally, NAFTA opens North America's financial services market, making more credit available at a lower cost. This is important as businesses seek to grow and expand—including the hiring of more workers.

And so let me summarize what I consider the main contribution of NAFTA. This agreement is really an instrument to make North America more competitive in the same way the Far Eastern countries and Europe are competitive. NAFTA will provide certainty. It allows us to take advantage of economies of scale, therefore lowering average production costs. It will multiply market niches, permitting firms that are not large to become specialists in a particular field by taking advantage of economies of scope. Importantly, it will widen the available choices of technology, lowering costs by allowing firms to choose the proper combination of technologies. And it will lower the cost of basic services that are so important to the productivity of firms in this region.

Bringing these five elements of competitiveness to North America is really the core of what NAFTA is all about. But as I mentioned earlier, there are two other issues that are important parts of the debate over this agreement: jobs and the environment. I would like to talk about them briefly.

About one week ago, the U.S. International Trade Commission released an impartial report showing that NAFTA will create jobs and boost economic output in all three member countries. The fear that jobs will be lost to Mexico is one that has been overblown and overused by NAFTA's critics. Free trade will create jobs in all three countries by allowing us all to export our goods and services freely within North America, and to export their goods in the world market because of our enhanced competitive position. The economy in Mexico is so small compared to that of the U.S. and Canada that it is impossible for us to cause a massive dislocation of jobs. The numbers just do not add up.

Certain business sectors have already undergone some adjustments, losing jobs to Asia. In part, this is the normal restructuring of economies and is unrelated to NAFTA. For example, some industries are adjusting to an economy that has become more high-tech and more service-oriented than it used to be. But this would be happening with or without NAFTA. By improving North American competitiveness, jobs will actually be returning to this continent, and new jobs will be created here in manufacturing, among suppliers, and in areas such as transportation.

Another important issue that is always featured in the NAFTA debate is the environment. In many ways this is the most frustrating part of the debate. While I have the highest regard for Canada's tradition of environmental protection, I respectfully say that an environmentalist in Canada or the United States could not care more about the Mexican environment than we Mexicans do. All citizens of Mexico want clean air and clean water for themselves and for their families. I certainly want a healthy environment for my family and my children.

Sustainable development is something President Salinas believes in very strongly, and something Mexican society demands. That is why I say NAFTA will improve Mexico's environment, not hurt it. Developed countries like Canada may take this for granted, but environmental protection requires considerable economic resources. A Princeton University study confirms this. It shows that when a country is very poor, there is no pollution because there is no industry. As a country builds its industries and per capita income starts to rise, environmental degradation becomes worse. That has been the recent history in Mexico. But, ultimately, a country reaches a turning point, growing to the level where it has the resources to devote to environmental protection.

Mexico is at that point now, with a per capita income of $3,500 to $4,000. As NAFTA promotes economic growth in Mexico and raises per capita income, we will see great environmental improvement. There is a direct relationship. Furthermore, the agreement itself contains strong provisions on the environment. It is perhaps the "greenest" multilateral trade agreement ever negotiated. Tough environmental policies approved by international bodies to which we belong will take precedence over NAFTA. And NAFTA specifically prohibits any country from loosening environmental rules in order to attract new investment.

These are some of the reasons why I think NAFTA makes a great deal of sense—creating jobs, improving the environment and making North America more competitive.

For Mexico to take part in this we must continue the dramatic economic turnaround our country has experienced in the past decade. Inflation is under control, the economy is growing faster than our population, our foreign debt has been reduced, more than 1,000 state-owned industries have been privatized and we are showing a fiscal surplus for the first time in a quarter of a century.

NAFTA will help consolidate these economic reforms, secure the confidence of the world's investors and allow Mexico's economic transformation to continue.

NAFTA and Brazil's Trade Policy Options

Donald V. Coes

L ET ME BEGIN BY SAYING that I speak for myself and not for the World Bank. I have been analyzing Brazilian trade problems since the early 1970s, and have lived there off and on since then.

Brazil is at an interesting juncture with regard to the options it now faces in its trade policy. Since it contributes more than half of South America's GDP, whatever Brazil decides will have very large consequences for trade and investment in the hemisphere. So let me begin by providing a background on Brazil's trade policy.

If we trace the trends back into the early post-World War II period, up until the '60s, we find that Brazilian trade policy was dominated by import substitution industrialization. And a lot was accomplished. It is fashionable for academics to take potshots at ISI, but given the size of the domestic market, it was possible for Brazil to attain some major gains in the 1950s and on into the 1960s. The kinds of policies that would obviously not work in Singapore or Luxembourg or Paraguay can play out quite well for quite a time, and they did in several major sectors— metals, automobiles, and a number of consumer durables.

In the 1960s, Brazil began to shift gears in a very interesting way. It moved from import substituting industrialization to more emphasis on export promotion. This method does not fit the textbook models of trade liberalization, in which you drop your import controls and allow an exchange rate reduction that favours exports. Instead, it tended to give export subsidies, both financial subsidies and credit subsidies, to the same sectors, in many cases, which were protected on the import side. So Brazil maintained its protection while at the same time becoming more outward-oriented. The correlation between protection on the import side and export subsidization is very high.

After 1982, however, it became more and more expensive to follow this particular trade policy. The fiscal incentives cost a lot in terms of foregone tax revenues; the credit incentives, particularly as inflation went up with subsidized and sometimes fixed nominal interest rates, became very costly. What we saw after Brazil was excluded from international capital markets, following the Mexican moratorium, was a trimming back on subsidies. Under considerable pressure from the United States in this period, Brazil began to consider other options in its trade policy. This was done in the 1980s, and partly because Brazil depended on trade policy as a balance of payments tool. Some of this was rooted in pessimism about the ability of the exchange rate to be used as the primary tool for balance of payments adjustment. As a result, they used trade policy, particularly control of imports, to try to regulate trade flows. There were a few successes here, but in terms of economic efficiency, this was a very expensive way to react to the kinds of external shocks that the Brazilian economy was subject to, both in the '70s and the '80s.

What we saw in the mid-1980s was the beginning of a period of intellectual ferment, and deep discussion of what Brazil's trade options should be.

Some of the discussions involved Brazil's relations with Argentina. In 1985, Brazilians and Argentinians negotiated a series of agreements that culminated in a larger agreement among the four countries that form the MERCOSUR, the Southern Cone common market. Brazil and Argentina formed the nucleus, and the deal was extended to Paraguay and Uruguay. Some of the political motivation for this agreement came from the transition to civilian rule in both Brazil and Argentina. It was in the interest of both countries to improve relations, to diffuse fears, and to remove the justification for greater military expenditures that came from poor relations between the two major South American economies.

In November 1985, Brazil and Argentina signed the first of their agreements, and these were followed by a series of agreements, most of them economic in content. Most of them paid lip service to freer trade, at least between these two economies. The interesting thing about this is that the motivation came from the two governments themselves. There was little support from either the corporate community or, for that matter, Brazilian academics, who were not particularly interested or involved in early discussions.

The discussions culminated in an agreement that eventually extended to the other two countries, which in comparison to NAFTA, or the earlier FTA, is really a very different animal. MERCOSUR is more of a statement of intentions. The final agreement is short, but the intent is much more ambitious than NAFTA, because it envisions a common market. It not only speaks of the free movement of goods, but also free movement of the factors of production.

In comparison with the much more voluminous agreements negotiated between the U.S. and Canada and subsequently the U.S., Mexico, and Canada, we are talking about an extremely short document when you take out the various quantitative appendices—under 60 pages. I do not wish, however, to sound too critical of the MERCOSUR agreement, and there are positive aspects that should be pointed out. In terms of trade diversion and trade creation, it is a fairly positive document. It binds countries to the lowest tariff of the external tariffs, and it provides for further reductions, which will reduce these trade barriers to zero by the end of 1994.

There is now some question as to whether elimination of tariffs will be attained, but the thrust of the agreement has certainly been positive. For example, among its other provisions is a kind of a most-favoured-nation clause, which in effect extends concessions granted by any member of the MERCOSUR to all the other members. No common external tariff can be higher than the tariffs in place before the agreement went into effect. In that sense, it has a positive spin toward less protection, and with some tangible results. Brazilian trade with Argentina has nearly doubled since 1987, and this is not the effect of a small base. It was one of the major trade flows within Latin America, even before the agreement.

The basic problem, though, is that Brazilian trade in general has not been, is not, and will not be, primarily Latin American in its orientation. There are some good reasons for this. The very structure of the transportation systems in South America has not been particularly conducive to trade within the region; one just needs to look at the rail system to see this. In some cases, shipping costs from some Brazilian ports to North America are lower than to other places in Latin America.

Traditionally, import and export routes have gone in other directions. Import substitution industrialization, not just in Brazil but in other Latin American economies, tended to make all of them less attractive markets to each other than would have been the case with more open trade policies. If you look at the structure of both its imports and its exports for the past decade and a half, you may note that Brazil has depended to a large extent on the rest of Latin America, except possibly Mexico, to generate trade surpluses that it has then spent for two purposes: to meet interest payments, and to finance its petroleum imports.

Thus, if you look at the structure of Brazilian trade and trade balances, you see trade surpluses with most of the world except some of the petroleum producing countries. This introduces an additional complication into negotiations with the rest of Latin America, which stems from the fact that many countries accuse Brazil of having to run a trade surplus with them in order to make payments outside the region.

In moving from a fairly closed economy to a more open one, in a more regional sense at least, Brazil faces a major problem. The aggregated size of MERCOSUR economies is slightly less than the size of the Canadian economy. This helps answer the question of whether Brazil really can view MERCOSUR as an attractive option in relation to membership in a much larger club, either a hemispheric one or otherwise a totally non-preferential arrangement.

The numbers speak for themselves. It is very difficult to identify a lot of products that Brazil could obtain more cheaply from members of MERCOSUR than it could obtain from outside. The other three members are in a similar dilemma. The one exception to this may be wheat. Argentine wheat is competitive at most times with other sources, including Canada. Removal of all restrictions would certainly be welfare-increasing from a Brazilian point of view, and presumably from a producer's point of view in Argentina as well, but the basic problem here is scale. That raises the question of "What now?" "Where should Brazil turn next?"

If we presume that NAFTA does go through, and countries such as Chile accede to the agreement, then Brazil faces the choice as to whether it too wishes to join. The issue will be divisive in Brazil. If you view MERCOSUR as primarily a political agreement (and there are good reasons for this), then Brazil may feel that it may have much more dominance, in fact almost a controlling voice, in the smaller group. From the point of view of economic efficiency I do not believe Brazil would do much better in the larger group. But certainly it may feel that there are threats to its sovereignty that may be much less severe in the smaller organization.

One option may be to allow Brazil to have the best of both worlds: continue with MERCOSUR as far as it will go (and I think that the dividends there are finite and certainly visibly limited) and join NAFTA if they can get in. Most important of all, Brazil is one of those countries that has a major stake in an open world trading system, in a non-preferential sense. And that is why it is disappointing to see the tendency to view trade policy (as I think we now tend to do in the United States and in Canada) in terms of what sorts of clubs we can form. Getting multilateral, non-preferential trade back on track may pay very big benefits to a number of countries, and Brazil is certainly among them

Any change in Brazilian policy, though, is going to face a number of the same problems that Mexico already faces. We are talking about a major shift in ways of doing business, the degree to which government is present in the economy, and in the whole style of administrative protection. If you look over the whole post-World War II period and consider all the sorts and forms of government policy and intervention that one reads about in the textbooks, you can find every single one of them in Brazil, and even a few that are not mentioned.

Brazil has had an extraordinarily activist trade policy for a long time. This has raised tremendous opportunities for rent-seeking, and I think one question that we cannot evade (and Brazilians today do not) is the degree to which corruption is favoured by the sort of intervention and the degree to which discretionary power within bureaucracy opens the possibilities for corruption. There is an old Brazilian saying: "For my friends, everything; for my enemies, the law." I think that captures the spirit of how people in a bureaucracy have viewed the law, when it offers as many niches and opportunities as was the case in Brazil. The thing that is worrisome right now is not the existence of corruption, which will not be absent anywhere, but the degree of lawlessness. The fall of the Colar government has brought this very much to the fore. Corruption existed on a scale that was unimagined even several years before. This is possibly going to be used by opponents of Brazil's entry into a larger group, and I am not sure it should be. Certainly, freer trade and pressure on Brazil to have fewer opportunities for the kind of rent seeking that does lead to corruption will be a much better solution than trying to freeze Brazil out, alleging that we cannot tolerate this.

The issue of corruption has certainly not disappeared in Brazilian politics, and may add difficulty to Brazilian trade negotiations in the future. In addition, the environmental issue promises to be a major irritant in negotiations in the North/South sense, with heightened Brazilian sensitivity. In Brazil, they are watching the Mexican negotiations quite closely, and I think that the stridency of environmental groups in both Canada and the U.S. may actually complicate rather than advance things.

Future Accession to NAFTA: The Cases of Chile and the MERCOSUR

Malcolm D. Rowat[1]

Background

Chile has undergone profound political, economic, and social change over the past two decades. A broad series of reforms have fundamentally redefined the role of the state, consistent with a private sector-led growth strategy. Chile was one of the first developing countries to reduce protection sharply through a pre-announced five-year program beginning in 1974. Through 1978, more than 250 firms that had been seized by the Allende government were returned to their original owners, and another 200 were sold. The bulk of the remaining public enterprises were restructured along commercial lines, reducing government subsidies and enhancing future privatization prospects. During the 1979-1983 period, the central government decentralized to municipalities the facilities, personnel, and administrative responsibilities for

---

1   The views expressed are solely those of the author.

delivery of education and health services. Private sector provision of social services was also encouraged, and most social security taxes were turned over to newly established private pension funds.

In 1982-83, domestic policies (the inconsistency of fixing the exchange rate in conjunction with a wage indexation policy, limited capital market development, and the lack of prudential regulations in the financial sector) combined with external shocks (the worldwide debt crisis, a fall in the price of copper, and the surge in oil prices) to generate a deep recession. After Chile's external indebtedness reached the equivalent of its GDP in late 1982, the government moved to address the most pressing issues, in particular the crisis confronting the financial and corporate sectors. Measures included the closure of some banks; the purchase by the Central Bank of the banking system's bad loan portfolio, subject to a scheduled repurchase by the banks from future profits; and rescheduling of the debts to viable companies and financial institutions at concessionary terms.

In 1985, the government accelerated the implementation of its medium-term structural adjustment program to increase real economic growth, improve savings and investment performance, and further strengthen the financial system. The government promoted a stable macro-economic policy environment through conservative fiscal and monetary policies, a relatively open economy, and strengthened external debt management. The success of privatization efforts during this period was helped by the deepening of capital markets through the expansion of pension funds and insurance companies, and by the provision of incentives to workers to participate in the acquisition of firms.

Trade promotion

The centrepiece of Chile's economic strategy over the past two decades has been the promotion of exports to the world at large without targeting particular regions (Figure 1).

This has been facilitated by a "competitive" exchange rate policy, aggressive marketing, and a vibrant private sector following the early privatization, and has been accompanied by a unilateral reduction in tariff protection to the point where, by June 1991, the tariff level stood at 11 percent, with virtually no quantitative restrictions. A summary of

Figure 1:
Composition of Chilean Trade and Exports (1960-1992)

Composition of Chilean Trade, 1991

	Imports %	Exports %	Trade %
United States	20.6	17.6	19.0
Japan	8.4	18.2	13.7
W. Europe	22.0	33.8	28.4
of which EEC	18.3	31.8	25.6
Latin America	26.7	14.4	20.0
Other	22.3	16.0	18.9

Export Shipment According to Country of Destination as % of Total Exports, 1960-1992

	1960-69	1970-79	1980-89	1990-92	1992-Nov
United States	29	11	21	17	16
Japan	9	14	11	17	17
Europe	52	48	38	35	31
Latin America	9	20	17	14	16
Other	1	8	13	16	18

Source: Central Bank of Chile.

Chile's export/import performance is given in Table 1, with a detailed breakdown of exports given in Table 2. While copper still accounts for the most important share (38 percent) of Chilean exports, what is apparent, particularly over the past five years, has been Chile's success in diversifying its export base to emphasize fruits and vegetables, fish (particularly salmon), wines, and pulp and paper. This has come at a

Table 1: Chilean Trade Performance

	Exports	Imports	Trade Balance
	(Millions of US$)		
1980	4,705	5,469	(764)
1981	3,837	6,513	(2,676)
1982	3,706	3,643	63
1983	3,831	2,845	986
1984	3,651	3,288	363
1985	3,804	2,955	849
1986	4,199	3,099	1,100
1987	5,224	3,994	1,230
1988	7,052	4,833	2,219
1989	8,080	6,502	1,578
1990	8,310	7,037	1,273
1991	8,929	7,353	1,576
1992	9,967	9,168	799

* Growth rates measured in 1977 pesos
Source: Central Bank of Chile.

time when Chile enjoyed has macro-economic stability and access to the international capital markets.

While Chile has enjoyed considerable success in its export endeavours, in recent years it has also kept a close eye on the evolution of regional and bilateral arrangements in Latin America. Chile had been a member of the Andean Pact (Colombia, Venezuela, Peru, Ecuador, and Bolivia) upon its formation, but withdrew in 1976 over a disagreement over economic policy (role of the private sector, investment, and trade liberalization) in addition to approaches to regional industrialization.

Table 2: Exports

		1986	1987	1988	1989	1990	1991	1992 (Nov.)
				(Millions of US$)				
TOTAL		4,191	5,224	7,052	8,080	8,310	8,925	9,171
1.	Copper	1,757	2,235	3,416	4,021	3,795	3,617	3,504
2.	Other main products	1,661	1,991	2,325	2,415	2,485	2,793	2,892
	Iron	88	101	110	124	141	157	128
	Nitrates and iodine	92	99	121	131	119	108	115
	Metallic silver	68	80	83	90	86	59	86
	Gold	64	69	97	76	84	55	59
	Fresh fruit	479	531	586	544	704	949	901
	Fish-meal	315	363	459	508	380	465	510
	Cut wood	64	86	97	90	159	163	119
	Logs and sanded wood	55	91	136	123	92	79	76
	Cellulose	82	102	101	83	98	102	101
	White cellulose	111	163	208	238	217	204	386
	Methanol	0	0	13	59	69	82	57
	Lithium	12	16	20	23	24	25	29
	Oxide and ferro-molybdenum	134	136	137	144	87	94	91
	Cold meat	97	155	159	184	228	251	234
3.	Other exports	773	999	1,310	1,644	2,030	2,515	2,775

Export Shares (%)

		1986	1987	1988	1989	1990	1991	1992
1.	Copper	41.9	42.8	48.4	49.8	45.7	40.5	38.2
2.	Other main products	39.6	38.1	33.0	29.9	29.9	31.3	31.5
3.	Other exports	18.4	19.1	18.6	20.3	24.4	28.2	30.3

Source: Central Bank of Chile.

Since that time, Chile has entered into "economic complementation" agreements with Uruguay (1985) and Argentina (1991) involving tariff reductions and the elimination of Non-tariff barriers (NTBs) on selected products. However, Chile has until now chosen not to become part of the Mercado del Cono Sur (MERCOSUR) on the grounds of the history of macro-economic instability with respect to some of the present members. Chile did, however, enter into an FTA with Mexico in September 1991 with the objective of eliminating most tariff and quantitative restrictions by the end of 1995 (some products would be put on a slower track and some excluded altogether). Safeguard provisions are included as are rules of origin, as well as some liberalization with respect to services. It is worth noting that Chilean exports to Mexico grew from U.S. $19.1 million to U.S. $46.9 million (a 144 percent increase) within nine months of subscribing to the FTA (mainly fresh fruits).

Despite Chile's diversified export structure and overall competitiveness, its trade strategy appears to be partly based on the need not to be "left out" of important regional arrangements that may prove costly in Chile's absence from the perspective of trade diversion, particularly where NTBs have become increasingly important. However, in the case of NAFTA, even though Chile's exports to the U.S. overlap to a considerable extent with those of Canada (e.g., copper, paper products), these products are already subject to low tariffs (fish products are the major exception). Nevertheless, virtually all countries, including the U.S., Japan, and the EC, employ tariff escalation techniques whereby tariffs are kept low on raw materials and raised on related processed goods (e.g., fresh fruit versus processed fruit).

Before the election of a democratic government in 1989, Chile had also encountered trade difficulties with the U.S. over such things as worker rights violations, which forced Chile out of the GSP temporarily. In addition, a U.S. embargo on Chilean fruit was launched over the "poisoned grapes" case, which, in hindsight, is generally accepted as a case of economic sabotage. Moreover, the U.S. applies seasonal tariffs during its own growing season on Chilean fruit, which can be seen as a form of protection. Finally, there is always the threat of anti-dumping proceedings, though this has occurred in only one case to date for Chile. These kinds of issues could probably be resolved more readily in the context of an FTA with an effective dispute resolution system, though the experience with the Canada-U.S. Free Trade Agreement (CAFTA) suggests that this may not necessarily be the case.

To resolve some of those difficulties, and in keeping with former President Bush's Enterprise for the Americas Initiatives (EAI), a U.S.-Chilean framework agreement was signed in June 1991, and former President Bush subsequently announced his intention to seek an FTA with Chile once NAFTA was completed. President Clinton appears to favour this view as well. While accession to NAFTA is a possibility, it appears more likely that a U.S.-Chile FTA would be the next step.

Taking NAFTA as a guidepost, a U.S.-Chile FTA would likely include, in addition to tariff reduction (minor) and removal of NTBs (potentially more important), agreements on services, intellectual property (though Chile recently amended its law to include pharmaceutical protection, the law still provides for compulsory licences, no "pipeline" protection, no coverage of biotechnology, and a patent duration of only 15 years), dispute settlement, labour, and the environment.

In the latter case, given Chile's poor record in environmental protection until recently (major pollution problems exist in the mining industry, pulp and paper, and fish-meal, in addition to severe water and air pollution, particularly in Santiago), environmental issues could become a major element in a U.S. FTA. In looking at such environmental issues, distinctions should be made between conflicts in regulatory/enforcement standards among countries on the one hand, and the indirect effects on trade of using environmentally unsound processes to produce a product (perhaps at lower cost) and/or the trading of hazardous products. These issues will now be the subject of potential side agreements under NAFTA, which should provide the model for how these issues will be addressed for subsequent accessions. A key point will be how environmental improvements will be funded. The World Bank recently granted a loan to Chile to provide financing for the establishment of an environmental institutional framework to address many of these issues.

Various Chilean studies[2] have estimated the trade impact of a U.S.-Chile FTA as involving an increase of 4.5 percent in exports and a marginal increase to the rest of the world (or an overall increase of $115 million per annum at 1991 prices) but within these totals, large increases would be recorded by industrial and agricultural exports (8.5 percent and 7 percent respectively).

However, equally important is expected to be the impact on foreign investment (both volume and higher rates of return) as a result of having Chile locked into binding commitments across an array of economic/legal/regulatory principles. These include protection of property rights, regulatory ground rules for utilities, competition policy, and capital repatriation, among others, which in effect legally commit subsequent governments and substantially reduce the risk to investors. Foreign direct investment (FDI) in Chile has already grown from U.S. $109 million in 1988 to U.S. $540 million in 1992.

Other FTA benefits would include further institutional upgrading, legislative reform, and particularly judicial reform. The latter involves better enforcement of laws through stronger court administration, better legal/judicial training, streamlining of procedural codes, use of alternative dispute resolution (ADR), and better information systems and infrastructure that would have unquantifiable but important effects.

From Chile's perspective, the advantages of bilateral FTAs are partly a function of the stalemated Uruguay Round (thereby preventing multilateral cuts in most favoured nation (MFN) rates in addition to reforms in numerous non-tariff areas), the possibility of trade diversion with the formulation of trade blocs, and Chile's need not to be left out, particularly if it hopes to increase the value added of its exports in the face of a pattern of tariff escalation on many of its primary exports. An FTA with the U.S. looks like the logical place to begin.

---

2   A good summary of the vast recent literature on this subject is contained in Velasco and Tokman, "Options for Chilean Trade Policy in the 1990s," January 1993, unpublished.

MERCOSUR

Latin America has witnessed many attempts at regional integration, with mixed results. In recent years, such initiatives or resurrections of old arrangements (e.g. the Andean Pact) have become more pronounced. The most recent of these (aside from NAFTA itself) concerns MERCOSUR.

The genesis of MERCOSUR lay in earlier agreements between Brazil and Argentina, including a 1986 Program of Economic Cooperation and Integration designed to reduce bilateral trade imbalances, through managed trade proposals that were codified under 17 protocols. Actually, most of the resulting expansion in intra-regional trade involved trade diversion from third countries. This disappointing performance was altered following a further bilateral treaty between Brazil and Argentina in 1988 that had more ambitious, across-the-board trade objectives that culminated in the Buenos Aires Charter in 1990, signed by the then new administrations of these two countries. In March 1991, Paraguay and Uruguay joined Argentina and Brazil in establishing the MERCOSUR, formalized by the Treaty of Asuncion, which became effective on November 29, 1991.

The objectives of the MERCOSUR include: (a) the free movement of goods, services, and factors of production by January 1, 1995;[3] (b) the establishment of a common external tariff (CET) which was recently announced to be at most 20 percent; (c) the co-ordination of macro-economic and sectoral policies; (d) harmonization of legislation; (e) reciprocity of rights and obligations among states parties.

Provision is made for additional membership from the Latin America Integration Association (LAIA) countries beginning five years after

---

3   The tariff reduction program begins on June 30, 1991, with a 47 percent tariff cut followed by a 7 percent reduction every six months to zero by December 31, 1994. However, each country has filed a list of product exemptions (ranging from 324 for Brazil to 960 for Uruguay), which must be removed at a rate of 20 percent per year beginning December 31, 1994, except for Paraguay and Uruguay, which have until the end of the following year.

the treaty's entry into force (November 1996), though exceptions are made for LAIA countries that are not members of a sub-regional or extra-regional association (e.g. Chile).

Institutionally, the treaty provides for a council to handle the political aspects of integration and a common market group that acts as the executive body (with a secretariat in Montevideo), but the intention is to keep the administrative structure modest.

The likelihood of the MERCOSUR achieving its objectives will be influenced by a number of factors. To begin with, there is a wide variation in the degree and approach to trade liberalization with Argentina[4] and Paraguay, the most advanced exemplified by the fact that both Argentina and Paraguay have average tariff levels (10 percent and 16 percent respectively) well below the maximum CET of 20 percent, with a few sectors at 35 percent, which suggests the possibility of trade diversion. Though Brazil's average tariff level is also below 20 percent, it does impose tariffs at considerably higher levels on common MERCOSUR products such as toys (40 percent).

Second, there has been a widely varied experience with macro stabilization programs. Argentina has succeeded over the past two years in controlling inflation, maintaining a fixed exchange rate, and running an operational fiscal surplus at the federal level. Brazil, in contrast, has continued to endure substantial macro-economic instability that seriously jeopardizes the prospect for the creation of a common market, particularly where harmonization of policies would also be required. In addition, there is a wide variation in market size among the four countries, which may hinder the likelihood of consensus on tariff and overall policy reform. A fallback possibility might be a MERCOSUR-FTA, given the above constraints including a perception that these countries may not be willing to give up sufficient sovereignty to form a common market.

---

4   Argentina imposed a tax on all imports in November 1992 as a temporary measure to offset the effects of a surge in Brazilian imports in 1992, which led to a substantial trade deficit; this has raised concern among MERCOSUR members, particularly Paraguay, that this represents a step backwards from integration objectives.

However, assuming that MERCOSUR becomes a reality by January 1, 1995, as least as an FTA, it is worth examining the implications of a U.S.-MERCOSUR-FTA on both parties, as well as for the rest of the region. The U.S. also signed a framework agreement with the MERCOSUR under the EAI in 1991. Table 3 provides a summary of 1990 MERCOSUR exports by region (including from each member country), which shows that exports to the U.S. ($9.4 billion or 20 percent of total MERCOSUR exports) are more than twice that of intra-MERCOSUR exports ($4 billion). What is also clear is that the great bulk of MERCOSUR exports to the U.S. are from Brazil ($7.5 billion or 80 percent) while Paraguay and Uruguay showed negligible results. However, unlike Chile's, MERCOSUR exports to the U.S. are distinguished by the fact that for all four countries, over 50 percent of their total exports to the U.S. represent manufactured goods and also that 39 percent of the MERCOSUR's exports are to the U.S., Mexico and Canada. Table 4 provides a breakdown by product of exports to the U.S., and a summary of conditions of access.

However, both Brazil and, to a lesser extent, Argentina, have been the subject of "unfair trade" retaliation measures by the U.S. under "Super 301" (restrictive import practices) or "Special 301" (inadequate protection of intellectual property rights).[5] While both countries have liberalized their import restrictions in recent years, both countries face NTBs in the U.S. on their exports, amounting to close to 30 percent of their total exports to the U.S. Of particular concern were anti-dumping and countervailing duty cases, and voluntary export restraints (particularly steel).

Recent estimates[6] suggest that (aside from Mexico) Brazil would be the prime beneficiary of either a multi-country or single exclusive FTA

---

5   Brazil is the only Latin American country ever to incur actual penalties for inadequate intellectual property protection (due to lack of pharmaceutical patent protection).

6   R. Erzan and A. Yeats, "U.S.-Latin American Free Trade Areas: Some Empirical Evidence," *The Premise and the Promise*, Saborio (1992), pp. 139-141.

Table 3: MERCOSUR Exports by Region 1990 ($ Millions and Percent)

Exporter	Total Exports	MERCO-SUR	Chile	Andean Pact	CACM	Mexico	Canada	United States	Other Western Hemisphere	Rest of World
Argentina	12,352.6	1,832.7	462.3	511.7	41.2	321.4	81.2	1,699.2	79.2	7,323.7
Brazil	32,266.0	1,249.0	713.0	921.0	131.0	416.0	733.0	7,551.0	309.0	20,243.0
Paraguay	958.7	379.3	—	—	—	—	—	39.4	—	540.0
Uruguay	1,693.7	599.3	16.4	16.4	1.1	32.0	13.1	165.2	2.9	847.3
MERCOSUR	47,271.0	4,060.3	1,191.7	1,449.1	173.3	769.4	827.3	9,454.8	391.1	28,954.0
(Percent)										
Argentina	100.0	14.8	3.7	4.1	0.3	2.6	0.7	13.8	0.6	59.3
Brazil	100.0	3.9	2.2	2.9	0.4	1.3	2.3	23.4	1.0	62.7
Paraguay	100.0	39.6	—	—	—	—	—	4.1	—	56.3
Uruguay	100.0	35.4	1.0	1.0	0.1	1.9	0.8	9.8	0.2	50.0
MERCOSUR	100.0	8.6	2.5	3.1	0.4	1.6	1.8	20.0	0.8	61.3

Note: Numbers may not add due to rounding.
Source: International Monetary Fund, *Direction of Trade Statistics* (Washington, D.C.: IMF, 1991).

Table 4: U.S. Imports from MERCOSUR and Conditions of Access to U.S. Market 1989 (%)

	Argen-tina	Brazil	Para-guay	Uru-guay*	World
U.S. Import Structure					
Foods and feeds	31.9	19.4	21.9	14.4	5.7
Agricultural materials	1.0	3.3	2.3	5.4	2.2
Coal and petroleum	13.2	8.5	0.0	0.0	11.4
Ores and metals	4.2	6.0	0.0	4.6	3.4
Manufactures	49.1	61.7	75.0	70.8	74.5
Non-classified	0.6	1.1	0.8	4.8	2.8
TOTAL	**100.0**	**100.0**	**100.0**	**100.0**	**100.0**
Conditions of Access to U.S. Market					
MFN duty-free imports	18.0	25.0	33.0	18.0	—
GSP duty-free imports	26.9	15.8	22.7	31.8	—
Tariff-paying imports	55.1	59.2	44.3	50.2	—
TOTAL	**100.0**	**100.0**	**100.0**	**100.0**	**100.0**
Weighted Tariff Rates					
Foods and feeds	4.1	11.1	3.3	0.8	3.0
Agricultural materials	1.2	0.0	0.0	2.8	0.7
Coal and petroleum	0.4	0.6	0.0	0.0	0.6
Ores and metals	0.0	0.3	0.0	0.0	0.6
Manufactures	3.3	4.7	4.5	11.3	4.5
All goods	2.9	5.8	3.3	2.5	3.6
Imports with trade of at least $50,000 paying tariffs equal to or higher than 5%**	22.5	27.9	27.29	43.1	—
Non-tariff Barrier Coverage Ratio	28.6	26.1	14.0	6.8	—

*Because exports of non-monetary gold contracted markedly between 1986 and 1989, comparison of trade (1989) and tariff data (1986) for Uruguay is misleading.

** 1986 trade weights

Sources: Based on *Commodity Trade Statistics 1989* (New York: United Nations, 1991); International Trade Division, World Bank; and *Boletin Commercial* (Washington, D.C.: OAS-CECON, 1990).

with the U.S., with incremental exports ranging from U.S. $760 million to U.S. $947 million per annum. Argentina, which has much more to gain under liberalized agricultural trade, particularly by increasing exports to the EC from a successful Uruguay Round, nonetheless could still increase exports by roughly U.S. $60 million per annum. Moreover, Argentina could be a significant beneficiary if Brazil reached agreement with the U.S. on an FTA after a MERCOSUR-FTA was already in place, since an expansion of U.S.-Brazil trade could lead to increased Argentine exports to Brazil. Uruguay and Paraguay would be marginal trade beneficiaries of U.S.-FTAs, though preferential arrangements for Uruguayan exports of textiles and apparel could be significant.

Thus, it would appear that Brazil would have the most to gain in Latin America in purely trade terms from further U.S.-FTAs. This could, however, have major implications on other Latin American countries. A U.S.-Brazil FTA would probably result in substantial displacement of Latin American exports to Brazil by those from the U.S., since most Latin American countries compete with the U.S. in regional markets over a wide range of products. Nevertheless, given Brazil's severe macro-economic problems, and its slowness in reforming other policy areas, this is not a likely prospect in the near future. The case for individual U.S. FTAs with one or more of the other three MERCOSUR countries would be more likely, but not in the immediate future.

Summary and conclusions

NAFTA represents a significant change in Western Hemisphere trade arrangements. It represents an agreement between developed and developing countries to reduce not only tariffs and other important restrictions, but also to seek to reduce barriers in areas still under negotiation in the Uruguay Round. These include financial services, intellectual property, textiles and agriculture and strong dispute resolution systems.

Chile and Mexico are the two countries in Latin America that have made the greatest advances in macro-economic adjustment, trade liberalization, privatization, and decentralization. Chile has launched a very successful and diversified (by region and product) export strategy. While it continues to face some NTBs in the U.S. market, its export performance runs the risk of being adversely affected if it is left out of

NAFTA or a U.S. FTA in the future, by virtue of some competition from Mexico and Canada in the U.S. market. Moreover, a FTA would bring added benefits in the form of increased investment, institutional upgrading, and the locking in of trade and policy regulatory reform that should provide additional incentives to potential investors.

MERCOSUR, on the other hand, appears to be a more challenging near-term possibility, at least in the form of a common market, particularly due to problems facing Brazil. An alternative may be for one or more of the remaining three countries in the group to seek entrance to NAFTA or to reach an FTA with the U.S. in the medium term. It appears unlikely that Chile would seek an agreement with MERCOSUR, but rather will most likely give top priority to a U.S. FTA or entrance into NAFTA.

NAFTA: Perestroika and Glasnost in Mexico

George W. Grayson

Introduction

L EE KUAN YEW, THE EX-PRESIDENT of Singapore, has argued that economic development leads inexorably to political opening. Once a
country reaches a certain level of industrial progress, he contends,
"you've got an educated work-force, an urban population, you have
managers and engineers. Then you must have participation because
these are educated, rational people. If you carry on with an authoritarian
system, you will run into all kinds of logjams. You must devise some
representative system."[1] This study examines the likely impact of the
proposed North American Free Trade Agreement (NAFTA) on
Mexico's authoritarian political system.

---

1   *The Economist*, June 29, 1991, pp. 16-17.

Mexico and the Soviet Union: contrasting styles[2]

The leaders of Mexico and the Soviet Union, like the Shah of Iran a decade before, faced an extraordinary challenge in the mid-1980's— namely, how to accomplish sweeping economic reforms without unleashing powerful political forces that could threaten the stability and integrity of their regimes.

Upon taking office in 1985, Mikhail Gorbachev plunged ahead with political reforms termed *glasnost* in hopes of achieving *perestroika*, the liberalization of a closed, inefficient command economy. As desirable as both changes were, they gave rise to uncontrollable forces that sparked ubiquitous dissent, chilled production, prompted an abortive coup d'état, scared off many outside investors, made the United States wary of furnishing huge amounts of foreign aid, and hastened the disintegration of the Soviet Union into the Commonwealth of Independent States.

In contrast, Carlos Salinas de Gortari, president of Mexico since 1988, and his predecessor, Miguel de la Madrid Hurtado (1982-1988) had the good sense to set priorities. They realized the imperative of achieving sustained economic growth before creating new channels (and widening others) for releasing the pent-up desires of peasants, blue-collar workers, shantytown dwellers, small businessmen, women, disenchanted elements of the middle class, and other segments of an ever more cynical population.

At first blush, the U.S.S.R. and Mexico appear so different as to make comparisons between the two nations seem ludicrous. To begin with, the Soviet Union, with 289 million people before its disintegration, had three and a half times the population of Mexico (88 million). Besides, its land mass was more than 11 times greater than Mexico's.

As in the Soviet Union, a single party, now called the Institutional Revolutionary Party (PRI), has dominated Mexico's political system for

---

2   This section draws heavily on the "Introduction" to George W. Grayson, *The Church in Contemporary Mexico* (Washington, D.C.: Center for Strategic and International Studies, 1992), pp. x-xii.

more than a half-century. Still, Mexico's government, in part because of its contiguity to the United States, is infinitely more open and pluralistic than the Rus, Mongol, czarist, and Communist regimes that dominated Russia or the U.S.S.R. for 1,000 years before Gorbachev assumed power. Historically, the Soviets sought to expand their borders, while Mexicans—traumatized by the loss of half their territory in the Mexican-American War—have concentrated on national integration and development.

These and other differences aside, striking similarities have characterized the two countries. They include bloody revolutions completed early in the century and the persistent trumpeting of the revolutionary mystique; large peasant populations beset by poverty and despair; pervasive state intrusion into economic affairs; sprawling, inefficient bureaucracies whose elites lived sybaritic lifestyles; and widespread corruption.

Salinas understood that he, like Gorbachev, had to confront enormously potent vested interests that benefitted from a hugely statist economy largely cocooned from external competition by tariffs and import permits. Thus, he moved rapidly to tumble protectionist barriers, privatize state firms, and dethrone so-called untouchable labour barons. He also enhanced tax collections, encouraged private industry, and launched negotiations for a free-trade accord with the United States and Canada. His reforms bear the sobriquet "Salinastroika"—a neologism based on the *perestroika* advocated by Gorbachev.

Rather than pursue two sets of ambitious reforms simultaneously, however, Salinas has emphasized rapid economic modernization complemented by carefully modulated, incremental political change. The centrepiece of the youthful president's program was a continent-wide trade pact. In his view, NAFTA would stimulate investment, attract state-of-the-art technology, promote exports, open the door to foreign loans, boost labour productivity and activate a domestic business community that has never been mistaken for Schumpeterian entrepreneurs. Although not a panacea, the trilateral agreement would spur sustained economic growth and help catapult Mexico from the Third to the First World.

Salinas made clear that widespread political changes would accompany Mexico's economic démarche. In his November 1, 1992 State of the Nation address, he said:

> We are promoting consensus among political parties for the improvement of the country's electoral instruments. New institutional channels and sustained efforts at dialogue, proved by our actions, allow us to make headway in settling differences. Constitutional amendments and new laws are opening up additional channels for the protection of human rights and the exercise of expanded freedoms . . . The processes of decentralization have been strengthened, thereby strengthening the States of the Republic through actions and decisions designed to improve the well-being of our countrymen.

The impact of economic liberalization on politics

Will NAFTA-impelled perestroika promote glasnost? Astute, veteran observers of Mexican politics argue that economic liberalization will expand the limited political opening accomplished by Salinas. They advance several reasons to support this conclusion.[3] First, economic progress enlarges the size of the middle class, which, in turn, serves as a powerful advocate for "political sophistication and democratic choice."[4] Second, experience in making decisions in the economic sphere generates "demands for greater choice in the political marketplace."[5] Third, multiple free-trade-inspired contacts with its democratic trading partners will diminish authoritarianism in Mexico just as Spain and Portugal's participation in the Economic Community fostered de-

---

3   For the most developed presentation of this thesis, see Sidney Weintraub and M. Delal Baer, "The Interplay between Economic and Political Opening: The Sequence in Mexico," *The Washington Quarterly* 15, No. 2 (Spring 1992), p. 187; and Luis Rubio, "El dilema liberal," *Vuelta*, No. 191 (October 1992), pp. 70-71.

4   Weintraub and Baer, p. 188.

5   Weintraub and Baer, p. 187.

mocracy in those once-authoritarian Iberian states. Fourth, market-focused policies go hand-in-hand with decentralization, which "inevitably diminishes the ability of the state to manipulate economic resources as a tool of political control."[6] Fifth, NAFTA will undermine the power of labour and peasant chieftains, denizens of the corporatist PRI's "dinosaur" wing, who view democracy as the political equivalent of fingernails clawing a blackboard. Fidel Velázquez, the nonagenarian leader of the five-million-member Mexican Workers Confederation (CTM), and other trade union stalwarts will suffer as the government encourages new labour organizations willing to include productivity and quality goals in their collective contracts.[7] Campesino leaders will lose out as a reform of the *ejido* or communal farm diminishes the dependence of peasants on a government that long supplied inputs, credit, and services for lock-step voting. Finally, liberalization diminishes opportunities for under-the-table pay-offs or *mordidas,* as market mechanisms replace discretion exercised by sticky-fingered bureaucrats.

The last factor is evident in the customs section of Mexico City's Benito Juárez International Airport. Before Salinas came to power, customs inspectors and their supervisors decided whose luggage they would scrutinize. Some affluent tourists and business travelers found it easier to "tip" inspectors a few dollars than suffer a lengthy, meticulous search of their belongings.

Democracy and the 1992 state elections

The 1992 elections provided an opportunity to determine the impact of economic changes on Mexico's political system. Voters in 14 Mexican states went to the polls during 1992, with 13 of the contests scheduled

---

6   Weintraub and Baer, p. 188.

7   For example, complementing the CTM's decline is the rise of the Federation of Unions of Enterprises Providing Goods and Services (FESEBES), led by Francisco Hernández Juárez, secretary-general of the Telephone Workers.

for the last half of the year. They cast ballots for governors (11 states), mayors (11 states), and state legislators (14 states).

The contests were extremely important to the ruling PRI for several reasons. First, like the nationwide congressional elections held in August 1991 in which the governing party ran strongly, they provided a referendum on the Salinas regime.

Second, several states attracted intense scrutiny because of past charges of corruption. For example, the name of Chihuahua—where a governor, 67 mayors, and 28 state legislators were chosen on July 12—had become synonymous with electoral fraud six years before. After the centre-right National Action Party (PAN) prevailed in municipal contests in towns containing 75 percent of the state's population in 1983, the PRI vowed to use whatever means necessary to retain the governorship in 1986. To this end, the ruling party allegedly manipulated electoral rolls, voted the dead (i.e., used the names of dead people on ballots), stuffed ballot boxes, encouraged multiple voting by flying squads known as "aviators," diverted public funds into campaign coffers, managed local news reports, and fiddled the results. Thus, its nominee, Fernando Baeza Meléndez, took office in the face of opposition party demonstrations, blistering criticism from the local archbishop, and acutely negative media coverage. The PAN candidate whom Baeza "defeated" ran again last year. The government seemed eager to erase the image of Chihuahua as an Augean stable of electoral venality. Similarly, the PRI faced stiff competition in Michoacán, the home state of Cuauhtémoc Cárdenas Solarzano, the major challenger to Salinas in the 1988 presidential race and head of the centre-left Party of the Democratic Revolution (PRD). Cárdenas insisted that the PRD lost ground to the PRI in the 1991 federal legislative elections because of corrupt practices.

Third, the government feared that violence in the 1992 elections might staunch the flow of loan and investment monies that have poured into Mexico in recent years.

Finally, the 1992 state and local elections coincided with the unveiling of NAFTA. Credible charges of PRI-sponsored fraud in these contests would cost the Bush and Salinas administrations votes in the U.S. Congress, where the pact had to attain majority support in both houses to be implemented. Salinas, in particular, could not risk the embarrassment at home and abroad that arises from elections crudely rigged by traditional politicos who, once in office, pilfer their states' treasuries. Such behaviour sparks condemnation from increasingly vocal opposition parties, as well as from foreign human rights advocates, public officials, and journalists, who paid little attention to Mexico before the 1980s.

The 1992 elections gave comfort to proponents of the thesis that economic changes ripple into the political system. Reforms were particularly notable in candidate quality and in the accuracy of official vote counts.

Compared to past administrations, PRI's gubernatorial nominees in 1992 were younger, better educated, more articulate, more closely linked to the state where they sought office, and possessed better negotiating skills. More attractive candidates, it was hoped, would triumph without resorting to the political "alchemy" long used to convert defeats at the ballot box into victories. Either during the campaign or once inaugurated, such candidates were perceived as more likely to negotiate effectively with opposition parties, the church, businessmen, and other interest groups. This skill seemed even more important than the ability to preserve intra-PRI harmony.[8]

Salinas and his entourage also recruited men who could deal with rapidly changing conditions in their states. In particular, they prized management skills. Overall policy objectives are still set in Mexico City, but the states must administer ever larger budgets for health, education, transportation, environmental protection, and other services. Indeed, greater decision-making has devolved to the states in at least two key areas: education and environmental protection. And with both the influx of foreign capital and the incentives for private firms to locate outside Mexico City, Guadalajara, and Monterrey, it is increasingly important that governors work effectively with the domestic and foreign entrepreneurs. This group is anathema to many old-guard *priistas*.

---

8   For this point, I am indebted to John J. Bailey, Professor of Government, Georgetown University.

The evolution in the attributes deemed appropriate for a successful governor weighed heavily on candidate recruitment. The Salinas team chose no army officers. Four factors explain their omission: the lack of suitable candidates; the poor performance of generals-turned-governors in Chiapas (Absalón Castellanos Dominguez) and Yucatán (Graciliano Alpuche Pinzón) during the de la Madrid administration; the armed forces' heavy involvement in narcotics trafficking; and a desire to avoid the stereotype of Latin American military officers in key political roles. The father of the nominee from Sinaloa (Renato Vega Alvarado) was a general, thereby preserving the PRI-military link. The PRI named only one dinosaur, Maximiliano Silerio Esparzo (Durango); he also happened to be the only representative of the party's peasant sector. The party nominated just two men associated with the CTM, neither of whom was a blue-collar worker: Sen. Enrique Burgos García (Querétaro), who served as a legal adviser to the federation but could not be considered a "labour" candidate; and Arturo Romo Gutiérrez (Zacatecas), a lawyer who has held several CTM posts, including secretary of education and social communication.

Apace with the decline in the number of recruits from traditional backgrounds was an increase in gubernatorial standard-bearers with experience in professions (accountant José de Jesús Macías Delgado in Chihuahua, public relations specialist Otto Granados Roldán in Aguascalientes, and media expert José Antonio Alvarez Lima in Tlaxcala); in business (Eduardo Villaseñor Peña in Michoacán and, in 1993, Rubén Figueroa Alconcer in Guerrero); and in the National Solidarity Program (PRONASOL) designed to spur local development (Manuel Cavazos Lerma in Tamaulipas and Diódoro Carrasco Altamirano in Oaxaca).

Widespread irregularities notwithstanding, official vote tallies generally jibed with pre-election public opinion surveys conducted by the government, newspapers, and private polling agencies. In the 11 gubernatorial contests, the PRI recognized the victory of a Panista candidate in Chihuahua, the scene of egregious fraud in 1986. This outcome raised to three the number of PAN governors.[9] Meanwhile, Villaseñor, the official party's winning candidate in Michoacán, "voluntarily" resigned the governorship amid protracted protests from the losing PRD nominee, Cárdenas, and their loyalists.

As encouraging as the candidates' credentials and the fairness of votes counts were, the 1992 contests raised serious questions about the impact of Mexico's *perestroika* and *glasnost*. To begin with, the revolutionary regime named the candidates from Mexico City, sometimes consulting with local leaders, rather than opening the selection process to rank-and-file participation. The major exception to the so-called *dedazo* or finger-pointing method of selection under Salinas took place in March 1991 when Colima held a primary election or *consulta directa a las bases* to select its candidate. Fearful that Deputy Socorro Díaz Palacios, a candidate favoured by Mexico City where she edited *El Dia* newspaper, would win the contest, several local aspirants united behind Carlos de la Madrid Virgen, a cousin of the former president. That de la Madrid emerged victorious seemed to represent a victory for grassroots democracy. But most PRI leaders condemned the primary because it was marred by fraud, divisiveness, and—perhaps, worst of all—loss of control by the party leadership over the selection process. Since then, only the *dedazo* has been used to select so-called "unity" candidates.

The outcome of the Michoacán elections also sparked concerns about advances in Mexican democracy. Mexico City's PRI chose the party's gubernatorial nominee after its pollsters asked state voters what characteristics they desired in the state's chief executive. The interviewers also asked respondents to assess various political figures. This research led to the choice of Villaseñor, an immensely wealthy businessman and dark horse, over such local political insiders as Armando Baillines and Ausencio Chávez. The naming of Villaseñor shocked many local *priistas*. They questioned his modest political credentials, his

---

9   The PRI recognized the mid-1989 victory of Ernesto Ruffo Appel in Baja California Norte, while installing as "interim governor" Carlos Medina Placencia in Guanajuato when the "victorious" PRI candidate stepped down amid charges of fraud in August 1991.

uninspiring style of campaigning, and his family's historic ties to the PAN.

Villaseñor captured an absolute majority (53 percent) of the votes cast burying the PRD standard-bearer (36 percent)—a Cárdenas protégé—and three also-rans. While the PRD cried foul, every major poll predicted a Villaseñor landslide, including those published in *El Norte*, Mexico's most respected newspaper. Even foreign observers agreed that the relatively tranquil election lacked the ubiquitous fraud that the PRI employed to crush the PRD in Michoacán's state and local elections two years before.

Although Salinas attended Villaseñor's inauguration, he forced the pork tycoon-turned-politician to step down. This move came after PRD militants occupied key government buildings in the state capital, organized marches, and inundated the media with "evidence" that their victory had been stolen. These protests came before a presidential visit to the United States, and Salinas apparently believed that strident, prolonged demonstrations would jeopardize NAFTA's prospects in the U.S. Congress.

The chief executive's pragmatic move constituted a setback to democratic principles. It placed in doubt the importance of elections, weakened the PRI (whose nominee was ingloriously removed from office), constituted a rebuke to the business community at a time when bridge-building was needed, and emboldened the PRD to employ disruptive methods in future elections, including the 1994 presidential contest. If the PRD resorts to violence next year, the government can be expected to respond in kind, particularly because Washington will have taken action on NAFTA.

The ouster of Villaseñor bolstered Salinas' record of having removed more governors than any president since Adolfo Ruiz Corines (1952-58). All told, 11 elected and two appointed governors have given up their posts. Those erstwhile state leaders who caused the greatest embarrassment (Leyva Mortera in Baja California, Manzanilla Schaffer in Yucatán, Neme Castillo in Tabasco, and Cosío Vidaurri in Jalisco) have disappeared from the political scene. Cosío Vidaurri held office when gasoline explosions ripped through 20 blocks in Guadalajara, killing some 236 people. There are rumours that he could be indicted; such action would breach informal rules of the game that have shielded ousted governors, no matter how venal or incompetent, from criminal prosecution.

Conclusion

As demonstrated in the 1992 gubernatorial contests, Salinas has continued to open Mexico's tightly controlled, hierarchical political system. To gain support for NAFTA, he has even promised to go beyond selecting more attractive candidates and insisting on fairer vote counts. He has pledged to furnish voters with photo identification cards and to allow foreign observers in next year's presidential election.

Still, it would be naive to expect Salinas or his successors to dismantle Mexico's highly centralized political system. The concentration of power in the presidency, so inimical to other North Americans, nurtures coherence, stability, and legitimacy in Mexico's 54-year-old regime. Its leaders worry that NAFTA will unloose centrifugal forces that they cannot control.

Constitutional Law, Trade Policy, and the Environment: Implications for North American Environmental Policy Implementation in the 1990s

Bradly J. Condon

Introduction

THIS PAPER COMPARES THE MANNER in which federal environmental regulations may be challenged under the North American Free Trade Agreement[1] to the way in which provincial environmental regu-

---

1   Canada, *North American Free Trade Agreement between the Government of Canada, the Government of the United Mexican States and the Government of the United States of America* (Ottawa: Minister of Supply and Services Canada,

lations may be similarly challenged under the Canadian constitution.[2] Under NAFTA, the issue is whether the true purpose and effect of an environmental law is to achieve an environmental objective or whether it is in fact a disguised barrier to trade. Similarly, constitutional law asks whether the true purpose and effect of a law is to address a valid constitutional objective or whether it deals with a matter that is beyond the jurisdiction of the enacting government. Both documents subject laws to legal tests that determine their validity on the basis of their subject matter.

The North American Free Trade Agreement

There are essentially two sides to the trade-environment issue. From an environmentalist's perspective, the central issue is how to make trade environmentally friendly. From a free trader's perspective, the primary focus is on making environmental regulations trade-friendly. The environmental perspective is being addressed under the trilateral "parallel accord" on the environment. Insofar as binding legal obligations are concerned, the NAFTA text concentrates solely on prohibiting green protectionism.

NAFTA limits the use of trade restrictions to implement environmental policy. Article 904(1) affirms the right of each party to set standards relating to environmental protection. Article 904(4) prohibits the implementation of those standards in ways that create unnecessary obstacles to trade. These provisions may be interpreted to apply a three-stage legal test to trade-restrictive environmental standards. The same test is implicit in Article 2101, which incorporates Article XX of the General Agreement on Tariffs and Trade,[3] and in Article 104, which

---

1992) [hereinafter NAFTA].

2   Constitution Act, 1867 (U.K.), 30 & 31 Vict., c.3 [hereinafter the Constitution].

3   General Agreement on Tariffs and Trade, opened for signature 30 October 1947, 61 Stat. A3, 55 U.N.T.S. 194 [hereinafter GATT].

permits the use of trade barriers pursuant to specific international environmental agreements. The test asks:

1. Does the standard relate to environmental protection? i.e. is the trade restrictive standard directly connected with an environmental program and primarily aimed at achieving an integral aspect of that program?[4]

2. If so, does the standard create an unnecessary obstacle to trade? i.e., are trade restrictions necessary to achieve the environmental goal?[5]

3. If trade restrictions are necessary, has the least trade-restrictive measure been chosen? i.e., is the degree to which trade is impeded proportionate to the environmental goal in question?[6]

If a trade restriction is not related to an environmental protection program, the implication is that its purpose is to protect domestic industry from competition and it will be ruled inconsistent with the NAFTA. If the restriction is primarily aimed at environmental protection, the analysis then proceeds to the second test. With the exception of measures taken under Article 104,[7] the second test regarding the

---

4   See NAFTA, Articles 904 (1) and 2101. GATT and FTA panels have interpreted the words permitting trade-restrictive measures "relating to the conservation of exhaustible natural resources" in GATT Article XX (g) to mean that such measures must be "primarily aimed at" conservation. The same analysis would apply to both NAFTA Article 2101 and Article 904(1) with respect to the meaning of the term "relating to."

5   See NAFTA, Articles 904(4) and 2101.

6   The least-trade-restrictive test is implicit in NAFTA, Articles 904(4) and 2101. NAFTA, Article 2101 incorporates GATT Articles XX(b) and (g), and applies to the entire NAFTA. Both GATT articles have been interpreted to implicitly apply the least trade-restrictive test.

7   Article 104 provides express permission to employ trade restrictions to achieve international environmental goals pursuant to specific international conservation and environmental agreements. Where there is a conflict between those agreements and NAFTA, those agreements prevail to the extent of the inconsistency.

necessity of trade restrictions is largely the same as that of the GATT. If it is unnecessary to use a trade restriction to achieve a particular environmental goal, the trade restriction must be replaced with a policy instrument that achieves the goal without restricting trade. However, if restrictions on trade are necessary to achieve the environmental policy goal, the issue then becomes whether the importing nation has chosen the least trade-restrictive means of doing so.[8]

If the importing nation has chosen the least trade-restrictive method of implementing its environmental policy, then the measure has succeeded in complying with the requirements of NAFTA. However, if there is a less restrictive method of achieving the goal, that method must replace the one that was challenged. This is precisely what occurred in a case under the Canada-United States Free Trade Agreement[9] respecting Canada's requirement that all salmon and herring caught off the British Columbia coast be landed at B.C. fish stations. The United States challenged this measure as an export restriction that was designed to favour Canadian fish-processing plants. Canada said the measure was necessary to ensure accurate data collection for the purpose of managing the resource and could therefore be justified under FTA Article 1201, which incorporates GATT Article XX(g), as a measure relating to the conservation of an exhaustible natural resource. The FTA panel found it was necessary to land only 80 to 90 percent of the catch in Canada to ensure proper data collection, not 100 percent. The panel reasoned that, since there was a less trade-restrictive means of achieving the conservation goal, the measure in question did not qualify as one "relating to"

---

8   This third test flows implicitly from the second. The drafting history of Article 904(4), when considered in conjunction with Articles 102(1)(a), 2101, and 104, indicates that its drafters intended that this test be employed in determining whether a trade restriction was necessary, but considered it unnecessary expressly to include the words "least trade-restrictive" in the final draft.

9   Canada-United States Free Trade Agreement, 22 December 1987-2 January 1988, Can.-U.S., 102 Stat. 1851 [hereinafter FTA].

conservation. Canada and the United States subsequently agreed to allow 20 to 25 percent of the catch to be landed outside Canada.[10]

The NAFTA rules are not concerned with what environmental policies should be, but rather how they are to be achieved. Trade restrictions may only be used to achieve environmental goals where they are the most effective means available. Thus, from a legal perspective, NAFTA neither strengthens nor weakens environmental protection laws.

NAFTA and the constitution

The federal government has the power to enter into treaty obligations, but their implementation as domestic law must be consistent with the division of powers between the federal and provincial governments under the constitution.[11] As a result, Parliament may not have the constitutional authority to enact legislation implementing international agreements where the subject matter falls within provincial jurisdiction.

NAFTA Article 105 provides that:

> The Parties shall ensure that all necessary measures are taken in order to give effect to the provisions of this Agreement, including their observance, except as otherwise provided in this Agreement, by state and provincial governments.

While the federal government may have sufficient authority under its trade and commerce power[12] to fulfill its obligations under Article 105 with respect to matters of international trade, the constitution

---

10   See "In the Matter of Canada's Landing Requirement for Pacific Coast Salmon and Herring," *supra*, note 4 and J. Anderson & J. Fried, "The Canada-U.S. Free Trade Agreement in Operation" (1991) 17 Can.-U.S. L.J. 397 at 403.

11   See *A.G. Can. v. A.G. Ont.*, [1937] A.C. 326, [1937] 1 W.W.R. 299, 1 D.L.R. 673 at 352 (P.C.) (the Labour Conventions case) where Lord Atkin stated, "the Dominion cannot, merely by making promises to foreign countries, clothe itself with legislative authority inconsistent with the constitution which gave it birth."

12   Constitution, Section 91(2).

provides little guidance regarding the manner in which the federal government may implement its NAFTA obligations with respect to environmental standards. Thus, in contrast to Article 105, NAFTA Article 902(2) merely requires each Party to "seek...to ensure observance of Articles 904 through 908 by provincial or state governments."

There are two ways the federal government may seek to ensure that provincial legislation complies with Canada's obligations under NAFTA with respect to environmental standards. Parliament could rely on its trade power to enact federal legislation implementing NAFTA that would override all provincial laws that are inconsistent with the federal legislation.[13] Alternatively, trade-restrictive provincial environmental standards could be challenged on a case-by-case basis as invalid intrusions on federal jurisdiction over international trade.

On matters affecting the environment or trade, in many cases, either level of government may legislate, one with respect to provincial aspects and the other with respect to federal aspects.[14] Provincial authority over property and civil rights enables each province to set environmental standards within that province.[15] Even where Parliament has validly enacted a single national standard, this will not preclude the provinces from establishing a variety of stricter standards.[16] When provincial

---

13 Under the doctrine of federal paramountcy, where there is a federal law and a provincial law that are, first, both valid and, second, inconsistent, the federal law prevails. Where overlapping jurisdiction exists, both orders of government are free to deal with the matter, but if federal and provincial legislation on the subject are inconsistent, the latter is regarded as inoperative to the extent of the inconsistency so long as the federal law is in force.

14 Under the double aspect doctrine, where a court finds that the federal and provincial characteristics of a law are roughly equal in importance, then laws of that kind may be enacted by either the province or Parliament. See *Hogg, supra,* note 11 at 317.

15 See *Hogg, supra,* note 11 at 737. See also, *A.G. Quebec v. Kellogg's Co. of Canada,* [1978] 2 S.C.R. 211; *Dominion Stores v. The Queen,* [1980] 1 S.C.R. 844; and *Labatt Breweries v. A.G. Canada,* [1980] 1 S.C.R. 914.

16 See *Hogg, supra,* note 11 at 737.

governments create trade barriers disguised as local environmental protection, however, the courts may view such legislation as an invalid attempt to regulate international trade.

Parliament has exclusive jurisdiction to regulate the importation of goods into Canada. In general, however, only a province may regulate the manufacture, possession, and sale of products inside that province.[17]

Because the constitution does not explicitly grant authority over environmental matters to either level of government, environmental legislation must be linked to one or more heads of power in Section 91 (for federal legislation) or Section 92 (for provincial legislation).[18]

The pith and substance doctrine is the constitutional equivalent of the "relating to" test of NAFTA Articles 2101 and 904(1). It classifies a law as "in relation to" a matter within federal jurisdiction or to a matter within provincial jurisdiction.[19] "Pith and substance" refers to the dominant or most important characteristic of the law in question.[20] In this regard, it is remarkably similar to the "primarily aimed at" test of trade law.

---

17 See *Citizens' Insurance Co. of Canada v. Parsons* (1881), 7 A.C. 96 (P.C.); *Caloil Inc. v. A.G. Can.*, [1971] S.C.R. 543, 20 D.L.R. (3d) 472 at 476-477, and Reference Re. Validity of Section 5(a) of the Dairy Industry Act (The Margarine Reference) (1948), [1949] 1 D.L.R. 433 (S.C.C.); affirmed [1950] 4 D.L.R. 689 (P.C.). Thus, while Parliament has exclusive authority to impose or eliminate tariff barriers to trade, its authority to regulate non-tariff barriers to trade, in the form of environmental standards, remains ambiguous.

18 *Friends of the Oldman River Society v. Canada (Minister of Transport)* [unreported] (S.C.C.) at 36; since reported at [1992] 2 W.W.R. 196. For example, the residual legislative power of Section 91 "to make Laws for the Peace, Order, and Good Government of Canada" gives Parliament jurisdiction over environmental matters of national concern. Subsection 92(16) grants the provinces jurisdiction over matters "of a merely local or private nature in the Province."

19 *Hogg, supra*, note 11 at 334; *General Motors of Canada Ltd. v. City National Leasing* [1989] 1 S.C.R. 641, 58 D.L.R. (4th) 255 at 275 at 275.

20 *Oldman, supra*, note 18 at 33.

Where the validity of a provincial statute or a particular provision thereof are in question, the steps in the analysis may be summarized as follows:

(1) Is the statute "in relation to" a valid subject?;

(2) If the statute is valid, is the provision both necessary and sufficiently integrated with the legislative scheme that it can be upheld by virtue of the relationship? If the provision in question has no relation to the regulatory scheme, then the question of its validity may be answered on that ground alone.

(3) Does the provision intrude on federal powers, and if so, is it the least intrusive means of achieving the legislative goal (i.e., does the intrusion on federal power outweigh the necessity of the provision to the effectiveness of the legislative scheme of the act)?[21]

If a provincial environmental standard were found to be a disguised barrier to international trade, it could be ruled *ultra vires* the provincial government as a matter in relation to international trade. However, if the standard relates to local environmental regulation, is a necessary part of a valid legislative scheme, and is minimally intrusive on the federal trade power, it would likely be *intra vires* the province to enact.

While the federal government could legally use the constitution to enforce compliance with NAFTA at the provincial level, political considerations may prevent it from doing so. However, the affected Canadian importer would also have legal standing to challenge provincial standards under the constitution, and may not be so constrained politically. However, the courts have repeatedly expressed concern over constitutional interpretations that could upset the balance of power between Parliament and the provinces. Thus, while constitutional arguments against provincial disguised barriers to trade are likely to succeed in clear cases, where there is doubt regarding the true nature of the standard in question constitutional challenges may fail on the grounds

---

21   See *General Motors, supra,* note 19 at 276-277.

that federal jurisdiction over environmental standards would be unduly enlarged.

Conclusion

Under both NAFTA and the constitution, environmental laws are judged by analyzing their subject matter and purpose. NAFTA says a law must relate to environmental protection to be considered a legitimate environmental law. Similarly, the constitution says a law must be in relation to a matter within the jurisdiction of the enacting government in order to be valid. NAFTA requires a trade restriction to be a necessary and integral part of an environmental scheme before it can be justified under the environmental provisions. Similarly, the constitution says a legislative provision that intrudes on the jurisdiction of another level of government must be a necessary and integral part of an otherwise constitutionally valid legislative scheme. NAFTA requires environmental regulators to use the least trade-restrictive means available to achieve environmental goals. Similarly, the constitution requires regulators to achieve constitutionally valid objectives by way of provisions that are the least intrusive on the jurisdiction of the other level of government. The result is that both the federal and provincial governments are obliged to avoid disguising trade barriers as environmental laws, the former under NAFTA and the latter under the constitution.

While the legal tests under NAFTA and the constitution are remarkably similar, there is one important difference between the two legal regimes. Genuine environmental laws are likely to withstand challenges brought under NAFTA as long as they only restrict trade to the degree that is necessary to achieve the desired level of environmental protection. Unfortunately, the same cannot be said for constitutional challenges to either federal or provincial environmental laws. Even those environmental laws that have no impact on trade may be struck down as unconstitutional if they pursue aspects of environmental protection that may only be regulated by the other level of government. Viewed from this perspective, NAFTA provides more protection for genuine environmental laws than does the Canadian constitution.

Section VI
Law and Dispute
Settlement

NAFTA and the Co-ordination of North American Commercial Law

Eduardo F. Ramirez

THE INTEGRATION OF MEXICO with the rest of North America produces eight areas of strain. Stress is appearing in laws affecting international trade, domestic commerce, liabilities, capital, labour, environment, natural resources, and democracy itself.

The focus of this paper is international trade and domestic commerce. Remember, the Mexican legal system derives from the civil law tradition, which is different from the Anglo-Saxon common law framework. An exchange, however, between civil law and common law has been a reality since the beginning of the modern era because of the interaction among people of different countries. Sometimes this relationship has come to be very close and abundant, as is the case between Quebec and the other Canadian provinces.

Surely, with NAFTA, a similar phenomenon will occur as economic interplay among the three North American partners becomes greater. To understand, forecast and, even more, to lead this process, the Canadian and the European experiences will be extremely useful. International trade is advanced by a harmonization of legal systems. During the 11th and 12th centuries, the western expansion of trade required the resurrection of the Roman Law (*Jus Gentium*) in order to provide a common legal scheme indispensable to businessmen of many different countries.

Similarly, the Mexican legal system has changed a lot during the past ten years because of the opening of a closed economy. Perhaps the first important change was the enactment of the International Trade Law of 1985, which contained, among other provisions, countervailing and anti-dumping duties. This law, however, has been little used until recently for three reasons: 1) lack of knowledge on the part of lawyers and entrepreneurs; 2) shortcomings of the law; and 3) an unwillingness on the part of government to set these duties (so as not to offset its policies against inflation).

This situation is expected to be rectified by the Mexican Congress with a new law that has already been discussed informally by some officials of the administration with selected entrepreneurial groups. The law will satisfy three main concerns: first, the dispute settlement panel system included in NAFTA requires the three countries to operate similar administrative systems to determine anti-dumping and countervailing duties, so that traders can receive the same treatment in any country of the region; second, the three countries must comply with Section 1907:3 of NAFTA, which outlines required characteristics of national laws to assure the proper transparency in the administrative procedure and to provide maximum procedural information to participants; and third, to satisfy explicit requirement in NAFTA, Mexico's trade remedy legislation must be amended in specific areas to conform with that of the other two partners.

Avoiding technicalities, I will deal with some relevant problems of the current statute that are supposed to be overcome by a new law. First, it is expected that the standard for legal standing to ask the government for determination of duties against illegal imports will be widened, in order to match the American one, and to introduce more fairness. Current law reserves the complaint process to representatives of larger firms in an industry (the top 25 percent). Furthermore, trade unions are deprived of this right. These restrictions discriminate against small and medium size industries and Mexican labour at a moment of great difficulty for these groups. They also place them at a grave disadvantage in comparison to similar groups in the United States.

Another important flaw in the current Mexican law is the handling and management of privileged and confidential information. We must note that this is not a negligible point of legal procedure. On the contrary, the sensitivity of this point is enormous insofar as it involves crucial information concerning costs and prices that could be of great importance for Canadian and American exporters.

In addition to these legal problems, there are other issues difficult to handle in the short run; for example, minimizing the time consumed by the administrative procedure to determine whether or not a duty is to be imposed. This is so because expediency requires not only knowledgeable lawyers and officials but also appropriate accounting systems with accurate and timely international statistical information. Even though advances have been made regarding statistics and access to international data bases, a lot is yet to be achieved in this area, and the state is expected to provide the necessary infrastructure, mostly for small and medium size companies. Nevertheless, solving these problems can lead to encouraging co-operation between the three countries.

The Mexican administrative agency with jurisdiction to decide whether or not a countervailing or anti-dumping duty is to be imposed is the Secretaria de Comercio y Fomento Industrial. The procedure that this agency follows is not standardized, at least in large part because it conducts investigations both to determine foreign dumping or subsidies, and to assess material injury. Unlike the United States and Canada, Mexico does not employ different institutions to do the job.

In all of this, the role that the trade unions are to play in international trade becomes increasingly crucial, so the international relationship between unions of the same and similar sectors in the three countries can bring unpredictable effects. For example, negotiation over interpretation of politically charged terms such as "social dumping" and "environmental dumping" might open new ways for international co-operation through non-government agents.

Where Mexican law is concerned, the "writ" or *amparo* is a real cornerstone of the legal system. Indeed, it permeates the whole legal structure as a paramount means to protect the Mexican Bill of Rights. One of its most remarkable features is, justly, its conclusiveness or final character. Consequently, this writ represents a chess piece difficult to move, or to co-ordinate with the panel system to settle disputes imbedded in NAFTA, because its authority conflicts with the supposedly final panel decisions.

Last, the new law will have to decide on a crucial dilemma: either it creates a new body called a "Tribunal of International Trade" or develops an appropriate legal framework for the "Federal Fiscal Tribunal" that currently has jurisdiction. The relevance of this choice is clear if we remember that the latter institution is the option that the panel systems will try to avoid as obsolete. An additional problem of creating a new tribunal would be the lack of a job for it. The current Federal Fiscal Tribunal has received no appropriate cases in the whole life of the law of international trade.

Domestic commerce

The current Mexican Commercial Code was enacted in 1884 and, despite a great number of amendments already introduced, it is clear that a complete new framework is needed, mainly with respect to contracts and commercial liabilities. Also, there are a lot of phenomena brought on by the technological revolution that are waiting for appropriate regulation by this code, for example, the transfer of funds by electronic means, communications to reach an agreement mainly by fax, etc.

Another outstanding issue is the Mexican Bankruptcy Law which was enacted at the beginning of the 1940s and obviously does not reflect the current situation. The commercial openness experienced in Mexico during the last decade has caused many bankruptcies. More, in the near future, are to be expected in some sectors. Therefore, an appropriate regulation should be a means to help a business in trouble.

Some data will suffice to demonstrate the need for new law. In the United States, bankruptcies filed annually amount to many thousands, but in Mexico, despite terrible pressure on small and medium firms, the total number of cases filed annually has hardly reached 200.

To conclude, I am going to refer to a relevant legal sphere: the new Antitrust Law that was enacted last December and will enter into force this coming July. We could speak at length about this law, because it is much more than a new law; it is a new kind of law for the Mexican system. This statute is very much in the common law style; it is brief and vague to some extent. This profile is understandable in a common law system that counts on the judges to create, so to speak, the concrete law. But in accordance with the Mexican civil law tradition, if the law does not establish certain parameters, neither the judging nor the administrative machinery itself can create it. So, in my view, the development of this law will be of great importance, and it may reflect some shift in the national legal system as a whole.

On the other hand, the significance of this law is now highlighted by two facts. The European Community has abolished anti-dumping and countervailing duties so as to rely only on anti-trust law for fairness in trade. It is not hard to imagine a similar long-run development in North America.

Despite the legal strains that the integrating process has generated in Mexico, about 75 percent of Mexican trade with the United States in both directions has been constant. The percentage of American investment has also been steady, and has recently increased. What does this mean for Canada? Mexico does have the necessary legal framework; otherwise recent progress would not be possible. Nevertheless, legal systems in all three partner countries need to be reviewed and adjusted to take advantage of NAFTA's full potential.

NAFTA, the Canadian Constitution, and the Implementation of International Trade Arrangements

Stephen A. Scott

Doing what one must

YOU DO WHAT YOU MUST. This, in a few words, sums up my view of the Canadian constitution's almost certain response—in the last resort, speaking through the Supreme Court of Canada—to the question of the federal Parliament's power to implement, as a matter of Canadian domestic law, international trading arrangements. These would include the North American Free Trade Agreement (NAFTA), entered into by and between the governments of Canada, the United Mexican States, and the United States of America, and signed on December 17, 1992. NAFTA contains this conditional, and somewhat ambiguous, provision as its entry into force: "This agreement shall enter into force on January 1, 1994, on an exchange of written notifications certifying the completion of necessary legal procedures."

"Necessary legal procedures," we should note, is ambiguous as between 1) procedures necessary for contracting the relevant international obligations, and 2) procedures necessary for their implementation in domestic law. Bill C-115, an act to implement the North American Free Trade Agreement, introduced into the Canadian House of Commons on February 25, 1993, probably implies that the government of Canada is proceeding on the former assumption. It does not, in general, enforce the agreement against the provinces. Perhaps this is so because NAFTA is so riddled with exclusions in favour of the parties' state, provincial, and local governments, especially for their existing non-conforming measures, that federal measures to compel provincial conformity may not seem immediately necessary. But enforcement against the provinces may become necessary; and, if it does, Parliament, in my view, will have the power to act.

The constitutional dilemma and the national imperative

NAFTA will be highly pervasive of the Canadian legal system, as indeed is the Free Trade Agreement between Canada and the United States of America—entered into by and between the government of Canada and the government of the United States of America, and signed in Ottawa on December 22, 1987, and January 2, 1988, and at Washington on December 23, 1987 and January 2, 1988—and, for that matter, so is the General Agreement on Tariffs and Trade, to a lesser but continually increasing extent.

To a greater or lesser extent, all of these international trading arrangements have an impact—often a very considerable impact—on matters that, in normal circumstances, are in Canada within the exclusive purview of the legislatures and governments of the provinces. Undertaking international obligations is a relatively simple matter. The federal executive of Canada can, on all subjects, bind Canada, in international law, by treaties and other agreements with foreign states. (On the prevailing view, a province has by itself no standing in public international law, and no capacity to make agreements recognized by international law.) The Canadian federal executive can both conclude and ratify an agreement. No legislative approval is legally necessary at any stage in the process of contracting an international agreement, though such approval is often in fact sought for political reasons (see Section 10 of Bill C-115). But implementation is another matter entirely. For treaties or other international agreements, regardless of their terms, are not in Anglo-Canadian law self-executing, save in the rare instances where the executive—which makes the treaty—itself has the power to carry it out and actually manifests in the treaty its intention to do so by means of the treaty itself without further executive or legislative action. Legislation is normally needed to carry out an international arrangement, and obviously this is so for the kind of trade agreements we are discussing, for they involve extensive changes in the law. How, then, can NAFTA be implemented?

On the one hand, the Canadian constitution, as it is read at present by the courts, does not allow the federal Parliament to rely on its power under Section 91.2 ("The Regulation of Trade and Commerce") to sustain legislation simply because that legislation happens to be addressed to economic or business activity. For, beyond undertakings of certain specific kinds (e.g., banks, air transport enterprises, broadcast communications, international and interprovincial transportation and telecommunications undertakings), only the provincial legislatures can, generally speaking, regulate the production and provision of goods and services in those transactions occurring wholly within their respective provincial boundaries, including control of what goods and services may be produced and provided, by whom, and to whom, and on what terms and conditions, as to price or otherwise.

On the other hand, apart from subjects that in any event fall within its legislative authority, the Parliament of Canada cannot, under the prevailing judicial orthodoxy, sustain legislation constitutionally simply because it is needed to perform international obligations owing to foreign states by virtue of treaties or other agreements entered into, on behalf of Canada, by the executive government of Canada.

Hence an apparent constitutional dilemma. The critical (and, I think, constitutionally decisive) reality is that more than a quarter of our gross domestic product enters into international export trade. The *OECD Economic Outlook* (No. 52) for December 1992 (published by the OECD in Paris) shows statistics on the value of exports of goods and services calculated as a percentage of GDP (in market prices) in the Group of Seven countries (1987 current prices except for Germany, which is based on 1991 current prices):

Country	Exports as a % of GDP	Country	Exports as a % of GDP
U.S.	8	Japan	10.4
Germany	29.7	France	20.6
U.K	25.3	Canada	26.1
Italy	17.9		

We are, whether we like it or not, a trading nation. While we have some measure of choice, the truth is that, in the end, Canada simply cannot stay out of international trading arrangements in one form or another. Nor can we confine the scope of these arrangements to those matters which, in Canada, happen to lie within federal jurisdiction. The day is long gone when international trade agreements were concerned only with import and export duties, as to which the federal Parliament's power is, in principle, exclusive. International arrangements address non-tariff barriers; increasingly they address services as well as goods; they even address government procurement and state enterprise. Therefore, inevitably, they address matters within provincial jurisdiction as well as those within federal jurisdiction.

There is, then, no way out. Canada must, as a matter of economic necessity, participate as a sovereign state in international trading arrangements. And the federal Parliament therefore must constitutionally be able, in the last resort, to impose implementing measures on the provinces, be they willing or not, and regardless of the normal distribution of legislative power, in respect of international trade agreements negotiated and entered into by the federal executive on behalf of Canada as a whole. This does not mean that Parliament need always impose them on the provinces as a first measure. Indeed, practically speaking it has some latitude to step in only after the failure of efforts to obtain voluntary provincial compliance. This is particularly so given the rather slow and ponderous character of the mechanisms to which signatory states must have recourse on breach. In fact, the posture of Bill C-115 *vis-à-vis* the provinces seems in the main to be one of "wait and see." In this respect, it rather resembles the Canada-United States Free Trade Agreement Implementation Act, S.C. 1988, c.65.

The least intrusive constitutional solution

Obviously the Canadian constitutional dilemma could be resolved with a broad brush either 1) by a wholesale reconsideration of the scope of the federal trade and commerce power—placing in federal legislative hands an overriding control of business activity—or 2) by a general reconsideration of the 1937 Privy Council decision on treaty implementation, *Attorney General for Canada v. Attorney General for Ontario*, [1937] A.C. 326 (Labour Conventions Case).

There are perfectly good reasons for doing either or both, and there have been judicial hints especially of the latter. But each would be highly sensitive in terms of the existing balance of authority within the federation. The latter path also involves textual problems, since to achieve the desired result the courts would be obliged to find implementation of federal governmental treaties to be a discrete and distinct legislative subject matter, which, since as such it could not fall within the list of provincial powers, would consequently lie within the federal residuary power. Federal residuary legislative power extends to "all matters not coming within the Classes of Subjects by this Act assigned exclusively to the Legislatures of all the Provinces" (Section 91 of the Constitution Act, 1867). Reliance on this power is not assisted by the fact that the 1867 Act (then known as The British North America Act, 1867) did in fact address treaty implementation. Proceeding on the assumption (perfectly understandable in 1867) that treaties for Canada would be made by the imperial government, Section 132 gave the Parliament and government of Canada "all powers necessary or proper for performing the Obligations of Canada or any Province thereof, as Part of the British Empire, towards Foreign Countries, arising under Treaties between the Empire and such Foreign Countries." Thus, the 1867 Act made specific provision for a federal power of treaty implementation, but only for "Imperial" treaties. As Canada, from the 1920s onwards, began to make its own treaties, the question arose as to whether Parliament could implement them insofar as they dealt with matters normally under provincial jurisdiction.

In its 1937 decision, the Privy Council refused "to strain the section [Section 132] so as to cover the uncontemplated event" ([1937] A.C. 326 at p. 350)—i.e., that the Canadian federal government would eventually make treaties. Their lordships refused also to treat "the implementation of federal-executive treaties" as constituting a discrete and distinct, and therefore residuary federal, legislative power. Section 132, in other words, was exhaustive. Though the Privy Council itself was divided at the time—and although the result has always been controversial in Canada and the courts have from time to time hinted at reconsideration—the 1937 decision has so far endured.

In my view, the least intrusive constitutional solution is likely to be the one preferred by the courts. This path does not require any real consideration of the trade and commerce power. Nor does it involve attributing a general power of treaty implementation to the Parliament of Canada. The key, in my view, lies in the very case that originated the long history of restrictive judicial interpretation of the trade and commerce power; that is to say, the 1881 Privy Council decision in *Citizens' Insurance Co. of Canada v. Parsons*, (L.R. 7 App. Cas. 96). The provincial legislation whose validity was there in question imposed compulsory conditions on all fire-insurance policies in force in Ontario with respect to any property therein. It was challenged as constituting a violation of the exclusive federal power under Section 91.2 of the 1867 Act ("The Regulation of Trade and Commerce"). The challenge failed. The legislation was upheld on the basis that not only did the province enjoy the necessary legislative authority (Section 92.13, "Property and Civil Rights in the Province") but that moreover its power to enact the type of legislation there in question was exclusive. Accordingly, Section 91.2 was held to have no application, whether to preclude the provincial legislation or to sustain similar federal legislation.

Speaking through Sir Montague Smith, their lordships observed (7 App. Cas. at p. 112):

> The words "regulation of trade and commerce," in their unlimited sense are sufficiently wide, if uncontrolled by the context and other parts of the Act, to include every regulation of trade ranging from political arrangements in regard to trade with foreign governments, requiring the sanction of parliament, down to minute rules for regulating particular trades. But a consideration of the Act shows that the words were not used in

this unlimited sense. In the first place the collocation of No. 2 with classes of subjects of national and general concern affords an indication that regulations relating to general trade and commerce were in the mind of the legislature, when conferring this power on the dominion parliament.

The key passage for our purposes is, in my view, the following (7 App. Cas. at p. 113):

> Construing therefore the words "regulation of trade and commerce" by the various aids to their interpretation above suggested, they would include political arrangements in regard to trade requiring the sanction of parliament, regulation of trade in matters of inter-provincial concern, and it may be that they would include general regulation of trade affecting the whole dominion.

The crucial words are, in the first passage, the phrase "political arrangements in regard to trade with foreign governments, requiring the sanction of parliament" and, in the second, the phrase "political arrangements in regard to trade requiring the sanction of parliament." The latter passage, though it leaves out the reference to "foreign governments," clearly refers to the former.

This seems to me to solve the immediate problem without any departure from established orthodoxy. It simply involves invoking a special sub-category—recognized since earliest days—of the federal legislative power conferred by Section 91.2 of the 1867 Act. It is of some interest that, in 1989, the Supreme Court of Canada (*General Motors of Canada v. City National Leasing*, (1989) 58 D.L.R. (4th) 255), sustained federal competition legislation—and in particular a civil damage remedy for loss or damage arising from prohibited conduct—under Section 91.2 as being valid legislation supportable under the established (if badly battered) rubric "general trade and commerce affecting Canada as a whole," which was another of the Privy Council's 1881 categories.

NAFTA, like the Canada-U.S. Agreement and even GATT, may well concern itself with a range of matters that go beyond the strict limits of what, in Canadian constitutional parlance, is usually referred to as international trade and commerce, which, as such, falls (along with interprovincial trade and commerce) under federal authority. Modern trade agreements are not concerned only with concretely defined barriers to international transactions, in the sense of cross-border movements of goods or services that are either carried out in fact or would be if they were not directly obstructed or impeded. They also address practices, which may occur entirely within a province or a country, having indirect implications for foreign trade, as by favouring in fact local products, even though ostensibly trade-neutral and directed to legitimate objectives. They also address investments and ownership of property within a province or country. But given the language employed by Sir Montague Smith in 1881, it does not seem pertinent to pursue abstruse conceptual distinctions between transactions constituting local trade on the one hand, and those constituting interprovincial trade on the other; nor between laws or practices directed at international trade and those that merely affect it incidentally. It is indisputable that we are concerned here with "political arrangements in regard to trade with foreign governments, requiring the sanction of parliament." That seems constitutionally sufficient.

NAFTA and the Canadian provinces

It is perhaps useful to cull from NAFTA the provisions that, to a non-trade specialist reader on first impression, strike the eye as being addressed more or less specifically to NAFTA's application to the Canadian provinces.

In Chapter 1, "Objectives," Article 105 reads, regarding the extent of obligations, "The Parties shall ensure that all necessary measures are taken in order to give effect to the provisions of this agreement, including their observance, except as otherwise provided in this Agreement, by state and provincial governments."

Chapter 2 is entitled "General Definitions." Article 201 contains two paragraphs. Article 201.1 provides that, for the purposes of the agreement, unless otherwise specified (*inter alia*): "territory means for a Party the territory of that Party as set out in Annex 201.1." Paragraph 201.2 states that "For purposes of this Agreement, unless otherwise specified, a reference to the state or province includes local governments of that state or province." Annex 201.1, entitled "Specific Country Definitions," defines "territory" to mean, "with respect to Canada, the territory to which its customs laws apply, including any areas beyond the territorial seas of Canada within which, in accordance with international law and its domestic law, Canada may exercise rights with respect to the seabed and subsoil and their natural resources."

Chapter 3 concerns "National Treatment and Market Access for Goods." Article 301 is as follows:

> 1. Each Party shall accord national treatment to the goods of another Party in accordance with Article III of the General Agreement on Tariffs and Trade (GATT), including its interpretative notes, and to this end Article III of the GATT and its interpretative notes, or any equivalent provision of a successor agreement to which all Parties are party, are incorporated into and made part of this Agreement.
>
> 2. The provisions of paragraph 1 regarding national treatment shall mean, with respect to a state or province, treatment no less favorable than the most favorable treatment accorded by any such state or province to any like, directly competitive or substitutable goods, as the case may be, of the Party which it forms a part.
>
> 3. Paragraphs 1 and 2 do not apply to the measures set out in Annex 301.3.

Annex 301.3, referred to in paragraph 3 of Article 301, enumerates such matters as "controls by Canada on the export of logs of all species"; and "controls by Canada on the export of unprocessed fish" pursuant to a series of specified provincial statutes, as amended on August 12, 1992.

Chapter 10, entitled "Government Procurement," applies in principle to provincial governmental "entities," but this is merely a commitment in principle subject to further negotiations, with the possibility in the meantime of "voluntary and reciprocal" liberalization, by state and provincial governments, of their respective government-procurement markets. Procurement by provincial government enterprises, so far as I can tell on a quick reading of Chapter 10, is not controlled by Chapter 10. I refer you to Article 1001 (Scope and Coverage), Article 1024 (Further Negotiation), Article 1025 (Definitions), Annex 1001.1a-3 (State and Provincial Government Entities), and Annex 1001.1a-2 (Governmental Enterprises: only listed enterprises are covered, but the Schedule of Canada includes no provincial government enterprises).

Chapter 11, entitled "Investment," contains a number of important provisions, notably in Article 1102 (National Treatment); Article 1103

(Most-Favored Nation Treatment); Article 1105 (Minimum Standard of Treatment); Article 1106 (Performance Requirements); and Article 1107 (Senior Management and Boards of Directors). Their application to Canadian provincial and local governments is controlled by Article 1108, which reads in part as follows:

1. Articles 1102, 1103, 1106, and 1107 do not apply to:

a) any existing non-conforming measure that is maintained by:

(i) a Party at the federal level, as set out in its Schedule to Annex I or III,

(ii) a state or province, for two years after the date of entry into force of this Agreement, and thereafter set out by a Party in its Schedule to Annex I in accordance with paragraph 2, or

(iii) a local government.

It is useful to note that the obligations under Chapter 11, including those which bar expropriation—unless it be for a public purpose, on a non-discriminatory basis, in accordance with due process of law and other guarantees, and with payment of compensation—give rise on breach to an arbitral-tribunal award resulting in monetary compensation or property restitution. Moreover, a party can pay monetary damages with interest in lieu of restitution. So the Parliament of Canada might well, at least in certain instances, prefer to cause the government of Canada to pay the pecuniary costs of provincial breaches—perhaps obtaining indemnity from the province—rather than coercing the province to perform specifically. Of course, it is generally true that the government of Canada could prefer to accept sanctions for Canada's provincially induced breaches of NAFTA rather than compel compliance by recalcitrant provinces.

Chapter 12, "Cross-Border Trade in Services," addresses, in Article 1202, National Treatment; in Article 1203, Most-Favored Nation Treatment; in Article 1204, Standard of Treatment; and in Article 1205, Local Presence. Articles 1206 and 1207 note that Articles 1202, 1203, and 1205 do not apply to the same measures as listed for articles 1102, 1103, 1106, and 1107 above.

Under Article 1207, "Quantitative Restrictions,"

1. Each Party shall set out in its Schedule to Annex V any quantitative restriction that it maintains at the federal level.

2. Within one year of the date of entry into the Force of this Agreement, each Party shall set out its Schedule to Annex V any quantitative restriction maintained by a state or province, not including a local government.

As regards application of Chapter 12 to the Canadian Provinces, I note also Article 1209 (Procedures); Article 1213 (Definitions), especially Article 1213.1 as regards non-governmental bodies exercising delegated powers. Let me announce here that I shall study very closely Annex 1210.5 (Professional Services), especially Section B—"Foreign Legal Consultants."

Chapter 14, on financial services, contains provisions closely analogous to those on services. In Chapter 14, I note particularly Article 1409 (Reservations and Specific Commitments), which specifically addresses the position of the parties' states and provinces.

The seven annexes to NAFTA contain the "Reservations and Exceptions" for Chapters 11, 12, and 14. Annex I concerns "Reservations for Existing Measures and Liberalization Commitments"; Annex II concerns "Reservations for Future Measures." Some of these provisions will be of special interest to Canadian provinces. For example, Annex II contains a reservation to the obligation of national treatment, arising under Article 1102, in respect to investment. Page II-C-2 reads:

> Canada reserves the right to adopt or maintain any measure relating to residency requirements for the ownership by investors of another Party, or their investments, of oceanfront land.

Students of the Canadian constitution will be familiar with the case of *Morgan v. A.-G. for Prince Edward Island*, (1975) 55 D.L.R. (d) 527, in which the Supreme Court of Canada upheld the legislative authority of a province to restrict landholding by non-residents. The reservation cited is narrower than the P.E.I. legislation, but no doubt the P.E.I. statute will in due course be protected under Annex I as an existing non-conforming measure.

Annex I contains a similar restriction for existing federal statutory provisions respecting restrictions on foreign landholding in Alberta. You will notice that there is a two-year period from the entry into force of NAFTA for parties to add to the present list in Annex I further existing state or provincial non-conforming measures (i.e. existing at the date of entry into force of NAFTA: see Article 201.1). This affects investment (see Article 1108.2) and cross-border trade in services (see Article 1206.2). It would be surprising if there were not a provincial stampede to protect their non-conforming laws.

The pending federal NAFTA implementing measure (Bill C-115)

Commons Bill C-115, entitled "An Act to Implement the North American Free Trade Agreement," was introduced into the House on February 25, 1993. It is, of course, not yet law; nor has it even been passed by the House of Commons. The bulk of the bill is contained in Part II, Related and Consequential Amendments, which adapts the body of federal statute law to the agreement. Nearly 30 federal acts are affected. Part I is entitled Implementation of Agreement Generally. Section 10 is very succinct. Under the heading, Approval of Agreement, it enacts simply "the Agreement is hereby approved." This, in my view, is simply a political statement of parliamentary approval. It is doubtful whether any legal consequences flow from it. Certainly it does not impose the terms of the agreement on the provinces. Far more explicit language is needed for that.

The only apparent instance of a provision coercive of the provinces is Section 20 of the act. Even this is only enabling; it empowers the federal executive—the governor general of Canada, acting by and with the advice of the Queen's Privy Council for Canada—to make regulations if they should appear necessary to enforce two articles of the agreement, and then only after consultation with the relevant provincial government. The two NAFTA articles in question concern certain alcoholic beverages.

The Canada-United States Free Trade Agreement Implementation Act, S.C. 1988, c.65, contained a provision, Section 9, analogous to Section 20 of Bill C-115. It covered Chapter 8 of the Canada-U.S. Agreement, "Wine and Distilled Spirits." It is interesting to see where, in the light of experience, the Canadian federal government expects trouble to arise.

Let me make a few other general remarks. If enacted, Bill C-115 will, in virtue of Section 247, only come into force—provision by provision—as ordered by the governor general in council, and only if he is satisfied that the other parties have taken satisfactory steps to implement the agreement.

Immediately preceding Part I are some provisions of general application. Section 6 appears designated to preclude private litigation to establish rights that arise under the agreement, insofar as the agreement has been made part of domestic law. Rights incorporated into domestic law are, in the normal course, justiciable; and Section 6 does not interfere with that justiciability, since those rights then arise under the relevant other (i.e. implementing) laws—not under Part I of Bill C-115, and not "solely under or by virtue of the Agreement." Section 6 is as follows:

> 6.(1) No person has any cause of action and no proceedings of any kind shall be taken, without the consent of the Attorney General of Canada, to enforce or determine any right or obligation that is claimed or arises solely under or by virtue of Part I or any order or regulation made under Part I.
>
> (2) Subject to Section B of Chapter Eleven of the Agreement, no person has any cause of action and no proceedings of any kind shall be taken, without the consent of the Attorney General of Canada, to enforce or determine any right or obligation that is claimed or arises solely under or by virtue of the Agreement.

Its terms apply, however, even to Section 20 (quoted above) and to regulations made under Section 20, despite the fact that these provisions would normally constitute a fully justiciable part of domestic law, and may even involve penalties (see Section 20(1); Interpretation Act, R.S.C. 1985, c. I-21, ss. 2(1) and 34; Criminal Code, R.S.C. 1985, C-46, as amended, s. 126).

Bill C-115 also provides (Section 3) that it, and other federal legislation implementing the NAFTA, are to be interpreted in a manner consistent with the agreement.

Section 3 would itself have been enough to justify scheduling the entire text of NAFTA to Bill C-115, cumbersome as that might be. That course was in fact followed in the 1988 statute implementing the Canada-U.S. Agreement, and is usual Canadian federal legislative practice when international agreements are given effects in domestic law. Instead, Section 2(2) of Bill C-115 simply requires that the agreement "shall be published in the Canada Treaty Series." Failure to make NAFTA part of the statute book impairs the access of the legal profession and the public to the NAFTA text, and involves issues of principle as well as practical inconvenience.

Industrial Policy, Subsidies, and Trade Law: Troubling the Waters of Trade

Brian R. Russell

> In these lay a great multitude of impotent folk, of blind, halt, withered, waiting for the moving of the water.
>
> For an angel went down at a certain season ... and troubled the water; whosoever then first after the troubling of the water stepped in was made whole of whatsoever disease he had.
>
> John 5: 3,4 King James Version

JOHN'S ACCOUNT OF THE MIRACLE at the pool at Bethesda provides a useful analogy to current U.S. subsidy practices and their role in international trade. Just as the sick and infirm of John's day waited anxiously at poolside for a miracle cure, so today, many companies and ideas await the introduction of some miraculous new government panacea designed to bolster their international competitiveness and assuage post-partum difficulties. The most recent example of this phenomenon is the decision by the Clinton administration to play archangel to the U.S. high-technology sector.

High-tech industrial policy

The instrument of government visitation was proclaimed by the president in a February 22, 1993, speech given to workers at Silicon Graphics Incorporated, a computer manufacturer located in Mountain View, California. In his speech, the president outlined a comprehensive plan for government assistance to U.S. high-technology companies. Technology for America's Economic Growth, A New Direction to Build Economic Strength (TAEG)[1] provides the details of what, on paper at least, appears to be an ambitious new mandate for government direction and subsidization of the American high-tech sector.

TAEG outlines an agenda for change in American technology policy. At an estimated cost of $17 billion over four years, the program calls for a major shift of military and other federal laboratory research priorities. Focusing on the creation of government-industry consortiums, the plan proposes a shifting of defence-related research to civilian technology and an additional dollop of federal spending to promote such things as computer-aided manufacturing, environmental technologies, and the so-called "information superhighway." The plan includes $1.3 billion to expand the role of the National Institute of Standards and Technology to include financial assistance for designated high tech projects, and a tax expenditure of some $6.4 billion over four years to make permanent the Research & Experimentation Tax credit currently set to expire this year. The Administration plans to take an active role in financing the development of an environmentally friendly automobile and to pump new funds into manufacturing extension centres designed to increase the diffusion of leading-edge technology to small and medium enterprises. Perhaps more surprisingly, the plan calls for the reform of anti-trust laws to permit joint production ventures. The SEMATECH model is extended beyond research collaboration to include manufacturing endeavours. This would seem to open the door to all sorts of collaborative efforts involving multinationals, some of which

---

1   Government Printing Office, Washington, D.C., 1993.

may smack of what used to be called oligopoly. Clearly, the administration has signalled a major foray into the high technology sector.

Whether or not the Clinton agenda constitutes what *The Economist* called "embarking on an overt industrial policy,"[2] it certainly raises serious questions about the role of government intervention in the economy. Certainly this particular bout of governmental largesse has been handled more skilfully than most of its predecessors. It is directed at a sector that is currently fashionable as the engine of economic growth, and it was constructed with the aid of many of the industries' leading private sector participants: As John Scully, CEO of Apple Computer Inc., noted, "We helped write it. How could we find anything wrong with it?"[3]

It is certainly not the case that targeting the high-technology sector was not going on before Clinton.[4] In fact, government assistance is a major part of the American business environment. A comprehensive review of all assistance programs from the federal and 11 state governments conducted by the U.S. Policy Studies Group at Dalhousie University suggests that the total value of U.S. federal and state government assistance to non-agricultural business was nearly $135 billion in 1989. Nonetheless, TAEG represents a significant upping of the federal ante in the high-technology sector.

Regardless of the relative merits of the approach, let us assume that the Clinton administration has decided to adopt some form of high-tech industrial policy and that TAEG is its manifesto. Such a policy appears to blend neatly with the managed trade strategy emerging from Washington. A government that believes it can target crucial sectors domestically that will drive economic growth is not likely to be any less sanguine about its ability to open or close trade selectively, based on

---

2   *The Economist*, February 27, 1993, p. 65.

3   *BusinessWeek*, March 8, 1993. p. 26.

4   Research conducted by the U.S. Policy Studies Group at Dalhousie University between 1989 and 1991 revealed 148 federal and state R&D programs aimed at assisting business nationally and in 11 selected states.

perceived self interest. This appears to be the current thinking. (Though one is, of course, entitled to a healthy scepticism about the ability of this or any government to make these prognostications with anything approaching accuracy.)

Trade law and domestic subsidies

How does this strategy on domestic subsidy policy correspond with the existing rules of international trade as set out in the GATT, the Canada-U.S. FTA, and the proposed NAFTA? The short answer to this question is, quite well. This reflects the fact that international trade law has traditionally given a wide berth to the question of domestic subsidies and has generally focused such attention as it has given the topic of subsidies on those specifically directed at increasing exports.[5] This approach is reflected in the GATT[6] in Article XVI(4):

> . . . contracting parties shall cease to grant either directly or indirectly any form of subsidy on the export of any product other than a primary product . . .

Article 11(1) of the Tokyo Round Code on Subsidies and Countervailing Duties makes explicit the Parties intentions:

> Signatories recognize that subsidies other than export subsidies are widely used as important instruments for the promotion of social and economic policy objectives and do not intend to restrict the right of signatories to use such subsidies . . .[7]

States are left to be masters of their own house with respect to assistance not specifically targeted at increasing exports.

---

5   For an excellent discussion of the export/import subsidy dichotomy see Hufbauer, Gary Clyde and Joanna Shelton-Erb, *Subsidies in International Trade*, (Cambridge, MA.: MIT Press, 1984).

6   *General Agreement on Tariffs and Trade*, 61 Stat. (pt.5), T.I.A.S. No. 1700, 55 U.N.T.S. 188.

7   *Agreement on Interpretation and Application of Articles VI, XVI, and XXIII of the General Agreement on Tariffs and Trade (Subsidies and Countervailing Duties), Basic Instruments and Selected Documents (BISD)* 26S/56 (1980).

Both the FTA and NAFTA are also timid on this question. Article 1907 of the FTA provides for the establishment of a bi-national working group to "seek to establish more effective rules and disciplines concerning the use of government subsidies" and to "seek to develop a substitute system of rules for dealing with unfair pricing and government subsidization . . ."[8]

This group was to have reported to the parties as soon as possible, and in any event to make its best efforts to develop and implement the substitute system of rules within seven years of the signing of the agreement. Failure to do so "shall allow either party to terminate the agreement on six months notice."[9] As envisioned, the entire Chapter 19 dispute resolution mechanism was to be an interim process to be replaced by a comprehensive binational law on dumping and subsidies. Such a system had been a major goal of Canadian negotiators in the agreement, but was clearly not on the table from the beginning for the U.S. negotiators. Binational dispute settlement panels were the resulting hard-won compromise. These have at least provided an impartial review body but they remain bound by archaic national trade remedy laws.

NAFTA[10] has watered down the FTA commitment even further. Under Article 1907(2), the parties agree to consult on:

a) the potential to develop more effective rules and disciplines concerning the use of government subsidies; and

b) the potential for reliance on a substitute system of rules for dealing with unfair transborder pricing practices and government subsidization.

Note the change in emphasis. The commitment to "seek to establish ... and develop" rules and a substitute system has become an agreement

---

8   Free Trade Agreement between Canada and the United States of America, Department of External Affairs, Ottawa 1989.

9   *Ibid*, Article 1906.

10   *North American Free Trade Agreement*, (Ottawa: Canada Communications Group-Publishing, 1992).

to "consult" on the "potential" for such agreements; not the agreements themselves, but rather the potential for them. The nebulousness of consulting on potential need hardly be commented upon.

Such reticence removes the parties at least one degree further from actual results, a condition to which they were never very close. Further, these consultations are to occur, not within the context of an ongoing, specified working group struck to examine the issues but apparently at a rather more generic level at which numerous other issues may divert attention and be traded off. Finally, any reference to a specified time frame is removed and any specific reference to lack of progress on these questions as grounds for abrogation is also absent. In short, the issue is placed so far on the back burner as to be out of sight.[11]

It has been suggested by some officials that the subsidies issue need not be addressed in the regional agreement in any case. According to this line of thought, which has prevailed for some time, the proposed subsidies provisions of the Uruguay Round of GATT negotiations[12] make acceptable arrangements on subsidies that could be incorporated holus-bolus into NAFTA once the Round is concluded. Were the current version of the draft code to be adopted, it could place substantial limitations on the ability of an administration to disperse funds to any specific high-technology project. Article 8.2(a) allows for:

> assistance for research activities conducted by firms or by higher education or research establishments on a contract basis with firms if:
>
> > the assistance covers not more than 50 percent of the costs of basic industrial research or 25 percent of the costs of applied research . . .

---

11   It should be noted that there is a legal question here as to whether the parties have succeeded in altering the commitments of Article 1906 and 1907 of the FTA. Article 103(1) of NAFTA affirms the rights and obligations of the parties under *inter alia*, the FTA. Article 103(2) goes on to provide that "in the event of any inconsistency between this Agreement and . . . other agreements this Agreement shall prevail . . ."

12   *Draft Final Act Embodying the Results of the Uruguay Round of Multilateral Trade Negotiations*, (Geneva: GATT Secretariat, December, 1991).

While it may be that this limit is too high for U.S. acquiescence (largely due to constraints on its own spending likely to be imposed by budget difficulties), it is nevertheless capable of being a significant factor in the individual case and is an undeniable restraint on U.S. freedom of action. Whether it is sufficient restraint to forestall the kind of federal generosity with which it is unlikely countries like Mexico can compete, or the type of industrial policy-making, suggested by TAEG, which mandates the preselection of successes (a function at which most governments have a notoriously poor record), is at best debatable. What is certain is that this restriction would be applicable to the type of high technology policy favoured by the Clinton administration and that other provisions of the subsidies chapter could have far-reaching effects in other areas and at the sub-federal level as well.[13]

It is true that the proposed Dunkel draft of the Uruguay Round Agreement contains the first attempts to restrain domestic subsidy policies and goes some distance toward providing a modicum of discipline. Whether or not one is of the opinion that these provisions go far enough, they are an improvement, and a substantial one. There remain, however, at least three major problems with allowing these proposals to serve as the NAFTA backstop. First, it appears that specific provisions of the subsidies code have become bargaining chips in the broader negotiations to conclude the Round and may be weakened or sacrificed. Second, Godot may never arrive. The fate of the entire Round is currently in doubt whether or not there is any agreement on subsidies. To date the parties have waited more than two years past the original scheduled conclusion of the Round. One is forced to wonder if it would not have been preferable to have used the time to have started on a Plan B should the Round collapse. No one seems to be prepared to deal with

---

13 The most notable of these from a Canadian viewpoint is the proposed restriction on regional development subsidies found in Article 8.2(b). In terms of scope, several articles of the draft would quite clearly limit the ability of states and/or provinces to implement certain types of subsidy policy (most notably Article 2.2). These provisions may come as a rude shock to a number of provincial and state bureaucrats charged with designing economic development policy.

this possibility even now. It is unlikely that frantic handwringing will suffice. Third, even if the Round succeeds and the subsidy chapter is approved extant, it is by no means the final word on the subject. This is particularly so in the context of a North American market that is becoming increasingly integrated in every sector. Much thought needs to be given to a system that goes beyond what can be achieved multi-laterally.

Conclusion

Where then does all this leave us? Essentially where we began, with an administration apparently disposed to try and target high-technology successes, and with any number of potential recipients clamouring for relief. To return to the parable, the crush at Bethesda was so great as to deny the most worthy his opportunity. No doubt there will be a similar caterwauling for Clinton "miracles." In the current undisciplined and wide open market for domestic subsidies, such cries will inevitably lead to a best-efforts attempt to satisfy the most vocal supplicants. Histori-cally, greasing the squeaky wheel has not been a terribly efficient strategy for economic growth, nor is any variation thereof likely to be. An environment in which nations are free to enter into unrestricted subsidy warfare limited only by their capacity to pay is neither efficient nor desirable. Given the size of worldwide deficits, and the varying degrees of available tax bases, such a policy is doomed to worsen national and global welfare. What is required is an agreed-upon set of rules which force nations to act more rationally and responsibly, bearing in mind their own long-run self-interest.

Regional agreements provide an ideal opportunity for this type of exemplary thinking. Unfortunately, NAFTA, while a step forward over-all, takes a backward step in an important area in which forward motion has been all too infrequent and tentative. Canadian, Mexican, and American policy makers need to reinvigorate the process envisioned in the FTA and begin to lead the rest of the world by example. The smaller negotiating group provides an ideal opportunity for innovative and ground-breaking thinking regardless of the status of the GATT propos-als. While we should not be Pollyannas, and must recognize that there are extremely high political sensibilities on these issues in all three countries, it is long past time that the process of change began in earnest.

The current spate of Canada-U.S. disputes on lumber, beer, and steel, among others, only highlights the importance of proceeding now. The current system is not good enough for the emerging North American market.

NAFTA Dispute Settlement Panels: Theory and Practice

Armand De Mestral

I KNOW THAT IN CIRCLES OF ECONOMISTS and trade experts, lawyers are considered parasites, but be assured that any knowledge I have of dispute settlement, I came by honestly. I am probably one of very few who has read the entire Canada-U.S. Free Trade Agreement. I had to read it because the provisions on dispute settlements begin in the preamble and run right through to the last annex.

The dispute settlement provisions that are envisaged in NAFTA were inspired by the General Agreement on Tariffs and Trade (GATT). One feature of the GATT over the past 40 years has been the development of a fairly interesting settlement process, which is half arbitration and half mediation.

In the same way that the FTA and NAFTA fit into the GATT matrix, a major part of the dispute settlement process is largely inspired by the GATT matrix. In the formation of panels—which are invited to study a problem and determine who is right and who is wrong and how a particular problem can be resolved—the FTA and NAFTA draw heavily on the GATT experience.

Indeed, at this point in the Uruguay Round of the GATT negotiations, there are a lot of new proposals that take the GATT dispute settlement processes somewhat further toward a more judicial and binding arbitration. There is almost a competition between the FTA and NAFTA and what has been happening in the Uruguay Round as to who will get there first in terms of the process.

Second, it is very clear that the NAFTA dispute settlement mechanism derives from the FTA process. If one is familiar with Chapters 18 and 19 of the FTA, the structure of the FTA, the role played by expert committees, by dispute avoidance, and the process involved in creating dispute settlement mechanisms, then one can understand very readily what has been done in NAFTA. NAFTA built almost entirely on what had already been done in the FTA regarding dispute settlement, but it has gone further.

Basically, the Canada-U.S. free trade model selected as its goal dispute avoidance, and not simply the setting up of a marvellous mechanism for resolving disputes and creating jobs for lawyers. Second, disputes and the dispute avoidance process are dealt with through the creation of many specific technical committees under every chapter in the agreement, not just the single dispute settlement chapters. This is built right into the structure of the agreement, and it is part of the ongoing implementation.

Third, we have in the agreement two specific chapters dealing with dispute settlement: one is Chapter 18, which is very similar to the GATT model, and then Chapter 19, which is tailored especially to disputes involving anti-dumping and countervailing duties or subsidies. The unique approach of this chapter in the FTA agreement involves the way the negotiators responded to their inability to reach common standards on laws governing large U.S. retaliatory legislation. Canada was not exempted from U.S. anti-dumping and countervailing laws, but Canada also saw the inclusion of Chapter 19, which created a special process of appeal on dumping or subsidies from decisions by American or the Canadian regulatory agencies to a bilateral tribunal.

The FTA also said that within five years both parties would try to work out common standards on dumping and subsidy laws. That process apparently never got off the ground. It was instead left to the Uruguay Round of GATT negotiations where, in fact, they have renegotiated a subsidies code, but have made little progress in abolishing anti-dumping duties.

In NAFTA, dispute avoidance and dispute settlement are extended more broadly. In fact, there are more specific dispute settlement commitments and even more dispute settlement procedures in NAFTA than there were in the FTA. As in the FTA, dispute avoidance procedures are woven through the NAFTA text, through virtually every chapter. More specific provisions are contained in four chapters: 11 on investments, 14 on financial services, 19 on anti-dumping and countervailing disputes, and 20 on the general dispute settlement process.

With respect to investments, this is one of the areas in the FTA where commitments are not subject to serious dispute settlement. The new NAFTA text, Chapter 11, which deals with investments, provides for an extensive dispute settlement, but instead of relying on Chapter 20, the general dispute settlement process in NAFTA, it was decided that the three countries would use a tribunal and arbitral process. That avenue has existed since 1965 and is known as the International Court for the Settlement of International Disputes (ICSID). It is an arbitral process that leads to binding arbitral decisions.

Chapter 11 of the NAFTA text specifies that if an investment dispute arises (other than the decision in a particular case not to allow a particular investment to proceed, let's say under existing Canadian investment laws) that question goes to the ICSID. The ICSID treaty takes precedence over others, and the decision must be respected by the parties. One of the interesting features of the ICSID is that it considers disputes between private investors and government as well as intergovernmental disputes.

Financial services are dealt with in Chapter 14, and here again the earlier FTA agreement commitments were very limited. In chapter 14 of the NAFTA there is a commitment to dispute settlement that did not exist under the corresponding chapter in the FTA. Instructions are to follow the process under Chapter 20, the general dispute settlement process, except that the people who would be called upon to form the panel are drawn not from the general group but from a group of financial experts. There is a special roster of financial experts so that the ordinary lawyer or trade expert will not be called upon. Financial services disputes are to be resolved by financial experts. Those who are aware that the trade world and the monetary world never meet will readily understand the subtle logic of this distinction. Bankers again submit themselves to dispute settlement, but with their own kind.

Chapter 19, the same number as in the FTA, deals with disputes arising from decisions of administrative tribunals in participating countries on dumping or injury from subsidies. I presume that everybody understands what is meant by dumping. It is also known as fair competition in a free market. A government believes that when you sell a loss leader it is good marketing. When you buy a loss leader that is dumping. We still treat foreign goods as somehow worse or inferior to our own, so if someone sells foreign goods more cheaply in our markets and this causes injury to local producers, this is dumping and is therefore bad.

If, under NAFTA, there is a finding of dumping or subsidized exports, in Canada, Mexico, or in the United States, that decision can be appealed by the injured party. Instead of appealing to the ordinary courts, as you would in Canada to the federal court, or the Board of International Trade in the U.S. or the appropriate court in Mexico, you appeal to a binational panel of five trade experts who take the whole court file and give a ruling.

This ruling must have the effect of law in that country. The ruling is directed to whether the domestic law was properly applied and implemented by the domestic tribunal. So, the ruling is not concerned with general international law, but is of a domestic nature. The question always arises, did the administrative tribunal apply its law in a proper fashion? This is the procedure followed today in Chapter 19 of the FTA.

As far as I know, there have been nine decisions and there are 12 or 13 cases actually running right now. Under the FTA, most of the decisions have confirmed the validity of the administrative decision. On occasion, they simply overturn.

My impression is that this system has worked relatively well and has done what has been asked of it in legal terms. The FTA system is simply carried forward to NAFTA, the only difference being that now you have a roster made up of three countries' nominees, each country having 25. When a dispute arises, the two countries involved will select two names from the roster, and the four in turn will name a chair. The panel is then complete. There is, as there was with the FTA, a built-in extra appellate that allows for what is called an extraordinary challenge in the event that the binational panel behaves in some egregious and improper fashion. There has been, in fact, one decision under the FTA by an extraordinary challenge panel made up of retired senior judges. There is another case presently proceeding.

The FTA Chapter 19 model was carried almost exactly forward into Chapter 19 of the NAFTA by simply adapting it to accommodate three countries. The wording of both dispute settlement chapters, 19 and 20, is designed so that NAFTA may be expanded to take in other countries.

Chapter 20 contains the general dispute settlement process. It concerns itself with any disputes over the application or interpretation of NAFTA not otherwise covered. I have noted three areas that would otherwise be covered by other processes. The general process, then, is this GATT-type model. It embodies a panel of five experts, who do not have to be lawyers and, under the GATT, are rarely trained in the law. The GATT uses three panellists while the FTA and NAFTA models use five. They are asked both to determine whether the treaty has been violated and whether the rights of either party under the treaty have been ignored or impaired.

General dispute settlement remains a dual process in that what is envisaged is both the determination as to the meaning of the treaty and recommendations as to how the particular dispute can be resolved. Under the FTA, there have been four decisions to date, and there is at least one more panel underway. FTA panels have operated very much like the GATT panels in the way they have interpreted the treaties.

The law of the GATT, the general multilateral law governing our international trade relationships, has heavily influenced the decision making framework used by the panellists in every one of the four disputes we have mentioned. Each country chooses two names from a roster of experts. The difference in NAFTA will be that if there is a dispute between, say, Canada and Mexico, Canada will chose the Mexicans and Mexico will chose two Canadians and the four will chose the chair. This was decided, I believe, at the Mexicans' behest. It is a positive step toward multilateralism and internationalism. I hope it will not lead to Canadians looking for two well-disposed Mexicans and Mexico looking for two well-disposed Canadians, as often happens in international dispute settlements before the International Court or international arbitration. Fairness will depend on the integrity of the panellists and the way each government behaves.

A final word. Although very close to the existing model, in NAFTA there could be language problems in its implementation. French is the official second language of Canada, and to my knowledge there has been no proceeding where all of the documents coming from Canada were in French and had to be translated and all of the hearings needed to be conducted in French. As far as I know, everything has been conducted largely in English.

Clearly it could happen, and maybe it will soon happen, that we will have an arbitration conducted in French and in English. With Mexico under NAFTA, it is certain that large volumes of documents which exist only in Spanish will have to be translated, and the hearings will have to be conducted bilingually. This is something of a technical question, but it may put a new spin on the way these dispute settlements are run. It may slow them down if they require translation of 10,000 pages of documents, or if 500 pages of new submissions are needed. This is a new issue that is not insuperable by any means, yet it has not altered how the panels have operated up to now.

Processes are fairly clear, but there are a number of other provisions throughout the NAFTA treaty on dispute settlement issues, including some right at the beginning that refer to certain environmental treaties. These treaties will have priority over NAFTA, and that could include their dispute settlement processes if they are spelled out.

Afterword—A Summary

Afterword

John W. Galbraith

FREE TRADE, OR THE MOVEMENT TOWARD IT, represents a reduction in the restrictions placed on individuals by governments (that is, a reduction in restrictions on commercial dealings with people living on the other side of some border). While restrictions imposed on oneself are generally resisted, restrictions imposed on others often have a certain attraction. Hence the potential for opposition to liberalizing changes that seem, to some, so obviously desirable.

But despite the scope for difference of opinion, we live in a time in which there is a great deal of support for liberalized trade arrangements, and not only on our own continent. One result has been a widespread, if very gradual, reduction in worldwide tariff levels through the GATT. Another result has been the formation of regional trading blocs, of which NAFTA (if passed into law) will be one example. We have had a good deal of discussion of the prospects for NAFTA passage; the mood of the conference, I would say, tends toward the view that passage (possibly with supplementary agreements governing, for example, environmental standards) is reasonably likely, but that the probability of difficulty has tended to be underestimated in the recent past. In any event, I will say no more about the predictions that have been made; we will know the outcome soon enough. What I will do is to suggest some general themes and ideas that emerge from the contributions that we have enjoyed over the past three days.

First, NAFTA represents a next step in the evolution of "our" trading bloc, which presently includes only Canada and the U.S. Implicit in this statement are the facts that NAFTA must not be viewed as anyone's idea of the best of all possible commercial and contractual worlds, nor as a final state for trade relations, nor indeed as anything other than progress toward an eventual goal of greater access, and openness, to markets in all countries. If NAFTA is equated with Cordell Hull's ideal of the elimination of all artificial barriers to international trade (if only within the confines of the North American continent), then false expectations have been raised. NAFTA, like the FTA in force between Canada and the U.S., exempts various classes of trade from consideration, allows some classes of restriction to persist, does not address the question of government subsidies, and perhaps most important is a regional arrangement that will create the trade diversion that follows from any system of regional preferences.

Of course NAFTA is most usefully compared not with the ideal state of the world but with the immediate alternative. From that angle, NAFTA brings much better access to a large market for Canadian and U.S. output, and substantially better access to a very large market, for Mexican output. Gains from specialization are available for division among citizens of the three countries; since we can clearly expect a large increase in demand for Mexican labour, these gains may well accrue disproportionately to those in the lower part of the continental income distribution (although it seems unlikely that we will see a similar reduction in income inequality within Canada and the U.S., as lower-paid workers' skills become relatively more abundant in those two countries). While there will be some trade diversion, for some countries this will be offset by the scope for the accession of new partners to the agreement in the future. The quick passage of NAFTA would be a precedent for rapid expansion of the free-trade area.

A second theme that emerged from the discussion is, as I want to emphasize, related to the first point that NAFTA is simply one step along the path to free trade among nations. That second theme concerns the difficulties that arise precisely because of the restrictions that remain in NAFTA, as well as the technical difficulty of resolving the myriad co-ordination problems, including co-ordination of laws and standards, that necessarily arise in an ambitious project such as this. To take one example from Michael Walker, consider the problem of defining rules of origin. If we have a product to be exported from Canada to the U.S. free of tariffs under the FTA, then it must be deemed a Canadian product. This necessitates formulating a rule for the percentage of content that must be Canadian, rules for making the calculation (e.g., is each component counted all-or-none or on the basis of its percentage content? Does interest on capital borrowing count as part of content?), and so on. It also requires that someone pay the cost of performing this potentially very lengthy calculation. But note that this problem arises precisely because the agreement is a restricted approach to free trade. If we had free trade among all regions of the planet, rules of origin would be unnecessary: there would no longer be any people outside the free-trade area whose products would have to be excluded. The same is true of the problem of trade diversion that arises because countries inside the bloc have advantages over those outside; in a world that had evolved toward general free trade, there would be no region outside the (single) bloc away from which trade would be diverted.

Not all technical difficulties in such agreements can be made to disappear by widening the free-trade net to catch more trading partners. There is pressure for co-ordination inherent in such arrangements, not only because similar legal and regulatory conditions in different regions make movement of goods and capital easier, but also because differences in conditions may put pressure on the government with more onerous regulation to ease its standards or lose capital. This co-ordination requires thought and adjustment. Carlos Braga and Eduardo Ramirez have given us two examples of such difficulties, in the efforts to co-ordinate intellectual property rights, and commercial law, among NAFTA countries. What is striking, however, is that co-ordination is possible, that progress can be and is being made.

These potential difficulties bring me, in any event, to a third theme that has run through the discussions: the relative merits of trade liberalization through regional trading blocs such as NAFTA, and the "multilateral" approach, through GATT, which attempts to make much wider reductions in tariffs, even if the reductions are less deep. The difficulty in co-ordinating the laws of three countries to facilitate trade and investment would be magnified hugely if an attempt were made to achieve the same level of co-operation among 20 or 120 countries. A lack of standardization may serve as a non-tariff barrier, as in the case of a lack of protection for intellectual property; the standardization will be much easier to achieve in negotiations among a smaller group. The same applies, no doubt, to the effort required to ensure the co-operation of governments at sub-national levels in each of the countries concerned: fewer participants implies fewer problems to overcome, and a higher probability of success.

In the short term, then, regional trading blocs may be a natural response to the inevitable difficulty of large-scale multilateral co-ordination. Regional trade blocs, again, need not be viewed as ends in themselves, but as a movement closer to an eventual goal of unrestricted trade. We may be able to reap a large percentage of the eventual gains from a regional bloc, while waiting for the eventual pay-off from GATT. Or, perhaps, it may prove easier in the end to move toward elimination of the last trade barriers through negotiation among five or six regional free-trade areas leading to offers of reciprocal privileges. The approaches exemplified by GATT and NAFTA can be seen, with some forecaster's licence, as heading toward the same goal, and therefore as complementary. And the optimal path for any given nation may well involve participation in both.